RICOCHET

CONFESSIONS OF A GUN LOBBYIST

RICHARD FELDMAN

BICENTENNIAL

1807

WILEY

2007

BICENTENNIAL

John Wiley & Sons, Inc.

Published by John Wiley & Sons, Inc., Hoboken, New Jersey
Published simultaneously in Canada

For general information about our other products and services, please contact our Customer Care Department within the United States at (800) 762-2974, outside the United States at (317) 572-3993 or fax (317) 572-4002.

Wiley also publishes its books in a variety of electronic formats. Some content that appears in print may not be available in electronic books. For more information about Wiley products, visit our web site at www.wiley.com.

Library of Congress Cataloging-in-Publication Data:

Feldman, Richard.
    Ricochet: confessions of a gun lobbyist / Richard Feldman.
        p.   cm.
    Includes index.
    ISBN 978-0-471-67928-8 (cloth)
    1. Gun control—United States.   2. National Rifle Association of America.
    3. Lobbying—United States.   I. Title.
    HV7436.F45 2008
    323.43dc22
    [B]
                                                                    2007002546

Printed in the United States of America

10 9 8 7 6 5 4 3 2 1

This book is dedicated to Harlon B. Carter, the man responsible for saving the Second Amendment freedoms for generations of Americans during a time in our country when gun ownership was on the road to extermination as a cherished and fundamental right. Equally important are the tens of thousands of local activists who make the "gun lobby" the true grassroots dynamo that it is. Money doesn't vote, people vote, or as we said in the sixties, "Power to the people" and, I should add, "away from the elites, wherever they dwell." I think Thomas Jefferson would have approved.

CONTENTS

ACKNOWLEDGMENTS

This book is my story of how I came to see the "gun issue" differently during my professional involvement with the gun lobby. My views were tempered by my understandings of and relationships with the various people involved. None of what follows could have been written without the guidance and assistance of the following people for which I am eternally grateful.

First I must thank my wife, Jackie, for putting up with me during this arduous process. My thanks to the following people for your insights, advice, and encouragement: Maryann Carter, Joseph Tartaro, John Aquilino, Rick Manning, John Adkins, Warren Cassidy, Paul Jannuzzo, Alan Gottlieb, Michael Saporito, Neal Knox, Richard Sorrentino, Jerry Preiser, Julie Versnal, Peggy Tartaro, Richard Gardiner, Robert Ricker, Robert Glock, Carol Bridgewater, Carlos "Los" Santizo, Rodger Iverson, Michael Lashbrook, John Anderson, Dave Tinker, Ron Stilwell, Paul Mollica, Irwin Nowick, Robert MacKinnon, Stephen Holbrook, Larry Pratt, Marion Hammer, Rick and Eleanor Sinnott, Keith McClellan, Merrill Gugarty, Philip Mattina, Al Rubega, Dave Marshall, Bill Ruger Jr., Bob Pemberton, Pat O'Malley, Mike Bussard, Dave Workman, Karin Levine, John Krull, Shirley Steffen, Anita Carson, R. T. Gregg, Sandy Edwards, Bill Chandler, Andy Molchan, Dave Kopel, John McClaughry, Congressman Bob Barr, Congressman Jack Brooks, Congressman Barney Frank, Edward Meese, William Bennett, and "Mr. X." My deepest thanks to all the current NRA staff who asked that their names not be included precluding retribution and shunning from their superiors.

NRA ANNUAL MEETING

pril 2003: Robert Glock drove the big BMW south on I-75 at a steady eighty-five miles an hour.

It looked like we'd make the normal seven-hour trip from Atlanta to Orlando in less than five. The flowering dogwoods of the Appalachian foothills gave way to flat miles of pulp pines and sprouting soybean. Then the first spiky palmettos of the coastal plain appeared. By 11:30 a.m. we were near the Florida line.

The four of us in the metallic green sedan were on our way to show the Glock flag at the annual convention of the National Rifle Association. The NRA is one of those American icons like the CIA or the NFL, for which an acronym automatically sparks recognition. When most people see the letters, "NRA," they think of the ongoing battle for gun-owners' rights—and the endless struggle to control gun violence.

But during almost twenty years' involvement with the National Rifle Association—both as a senior political agent and then as an executive director and chief lobbyist of the American Shooting Sports Council (ASSC), the firearms industry—my image of the organization had radically changed. Once, I'd naively viewed the association as the resourceful advocate of citizens' Second

Amendment guarantees to "keep and bear arms." But I'd been forced to recognize that, despite its sacrosanct facade, the NRA is actually a cynical, mercenary political cult. It is obsessed with wielding power while relentlessly squeezing contributions from its members, objectives that overshadow protecting Constitutional liberties.

And now, after a bitter estrangement of four years, I was about to encounter the NRA again. I'd meet the executives, the officials, and the loyalists with whom I had shared so many triumphs, but who had ultimately branded me a traitor. Watching the flat, semitropical landscape roll by, I recalled the analogy former executive vice president Warren Cassidy had used to describe the NRA. People would gain a true understanding of the National Rifle Association, Warren had said, only if they thought of it as "one of the world's great religions."

In fact, the fervor of its activist members is just as inflexible as that of Muslim, Christian, or Jewish zealots. But the organization's present leaders have contemptuously manipulated those passions to consolidate political power and keep the money stream flowing steadily. For loyal rank-and-file members, however, their zeal blinds them to this reality.

But, according to orthodox NRA doctrine, I had committed the heresy of compromise, a sin for which I would be eternally damned. My transgressions were grave: I had openly cooperated with the "jack-booted thugs" (one of the NRA's favorite epithets) of the Bureau of Alcohol, Tobacco, and Firearms (BATF), I had sacrificed at the highest altar of the "gun grabbers" (another favorite NRA slur)—the Rose Garden of the Clinton White House, and I had been tempted to negotiate reasonable settlements to imminent municipal lawsuits against gun manufacturers. The fact that I had valid, practical reasons for all of these actions, which would have strengthened the rights of law-abiding gun owners while dampening the level of acrimony in the great American debate over firearms, just increased my culpability in the eyes of the NRA leaders. They weren't interested in actually solving problems, only in fueling perpetual crisis and controversy. That was how they made their money.

In a few hours I would be mingling again with those leaders and the throngs of the faithful.

"The Sunshine State," Robert Glock announced as we sped past the Florida welcome center. "Why, then, is it cloudy?"

Tall and dark-haired, Robert Glock was an urbane Austrian who spoke precise English with a slight Tyrolean accent. Working for his father, Gaston, Robert had taken over the leadership of Glock's rapidly expanding American operation a few months earlier. I was Robert's consultant, easing his entry into the often-confusing world of guns in this country.

"Hey, the sun's coming out up ahead," Chris Edwards, director of the Glock Sports Shooting Foundation and chief of special projects, said from beside me in the wide backseat.

"Pool time," Robert's girlfriend, Carolyn, added cheerfully from the front seat.

I was thinking of how nice it would be to have a frosty Amstel in the Florida sun beside the pool at the Peabody Hotel. But then I felt a chill of apprehension as I recognized the possibilities that pleasant scene might hold. The pool deck was bound to be thick with NRA insiders. Thursday afternoon of the convention week was traditionally a time to relax, a break between the committee meetings and closed-door sessions and the upcoming weekend events for the general membership. The Peabody, just across the street from the sprawling Orange County Convention Center, was the hotel of the NRA "Official Family," the coterie of committee and board members and senior leaders—including Executive Vice President Wayne R. LaPierre Jr. and Chris Cox, who ran the NRA's powerful lobbying arm, the Institute for Legislative Action (ILA). Many of the people I was apt to encounter at the hotel, such as "the Colonel," Robert K. Brown, the publisher of *Soldier of Fortune* magazine and an NRA board member, hated my guts. In their eyes, Richard Feldman showing up at the Peabody on this pleasant April day would be like Judas Iscariot appearing in St. Peter's Square on Good Friday.

Or, in the parlance of Long Island, New York, where I grew up, hocking a loogie onto the Ark of the Covenant.

The coming confrontation triggered anxiety and anticipation. I had never shied away from a fight, especially when I was right. And I knew that I had never abandoned the cause of the Second Amendment. Rather, the NRA itself had deserted its fundamental principles and had willingly jeopardized its members' constitutional rights in order to preserve and further its political and financial power.

• • •

We entered the Peabody's lobby just as the traditional midday duck parade was ending. A small flock of mallard hens and one drake strutted along the red carpet to the beat of a Souza march and flapped into the stone fountain. The crowd around the registration desk regrouped after the show. But a tanned, patrician couple in Mephisto shooting boots and matching tailored khaki shirts with Virginia Tidewater Hunting Club logos stayed where they'd been, watching the paddling mallards with less than benevolent eyes. They looked like old money, NRA stalwarts who probably owned a five-thousand-dollar chocolate Labrador retriever with field champion bloodlines, and who hunted with custom-made Perazzi shotguns worth a lot more than that.

Hunters and gun hobbyists like them, including their middle-class and blue-collar counterparts, once had made up the core membership of the NRA. Before the 1970s, the NRA had been a relatively small, basically nonpolitical association of hunters, shooting sports enthusiasts, and gun collectors. Today, with a membership of around 3 million, the association is probably the single most politically active lobbying group in the country. And the quaint interests of the wealthy and working class waterfowl hunters have become a much lower priority on the National Rifle Association's agenda.

• • •

On the pool deck in search of a beer and a sandwich, I was still feeling apprehensive about the people I might encounter there. As if to verify my bout of nerves, I almost ran straight into Kayne B. Robinson, the first vice president of the NRA. He was dressed in his habitual blue suit, with carefully water-combed short hair and his trademark gold-rimmed glasses. Kayne produced a cold, thin-lipped scowl when he recognized me and strode past silently. That's what the Brits call cutting someone dead. *Jeeze*, I thought, *this is gonna be tough*.

But then, Mary Rose Adkins walked up, smiling. "Hi, Richie," she said. "Nice to see you again." We were still friends, and obviously the NRA's official animus toward me didn't cut much ice with her. Then Steve Halbrook, an NRA attorney whom I'd known for years, clapped me on the back and said, "It's great that you're back, Richie."

So, I realized that there might be a pattern here. Senior NRA officials like Robinson adhered to NRA dogma that proclaimed me a heretic who must be shunned. But, beyond the Byzantine inner sanctum of the senior association executives, the NRA still had its share of decent human beings with whom I had worked closely for almost two decades.

Maybe I'll survive this convention after all.

•   •   •

That evening at the Glock party in the Peabody's best dining room, I ate with former U.S. congressman from Georgia Bob Barr, and his wife Jeri. I'd moved to an area of Atlanta, which Bob had represented when I'd taken over the fledgling ASSC in 1991, and he'd become one of my strongest supporters. Bob Barr was also known in the media as "the NRA's representative" in Congress because of his dependable position as a pro-gun advocate. After his defeat in the 2002 congressional elections, Bob continued to easily win election to the NRA's board of directors. The NRA still valued him highly as an adviser because he had fashioned the House campaign to defeat the extension of the 1994 assault weapons ban when it came up for renewal in 2004. When the NRA members saw that "traitor" Richard Feldman hobnobbing over a fine Merlot with Bob Barr and conferring with Robert Glock—a rising star in the firearm industry—the knickers of more than a few members of the NRA "Official Family" seated around the tastefully decorated restaurant must have twisted.

I glanced at a big table in the corner where several high-ranking NRA women were seated. There was Marion Hammer, immediate past president, seated next to Mary Corrigan, executive assistant to Wayne LaPierre. When their dinner broke up, Mary and several of the women filed silently past our table, avoiding eye contact with me.

But Marion was obliged to pay her respects to the Barrs. She was friendly to them and to Robert Glock but cool and formal to me when she reluctantly shook my hand. The NRA's orthodox canon still prevailed. I had been excommunicated and had become virtually a nonperson in the eyes of the faithful.

After dinner, I noticed Roy Innis, the prominent civil rights leader and chairman of the Congress of Racial Equality, eating alone at a small table. He was the only black person seated in the room; the other African Americans were waiters and busboys. In his late sixties, Roy was fit and vigorous, his neatly trimmed beard and lively, intense eyes gave him the appearance of a charismatic southern preacher or a senior African official in some alphabet soup UN agency. Roy was a longtime NRA board member and the chairman of the Urban Affairs Committee. He and I had worked hand-in-hand in 1985 during the media firestorm that erupted after Bernard Goetz (the "Subway Vigilante") shot four black teenagers who were attempting to mug him on a New York City subway. The fact that Roy was a pillar of the civil rights struggle, and yet was a pro-gun Libertarian and a defender of Goetz, confused a lot of liberal talking heads and TV producers who preferred to categorize people by inflexible simplistic formulas.

"Richie Feldman," Roy proclaimed in his rich baritone voice. "Sit yourself down here and have a glass of this nice wine."

Roy was genuinely pleased to see me, and that went a long way toward smoothing any feathers ruffled by a Kayne Robinson or a Marion Hammer. After Roy filled my glass, he fixed me with his prophet's gaze. "It's *so* good to have you back. You know, with all the work you've done in cities, I really want to have you on my committee."

Obviously, Roy assumed that I was about to don the official cloth of the NRA again. He had no way of knowing I was down here as a consultant and squire to Robert Glock.

"Roy," I said, lifting my open hand. "I'm not really interested in getting back into the NRA's official family. There's just too much bad blood between the senior people and me. It would never work."

Despite his Old Testament persona, Roy Innis possessed an astute and practical political mind. He nodded gravely. "You're right, Richie. But that's a real shame."

●   ●   ●

The next day I joined Robert Glock and Chris Edwards in the vast Exhibit Hall of the Convention Center. More than thirteen hundred large corporate pavilions and small booths filled the area. They ranged in size from the wide-open, multimedia displays of major international gun makers such as Beretta U.S.A., Colt's, and Heckler & Koch, all the way down to the inexpensive, narrow cubbyholes for niche advocacy groups and niche marketers. Alongside such renowned manufacturers as Remington and Browning were groups like the Fifty Caliber Shooters Policy Institute, which promoted the ownership of large-caliber, military-style weapons. Next to them, specialized merchants like the Concealment Shop, of Mesquite, Texas, hawked customized purses, vests, and belts to carry hidden handguns.

The Glock exhibit was large and centrally located, staffed by employees in neat black polo shirts with the company logo. As we made our way down the crowded aisles, I greeted industry acquaintances who had been my members and clientele for ten years in the ASSC. They were all glad to see me and pleased to meet Robert Glock. The Glock semiautomatic handgun with its trademark dull black polymer grip and frame was rapidly capturing a huge share of the lucrative American law-enforcement market. In fact, 80 percent of police departments that made the transition from revolvers to semiautomatics chose Glock. Cops loved Glock pistols because they were completely reliable, available in a variety of calibers such as 10 mm and .45, and possessed a unique internal safety system that allowed the shooter simply to raise the weapon and squeeze the trigger to fire. In street gunfights over the years, too many officers had been killed or wounded as they fumbled to release the external safety of their weapon. In the world of guns as throughout industry, success based on a quality product bred respect. And Glock was respected.

As we wove our way among the displays of handguns, rifles, and shotguns, I explained again to Robert that this was a "tire-kicker" event. Companies large and small showcased their products for industry colleagues and NRA members, as well as for the thousands of wannabe "gunnies" who couldn't afford to buy very many but just liked to hoist a collector's edition of a World War II M-1 Garand rifle or a long-barreled .44 magnum ("C'mon, make my day") Dirty Harry revolver. No guns or accessories were sold at the NRA convention. The exhibitors took no orders. Company prestige and pride were the commodities of trade here.

I followed Robert's lead and wore my best dark, conservatively tailored chalk-striped power suit. I had also defiantly displayed on my left lapel the distinctive burgundy-and-gold NRA endowment member pin. This was a statement: I had not abandoned the association; it had turned its back on me. As we walked the floor, I noted that the visitors we passed differed in subtle ways from the people I had seen at my last convention four years earlier. There were the expected clutches of fellow "suits," firearms industry executives, members of the NRA official family, and ubiquitous consultants—many of them attorneys like me. Then there were large numbers of white middle-class NRA members tastefully but casually dressed, a few wearing polo shirts with the embroidered logos of hunting or gun clubs.

What I did *not* observe were the bunches of walking bumper stickers in provocative T-shirts emblazoned with defiant slogans such as, "From My Cold, Dead Hands" made famous by NRA president Charlton Heston. In years past, inflammatory T-shirts pushing Second Amendment rights to extremes had been much more in evidence. Nor were there many of the often shifty-eyed "camo people" who represented the paranoid world of the militia movement. There'd been a period in the mid-1990s when longtime uncompromising zealot "Toxic Tanya" Metaksa—who at the time was the executive director of the ILA—had reportedly courted the militias in their dubious battle against the New World Order. But Oklahoma City had changed all that. Like all successful power lobbies, the NRA bent in the political wind: and now, the putative warriors of the militias were no longer welcome in the NRA.

But there were still a few bubbas strolling the exhibits, clutching their plastic bags of freebies to their hefty bellies. I was always amazed that there were actual humans inside those mounds of adipose tissue. The media, of course, invariably zeroed in on the camo (camouflage) people and the bubbas to get B-roll footage for the six o'clock news. But that was just professional laziness. These outlandish characters had never been truly representative of the NRA membership. A clean-shaven Wal-Mart assistant manager from Akron or a well-dressed dentist from Sacramento did not provide such archetypical good visuals or reinforce stereotypes.

As we moved through the crowds, I recognized once again that the media analysis of the National Rifle Association invariably missed the mark—to the cynical glee of the NRA's leaders. They thrived on unfair treatment from the "liberal antigun" establishment media, which provided invaluable fodder for the fund-raising drives in support of the NRA's semiannual crisis du jour.

The fact was that an interest in and an attachment to guns were definitely not extremist in American society. There were more than 200 million privately owned firearms in the United States. People continued to buy rifles, shotguns, and an ever-increasing number of handguns (the tidal wave of fear generated by 9/11 caused a huge spike in pistol sales, which has only recently subsided). For the millions of law-abiding Americans, the constitutional right to own a gun was a vital facet of citizenship.

But, preoccupied with the demands of contemporary life, people like those mingling among the exhibits did not have the energy to follow the shifts and nuances of complex gun policy at the local, state, and national level. Just as they trusted the National Cancer Institute to invest wisely in productive research, they believed that the professionals of the NRA worked diligently to protect their interests as gun owners.

As LaPierre's predecessor, Warren Cassidy had acknowledged this belief was akin to religious faith. And as I strolled past the displays of six-shooters and lever-action rifles at the Wild West Guns booth and the replica Civil War muskets at the Dixie Gun Works, I realized once again that an NRA national convention was more like a pilgrimage than a trade show.

●   ●   ●

The next afternoon, Chris Edwards met with the chief of Governor Jeb Bush's security detail to discuss the recent Florida Department of Law Enforcement's transition to Glock handguns. Chris had helped outfit the governor's bodyguards with weapons specialized for their particular requirements, and suggested that Robert Glock would like to meet Jeb Bush before the annual members' banquet, where the governor was to be the keynote speaker.

"The governor would be very pleased to meet Mr. Glock," the state police captain said.

It was arranged that Robert would pay his respects and have a picture taken with Governor Bush—a standard political grin-and-grip—at the exclusive VIP reception before the banquet.

Robert invited me along as part of the company delegation. Walking across the street from the Peabody to meet him and Chris in the convention center, I ran into Maryann Carter, the widow of Harlon Carter, the father of the modern NRA. He had undoubtedly been the single most influential modern NRA leader. In the 1970s, Harlon had decisively completed the transformation of the association from a confederation of sportsmen and gun buffs into the disciplined political juggernaut it is today. He had been my mentor when I'd gone to work as a young NRA political operative in 1984. Beyond our professional relationship, Harlon, Maryann, and I had become close friends. Now Maryann Carter was the undisputed grande dame of the National Rifle Association. So a lot of heads were turned as we strolled, arm-in-arm, into the convention center.

My renewed confidence wavered, however, when I met Robert and Chris outside the door of the small VIP reception room. This was the *sanctum sanctorum*, the Holy of Holies, of the NRA. Inside were all the people who had made my life hell for the past four years. I really did not want to confront them close up and personal.

"Look," I said to Robert, "why don't you and Chris go in, and I'll just meet you later. I'm too recognizable. I don't want to cause a scene."

Robert gripped my shoulder. "No, no, Richard. You come in. You're part of the team."

At that point, the tall, rugged, state police captain, who looked typecast for the role, came out smiling and shook Robert's hand. "This way, sir. The governor is looking forward to seeing you."

I walked to the right of Robert and Chris. As soon as I entered the reception room, I saw Wayne LaPierre and his wife, Susan, holding court at one end of the white-draped refreshment table. Although the room was small, the lighting was subdued and I couldn't tell from the doorway whether Susan was wearing one of her designer dresses that had increasingly become her trademark. Her haute couture had caused a stifled groundswell of discontent among the traditional conservative higher-ups in the official family. It was one thing to make a killing in a nonprofit, membership-funded organization. But it was another thing altogether to flaunt it.

Glancing toward Wayne, who looked like a sleek, well-tailored, and complacent CEO—which of course he was—I wondered what the reaction would be among the Texas oil-patch roughnecks, Oregon Wal-Mart employees, and New Jersey truckers if they learned how much he earned. Would they keep sending their hard-earned thirty or forty bucks every time they received another a fund-raising letter with Wayne's computer-affixed signature pleading for donations to quell some dire crisis if they knew that he was among the highest paid leaders of any tax-exempt organization? His official annual compensation package totaled *only* about $900,000, but he purportedly received lucrative royalties on the NRA's bestsellers allegedly ghost-written by the NRA's public relations department. And Susan was a well-compensated association consultant.

I was just sizing up Governor Bush's entourage at the other end of the refreshment table when a woman's strident voice cut through the cocktail murmur.

"*He's* not allowed in here!" It was Andra Fischer, Wayne's private office manager and general factotum. Among her responsibilities was ensuring that these ceremonial events ran smoothly, which meant excluding gate-crashers like me. Especially like me. Glaring first in my direction, then at the state police captain, Andra added in the same raspy tone, "This is an *NRA* reception."

The chief of the security detail leaned down, frowning at her, and then nodded at the Glock party. "These people are here at the governor's request. He wants to meet them."

Now, everyone in the small room could hear what was going on, but wouldn't acknowledge the indecorous confrontation. Andra stood her ground, quivering with outrage. "Well, he's not allowed to be here. Richard Feldman can't stay. This is a private reception."

State police captains who command governors' security units are not used to following the orders of civilians. "Look, lady," he said bluntly. "You can take that up with the governor. I'm escorting these people to meet him."

Andra stepped aside but glared at me. It was impossible for the small group of VIP guests not to have heard every word of this unpleasantness.

As Robert and Chris followed the captain to shake hands with Governor Bush, I hung back, not wanting to cause any more trouble than I already had. But in the glare of the photo strobes, I scanned the tense faces of the NRA's hierarchy. Not so many years before, I had been their valued colleague and trusted ally. I had contributed to several of the association's notable public relations and legislative successes. Now I was a pariah. As I stood there, isolated on the thick blue carpet, my mind cast back to the long, improbable train of events that had brought me here.

2

THE DREAM JOB

ashington, Monday, June 18, 1984: A mailroom cart crammed with Public Telecommunications Facility Grant applications filled half my workspace on the fourth floor of the U.S. Commerce Department. The narrow metal desk was covered with files from a National Public Radio (NPR) station in the Midwest that wanted Uncle Sugar to foot the bill for a new antenna tower.

The NPR station was in the district of an influential House member, so the grant was a done deal. I just had to plow through the boilerplate, to make sure that the bureaucrats complied with relevant statutes.

It was only 10:30 a.m., still an hour and a half to lunch, but I couldn't tell if it was day or night in this windowless inner corridor.

I missed my corner office. For a year, I'd worked as the special assistant to Bernie Wunder, assistant secretary of commerce for communications and information. Being a Schedule C Reagan Administration political appointee, I'd rated a big office next to Bernie's on the northwest side of the building with a window overlooking Pennsylvania Avenue and the Rose Garden.

Being Wunder's go-to guy for the rest of the department, other agencies, and Capitol Hill had been challenging and engrossing. But Bernie left for the private sector in 1983, and the new man who came in from the Federal Communications Commission brought his own people. I was shunted off to this make-work job in the office of the chief counsel.

And here I sat, just another anonymous civil servant in another overstaffed agency. I'd slipped through the event horizon of the Beltway black hole. I could probably occupy this same closet office until I retired with a gold watch and a comfortable pension. That might have been an attractive prospect for an unadventurous thirty-something lawyer.

I was bored and frustrated, but didn't know where I'd end up "on the outside."

As I turned a page in the public radio station's thick grant application, I realized that the descriptions of "propagation capacity" and "polyphasor coax" properties of antennas might as well have been written in Mongolian. Six more pages to review.

Is this why I sweated through three years at Vermont Law School?

Twenty minutes later, I closed the file. Instead of retrieving another grant application from the cart, I removed my bar review notes from the drawer (camouflaged inside a manila grant folder) and went back to mastering the nuances of public contract law in our nation's capital. Once I passed the D.C. bar, I would have options beyond feeding at the government's trough.

But I'd always hated contracts. And these "give and convey to all parties singular . . . estates, interests, rights, claims, titles" were stultifying. What was worse, the "maximum amperage rating" of the NPR station or this crap?

I sat back and examined the walls of my cell. The fact was that I'd studied the law to gain entry into a life of politics. And it had been my passion for politics that had drawn me to Washington in 1982. I'd never been what Bill Clinton would later call a "policy wonk." But I definitely was a *politics* wonk, and had been since eighth grade in Lawrence, the wealthy, predominantly Jewish, New York suburb on the south shore of Long Island.

That first taste of politics had been in 1965. William Buckley, the erudite publisher of the *National Review*, was running for mayor of

New York on the new Conservative Party ticket against liberal Republican John Lindsey. I'd spent a day in the city, stuffing envelopes at Buckley's Manhattan campaign headquarters, and had the thrill of shaking his hand. He'd even displayed his languid, lopsided grin—old money Ivy League—and patted me on the shoulder. "Thanks for stopping by to help us out, Richard." *He knows my name*, I thought with a rush of pride, not yet recognizing the politician's skill of scanning a room for stick-on name labels.

Bill Buckley lost to Lindsey. However, I was hooked on the drama and tension of electioneering and politics.

The following year as a freshman at Lawrence High School, I served as a volunteer for the reelection of Republican state senator Norm Lent. The duty of handing out campaign brochures while Lent shook hands with commuters at the Lawrence and Cedarhurst Long Island Railroad station on chill fall mornings was not demanding.

For my parents, my pulling on a good sweater and shining my shoes before sunrise to distribute campaign literature was better than playing in a band and smoking—either tobacco or marijuana.

Health, mental and physical, was a priority in my family. My dad, Joseph Feldman, M.D., was a child psychiatrist. He treated patients one town away in Woodmere in an office that had its own private entrance and had walls lined with bookshelves. Selma Feldman, my mother, had spent four years as a social worker in Brooklyn. Growing up, I thought we were lower middle class because Dad drove an Oldsmobile while the neighbors had Caddies or Mercedes and even a few Rolls.

Mom and Dad, dedicated independents, encouraged me "to get involved" in the community. They were Jacob Javits supporters, moderate, pro business, and Nixon even then seemed like a moderate.

I didn't need a lot of encouragement. As a junior in 1968—the truly seismic year in a decade of cultural earthquakes—I beat several competitors to become the school's coordinator for the Nixon-Agnew campaign. That spring, most of my fellow students were Bobby Kennedy Democrats, with some leaning toward Senator Gene McCarthy. By September, Kennedy was dead and McCarthy was politically moribund. I distrusted Democrats and felt that the establishment party candidate, Vice President Hubert Humphrey, would simply continue Lyndon Johnson's bankrupt policy in the geopolitical train wreck called the Vietnam War.

Richard Nixon had announced a "secret plan" to end the war. I was all for that.

Nixon won. The war continued. I learned an important lesson about the relationship between campaign promises and reality.

But I'd gained entry to the sub-subbasement of a political party. In 1970, as a freshman at Boston University, I threw myself into student politics with a little more enthusiasm than I devoted to my classes. But the sixties had not yet ended, despite the date on the calendar. The war still churned on in Indochina. The draft was still in effect, and liberal academics almost never gave failing grades to young men facing conscription—no matter how dismal their performance in class.

There were antiwar and antidraft demonstrations practically every day on the sidewalks in front of the Mugar Library and the Student Union on Commonwealth Avenue. But there were also the feminist demonstrations with their chanting-shouting snake dances and mock bra-burnings. I was all for that. Black Panthers paraded, glowering under bushy Afros and berets, protesting the "racist war" and worldwide "imperialist aggression." I was dead set against the war but couldn't accept the prevailing lockstep mentality that ordained all "youth" must unquestionably embrace the complete catalog of leftwing causes.

In other words, I didn't need some stoned-out longhair telling me how to think. Or act. I had long hair like the rest of them—short-haired guys didn't really get to enjoy the Sexual Revolution—but I still had a brain.

Fortunately, there were a lot of independent thinkers among the student body. Using the organizational and speaking skills I'd honed in high school, I was elected freshman class president in the college of liberal arts—My "Get out the Vote" campaign worked!

My old Republican Club in Lawrence invited me to attend the February 1971 Young Republican Leadership Training School in Washington. When I arrived in D.C., I was eager to hear the speech of a California congressman, Paul N. "Pete" McCloskey. He was a highly decorated Marine veteran of the Korean War—congressional co-chairman of the first Earth Day—who was pro military but by now firmly against our misadventure in Vietnam. Then I discovered that the day before the program began, the GOP withdrew its invitation for McCloskey to speak because he had stood in the well of the House and introduced a bill of impeachment against Richard Nixon over his just-revealed secret bombing of Cambodia. Always a scrapper, McCloskey decided to deliver a rump speech outside the conference at the Twin Bridges Marriott. I was much more interested in hearing him than in receiving turgid instructions from smug party workers.

Pete McCloskey was an obviously sincere, skilled, and "vigorous" speaker in the JFK style. After the speech I shook his hand, telling the Congressman, "If I move to San Mateo, you've got my vote."

As my freshman year ended that May, I learned that McCloskey had decided to run against Nixon in the 1972 election, and was organizing a campaign office and recruiting volunteers for the all-important New Hampshire primary. The first weekend in October, I hitched a ride with another student up to Concord to check out McCloskey's operation.

Mike Brewer, the campaign manager, shook my hand and introduced me to the paid staff and the volunteers, who included a couple really hot-looking girls. That fall I made the trek back to Concord three times, staying longer on each visit, and getting more involved in the fascinating mechanics of planning and organizing a real political campaign. This was a lot more exciting than campus politics. In January, I decided to take the spring semester off and work full time for Pete McCloskey. My parents, who by now were thoroughly disenchanted with Nixon, gave their grudging approval.

To my pleasant surprise, Brewer assigned me to run the Manchester campaign office. I was twenty years old, and my hair was short. I wore a tie and a wrinkled wash-and-wear shirt. The campaign could afford a salary of thirty-five dollars a week, just enough for a Dunkin' Donuts breakfast and lunch and dinner at the local Howdy Burger. I was running on caffeine, cholesterol, and adrenaline. Reporters from the *New York Times* and the *Boston Globe* would show up at our Hanover Street office asking for "Mr. Feldman." Hunter Thomson, from the *Rolling Stone* dropped in. He looked a little under the weather and picked up some information on Pete's scheduled appearance with Paul Newman later in the week.

That night when I went to bed after midnight, I lay there thinking, *I never want to do anything else.* But politics is about winning and losing. And we lost the New Hampshire primary. Pete's campaign had flared, and then died. But the political bug had bit me hard.

Back at Boston University that fall, I became the president of the College Republicans and kept my hand in student politics. But my independent streak led me to what became a well-publicized confrontation with the SDS-dominated student mob.

In May 1973, the United States Marine Corps—which rarely avoided frontal assaults—decided it was a good idea to send a recruiting officer to the Boston University campus. This was no doubt less dangerous than advancing across the lagoon at Tarawa against Japanese machine guns—but probably about as noisy. The antiwar crew called for a "monster demo" and marshaled enough bull-horn-toting, foul-mouthed, egg-throwing students to blockade access to the Marine recruiter in "the Castle"—the alumni house on Bay State Road.

"This is bullshit," I told my roommate, Rick Peterson. The First Amendment right to free speech and to assembly did not mean that a bunch of radicals enjoying student draft deferments could deny everybody else on campus access to the recruiter.

I wasn't the least bit interested in joining the Marines. But I was determined to show the recruiter—and the entire campus—that Captain Michael Collier had the constitutional right to perform his duty.

I consulted the twenty-eight-year-old dean of students, a philosophy professor named William Bennett. As freshman class president, I'd developed a friendship with Bennett based on mutual respect and trust, as well as on shared political values. I called Bill at President Silber's office the night before the interviews and told him, "I'm not about to quit school and become a Marine, but I don't want some mob telling me I can't speak to the recruiter."

"Since you'll be the Marine recruiter's first, and probably only, interview," he said, "I'll escort you through the police lines. It may be a nasty demonstration, outsiders are coming in."

The cordon of the campus cops and the Boston police department's officers, helmeted with gasmasks strapped to their hips, was having trouble containing the demonstration. The obligatory "Pigs off campus" chants echoed from the stonewalls of the political science building across the street on Bay State Road. This is a bit more than I bargained for, I thought, as Bill Bennett and I approached the crowd that surged around the steps. But the cops had kept the sidewalk open, and we made it through with no physical injury.

I chatted with the young captain, noting the rows of Vietnam campaign ribbons on his chest, and then Bill and I left. So far, it had been a nonevent. But on leaving, I saw that the picket lines were now solid, and the mob was determined not to let another student enter. *Well*, I thought, *I got through once, why not again?*

"Forgot to ask the captain a couple questions," I told Bennett, turning around.

He rolled his eyes, but then grinned, realizing that I intended to fully test the principle of free speech. As we passed back through the line of cops, an SDS woman with unshaven legs tried to jab the stick of her protest sign into my groin.

"Motherfucker!" she screeched.

I'd been taking karate lessons for a couple of years and I reacted automatically, delivering a swing kick to her jaw. She and her sign went flying. The cops closed in. That evening, I watched the whole confrontation broadcast on WBZ, the local CBS station. With my grade point average in the basement, a change of campus was indicated. For my last two years of college I transferred to Union College in Schenectady and worked hard on a B.A. in American Political Science. The effort bore fruit. By actually studying and eschewing politics and beer parties, I discovered that earning A's and B's wasn't all that difficult. To my parents' delight and surprise, as well as my own, I made the dean's list during my first year at Union.

But still I couldn't avoid all involvement with politics. During the 1974 session of the New York State Senate in Albany, I worked as a legislative intern for Senator Norm Levy who chaired the labor committee. In the smoky, shirtsleeve, let's-cut-a-deal atmosphere of the committee rooms, I witnessed firsthand the truth of the adage that "You probably don't want to see how sausage is made—and you sure don't want to see how laws are made." (Though both can be tasty.)

I wanted to give law school a try—eventually, but I didn't bother taking the LSAT exam. I needed time away from books.

Back in Boston, a newly minted graduate in the middle of a recession, I didn't find lines of corporate recruiters at my apartment door. And I had to make a living. So I landed a job as an investigator with the Commonwealth Attorney General's office. I was assigned to the Consumer Protection Division. My caseload involved pretty tame stuff . . . usurious car loans, shoddy vinyl siding, and bogus life insurance. But I learned a valuable lesson: Just as private attorneys liked to rack up billable hours, lawyers employed in a bureaucracy would stretch out a case to fill the forty-hour week. They were more interested in looking busy, proving they were earning their salaries, than in resolving the dispute.

Even though my goal remained law school, I couldn't resist the lure of politics. Mutual friends introduced me to Republican state representative Jay Healey from the Montigue district of western Massachusetts. Soon I was working in one of America's oldest statehouses, a legislature even more convoluted than that in New York State in Albany where I'd been an intern. Political alliances, I came to realize, were almost always founded on practical quid pro quos, rarely on principles.

The Massachusetts House of Representatives churned out hundreds of bills each session, just like Oscar Mayer produced wieners. Laws and sausage.

But the great majority of those bills never became law because their sponsors had no intention that they reach a final vote. This activity was ornamental, window dressing to appease voters in the home district. Representatives' and senators' newsletters and press releases invariably bore headlines like "Representative John Doe (or Senator Mary Roe) has introduced important new legislation on an issue of vital interest to citizens of (fill in the blank)." The ratio between bills introduced and the final enacted law was probably about ten to one in the statehouse. Another dose of reality. (Years later I would realize that this charade prevailed—in spades—on Capitol Hill in Washington.)

I was getting my true education in political science.

But there were politicians in the statehouse clearly dedicated to their calling for whom deal making was a means to an end, not the end in itself. One member who impressed me with his intelligence and skill was the deputy minority leader, a representative from Holbrook named Andy Card.

"That guy's going to go far," I told Polly Logan, the Republican National Committeewoman, after spending an afternoon with Card and his staff, discussing the politics of the budget process.

Twenty-some years later, when Andy Card became President George W. Bush's White House chief of staff, Polly called to remind me of my prediction.

In Boston, I met Middlesex County sheriff John Buckley—no relation to publisher William Buckley. The sheriff was running for governor in the 1978 election and needed a full-time advance man-driver-cum-general factotum. Buckley was liberal to moderate, best known as the co-founder of People vs. Handguns. The group, which had the backing of several prominent law-enforcement officials—but not of rank-and-file officers—had sponsored a referendum to ban private ownership of handguns. This effort was based on the premise that revolvers and semiautomatic pistols had no legitimate purpose in the hands of citizens. Once privately owned handguns were banned, Buckley's group reasoned, "getting guns off the street" would be a relatively straightforward undertaking (and violent street crime would evaporate).

To me, this seemed like a reasonable proposition, even after the referendum was voted down—largely through the efforts of the National Rifle Association's grassroots activists.

I loved working for Buckley. I set up rallies and speaking engagements around the state, drove his big tan Plymouth Fury III with its two-way radios, mobile telephone, and siren lights. Part of the job was acting as a liaison with the local press, a skill I thought I'd mastered as a college kid managing Pete McCloskey's campaign office in New Hampshire.

But one day in November 1977, I tripped, sticking my foot in my mouth. An often-frustrating, albeit necessary aspect of any gubernatorial campaign was having the candidate pay homage to the local party organizations. The small-town Republican committees Buckley (and I) had to deal with were usually comprised of hidebound retirees, including suspicious octogenarians who considered Dwight Eisenhower far too liberal. Many of them opposed any government control of firearms. Worse, they were nitpickers who insisted on controlling every piddling detail of Buckley's appearances. That evening, in frustration I told a reporter from the *Middlesex News* that the Republican town committee members were "a bunch of old fogies."

Those words appeared in the paper the next day, quoting "Buckley campaign official Richard Feldman."

The sheriff called me in. "Sorry, Richie. I've got to let you go."

I was out of a job.

Law school looked better all the time.

But I needed some more legal-related experience to pad my application.

Back in Boston, I saw an ad in the *Herald* announcing an opening for a deputy tax collector at city hall in Cambridge; "clean record required, appointment as City Constable necessary," the ad read. Serving as a cop would probably look good to law schools, I figured. So I took the MBTA to Central Square and filled out the forms to become a "city constable."

Once I was accepted, the city manager encouraged me to join the auxiliary police force, which I did. The job entailed studying criminal statutes and department regulations. As an auxiliary officer, I also learned how to shoot a .38-caliber, four-inch barrel Smith & Wesson police revolver.

To my surprise, I scored well on the firing range. And— more surprisingly—I loved the feel, the *heft* of the gun. I rationalized this emotion with my earlier sympathy for John Buckley's efforts to get guns off the street. This pistol was the necessary tool officers carried to protect citizens. Strapping on my holster to report for duty would soon feel natural, if a little weird, given my background.

In the peaceful suburbs of Long Island, I'd had next to nothing to do with firearms. Nice Jewish boys played golf and softball; they didn't shoot sparrows with BB guns or hunt rabbits with a .410 shotgun. But I'd fired my first firearm when I was twelve in July 1964, at Camp Mac-Kee-Nac in Lenox, Massachusetts.

Bill Chandler, a stocky, brush-cut Marine vet was the camp's rifle instructor. Bill wore a sleeveless shooter's vest that bore the crimson patch of the National Rifle Association, a bald eagle soaring above a stars-and-stripes shield, a pair of crossed sporting rifles clutched in its talons. Bill rattled off Marine jargon like "Listen up, men." We all held him in respectful awe.

During my month at camp, I investigated the mysteries of the Remington 22-caliber bolt-action target rifle, taking as much extra-range practice as Bill offered. Under his patient tutelage, I mastered the alien skill of marksmanship.

I would never forget the comfortable, yet exciting ritual of the range, six boys sprawled on the kapok mats, cradling their rifles, waiting in the cool sunshine for Bill's order.

"Ready on the left . . . Ready on the right . . . Ready on the firing line . . . Unlock. Five rounds. Commence firing."

The rifles cracked. The exotic scent of cordite gunpowder drifted in the air. I sighted the bull's eye and squeezed—not pulled—the trigger. A white spot appeared in the ten ring of the target. Magic.

That summer I earned a Sharpshooter badge with four bars—my specialty being the sitting firing position at fifty feet.

My other abiding memory of camp was spending my free time after dinner in the stuffy lodge hall, hunched before the fuzzy black-and-white TV screen. For some unknown reason, the drama of the Republican National Convention in San Francisco fascinated me. Would conservative senator Barry Goldwater snare enough delegates to win the nomination from his archrival, the liberal Nelson Rockefeller? Goldwater won, of course, and went on to lose the general election to LBJ. But innuendos of Rockefeller's extramarital sex—a topic of great interest to a pub-escent lad—sent a subliminal message that real-world politics had wheels within wheels under layers beneath layers that could be very intriguing.

I came away from that summer at Camp Mac-Kee-Nac with a weird, but unshakable, mental connection between guns and politics.

Then, as a constable in Cambridge thirteen years later, I began to realize that this connection was grounded in reality. There were lots of guns and a lot of politics in Cambridge, even if both were kept hidden much of the time.

Once you left Harvard Square, the neighborhoods became shabby and dangerous. I spoke to a Portuguese immigrant who owned a small grocery store on my beat one sleety afternoon. He had been robbed at gunpoint three times in little over a month.

"Why don't you buy a pistol for your own protection?" I asked, beginning to recognize that—despite John Buckley's good intentions—it was impossible for the police to provide adequate security for every threatened citizen.

"I tried," the man said, "but the police chief, he don't let me."

I knew that there had to be something wrong here. When I got back to the station, I ran a criminal background check on the shopkeeper. His record was completely clean, not as much as a parking ticket.

So I went to my lieutenant. "Why won't the chief sign off on a firearm's license so that guy can buy a gun? He certainly needs one."

"Oh, you know," the lieutenant said, one cop to another. He was a burly Irishman with a broken nose and a complexion like raw sirloin.

"Well, no, I don't know, Lieutenant."

"Hey, that guy hasn't lived here a long time. He's one of them Portugees, just off the fuckin' boat. The chief doesn't believe people like him should have guns."

This explanation stuck in my craw. The shopkeeper was a naturalized American citizen, with the same rights and responsibilities as the lieutenant and me. The criminals who robbed hardworking small business owners on my beat certainly had no trouble obtaining guns. But the decent, law-abiding citizens did not have that same opportunity.

The concept that police could not and *would* not protect their fellow citizens began to erode my well-ordered liberal Republican worldview. For years, I'd instinctively accepted more stringent gun control—at all levels of governmental jurisdiction—as the principal and most effective means of combating street crime.

A few weeks after my conversation with the lieutenant, I woke up in my Fresh Pond duplex to a troubling epiphany: That shopkeeper had the constitutional right to defend himself and his business, to take the law into his own hands in the form of a legally licensed handgun.

Oh, no, I thought, *I'm becoming pro-gun.* The revelation took some getting used to.

With a record as an investigator at the attorney general's office, as a Cambridge cop, and as a bona fide campaign aide, I submitted a slew of law school applications in February 1979. I was pleasantly surprised that the new Vermont Law School in the state's central resort area sent me the first acceptance letter. I'd lived in cities or suburbs all my life. It was time to widen my horizons.

South Royalton, Vermont was a picket-fenced, white-steepled town surrounded by hills of sugar maples, with a population around two thousand. The Vermont Law School was the state's first, and one of only two rural law schools in the country. It attracted a lot of skiers and hunters.

Because the school was new, the student body had no traditions. Almost all of my class was from outside Vermont. And the small New England town seemed downright exotic. So did the state's rock-ribbed New England ethos of individual rights. One of my class-mates, Paul Mollica, a burly guy from Brooklyn and Poughkeepsie, let me know just how exotic Vermont was.

One September afternoon leaving class, Paul asked, "Hey, Richie, what kind of piece do you carry?" Paul discreetly let it be known that he owned an extensive gun collection.

"Piece?"

"Your gun. What kinds of guns do you own?"

"I . . . I *had* a .38 when I was a Cambridge cop," I explained. "But I don't think I need a gun up here."

Paul put his hand over the front pocket of his jeans to show the outline of a .38 snub-nosed revolver.

"You may or may not *need* a gun here, Richie," he explained, as if talking to a child. "But it's your constitutional *right* to own and carry a gun. Vermont has some of the best firearms laws in the country. Why do you think I came to this school?"

The next day was Saturday, no classes. Maple leaves were beginning to turn, the sky was sparkling. I did feel free. Suddenly I remembered that skinny, stressed-out Portuguese immigrant trying to run his shop on the dangerous streets of Cambridge.

I drove my '72 LeSabre Custom up I-89, letting the four-barrel 350-engine roar. At the exit to Randolph, I followed Paul Mollica's directions. Ten minutes later, I parked in front of the Snowsville General Store, which had an old enamel sign in the window: "Guns 'n' Ammo."

"I'm looking for a revolver," I told the owner, a taciturn Yankee with a pinched face.

"Ayy-up," he said. "We got 'em."

Ten minutes later, I walked down the store's creaking wooden steps with my own .38 police special—a short-barrel detective's Model 15—stuck in a holster concealed beneath the flap of my windbreaker. The $130 cash transaction had been simple, requiring a one-page federal Bureau of Alcohol, Tobacco, and Firearms (BATF) form to sign, and a cursory glance at my Vermont driver's license. There had been no state registration, no check of my criminal record. And then, legally carrying a "concealed firearm," I exercised my right as a free, albeit transplanted, Vermont citizen.

Paul Mollica beamed proudly and gave me a spine-bruising bear hug when I showed him my revolver.

Guns became a favorite hobby, the in thing, among several of my classmates. We all liked the sense of freedom that virtually unrestricted gun ownership gave us. Packing a loaded gun to class was without doubt the quintessence of freedom.

Soon, there was a tight group of students who not only owned guns, but also met regularly to shoot them. There was no firing range in South Royalton, so our "gang," Paul Mollica, Phil Mattina, and Paul Jannuzzo, gathered on a wooded hillside near the small frame house I shared with eight other students, right down from the Jersey barriers marking a curve on I-89. We shot pistols, rifles, and shotguns, sometimes blasting our way through several boxes of ammunition. Because this was Vermont, none of the locals complained, least of all the local police. Paul Mollica was the most experienced "gunnie" in our group and, purist that he was, insisted on stringent safety measures. One of them was no beer before or during our shooting.

After a few weeks of this, my downstairs housemate, Merrill Gugerty, freaked out that I kept a loaded gun in my room, and voiced his concern to our landlady, Mrs. Rita Jacobs.

She grinned at Merrill, patted him on the shoulder and shook her head. "Don't worry, son," she said. "Everybody has guns up here."

Gugerty, an Irish American from Locust Valley, Long Island, and a devotee of John F. Kennedy, remained skeptical. But over the next three years, we converted him. At first he would come and watch us shoot, and finally he accepted a gun to try his hand. In our third year, Merrill was so hooked on guns and on shooting that he borrowed several hundred dollars from the law school's student emergency fund and bought a Ruger Mini 14 semiautomatic rifle, the kind of gun that would later be classified as an "assault weapon."

When Paul Mollica realized that my interest in guns was more than a fad, he took me aside one lunch hour and presented an application form for membership in the National Rifle Association. "If you're serious about your Second Amendment rights, Richie," he said, "you'll join the NRA."

I joined. And despite the study load, I sat down and read in one sitting the copies of *American Rifleman* that I had received as a new NRA member. I was intrigued by the political sophistication of the association's executive vice president, Harlon Carter, and the political exploits of the Institute for Legislative Action.

Owning and shooting handguns and rifles would become the trademark of our class. In our last year, a bunch of us—both male and female—gathered, fully armed, for a class photo in front of "Main," the former South Royalton High School where all our classes were held. We dubbed this photograph "Lawyers, Guns and Money," after the haunting offbeat song by cult rocker, Warren Zevon. "Send lawyers, guns and money . . . The shit has hit the fan."

But I knew that passing my courses and shooting guns would not get me back to the world of politics that I loved so much.

Since South Royalton was so isolated, we initially had no opportunity to meet and hear public figures. I volunteered to create and direct a distinguished lecture series, through which the school would invite speakers. I received the green light and a budget, but I had to scramble to find a suitably distinguished first speaker. A desire to spark a passionate debate led me to invite Sheriff John Buckley, who was then stumping for John Anderson's third-party presidential campaign. And when Buckley presented his heartfelt case *against* private handgun ownership—to an audience that included at least six or seven students legally packing concealed pistols—the debate was warm, indeed. Paul Mollica was livid; I might as well have asked the Antichrist to address a Vatican congress.

Partly to placate Mollica, partly to present a balanced perspective, I called the NRA's headquarters in Washington and requested a speaker. Their Information and Member Services Division recommended Richard Gardiner from their general counsel's office.

Gardiner's speech was much less passionate than John Buckley; in fact it was dry, cautious, and thoroughly lawyerly. But he was persuasive in presenting the NRA's defense of immutable Second Amendment rights.

Paul Mollica was ecstatic. "Richie," he said, threatening me with one of his crushing bear hugs, "you're a good man."

During this time I had been following the political news about John McClaughry, a prominent Republican intellectual and a transplanted Vermonter who had built his own log home in Kirby. I'd met John working on the McCloskey campaign and had been very impressed by his mind and by his philosophical outlook. A former nuclear engineer with extensive public policy expertise, McClaughry was a staunch supporter of frugal, decentralized government, private property rights, and personal responsibility. He was also an articulate advocate of the Second Amendment.

After working as a speechwriter on Ronald Reagan's 1980 presidential campaign, McClaughry became a senior domestic policy adviser in the White House. In the summer of 1981, John kindly arranged an internship for me at the National Telecommunications and Information Administration, which was led by Assistant Secretary of Commerce Bernie Wunder, a Vietnam vet and brilliant attorney. Working at that level of the bureaucracy was stimulating.

Back at law school, I realized that McClaughry was just the kind of renaissance mind that I wanted for the lecture series. Always gracious, John agreed to speak on September 24, 1981. When he addressed the several hundred people jammed into Adam Quincy Hall, McClaughry was no doubt the smartest and most articulate person in the room.

I must have impressed John McClaughry because, when he decided to challenge incumbent Republican senator Robert Stafford in the 1982 primary, John called.

"Richie," he said. "Think you might be interested in running my campaign next spring?"

Like many memorable campaigns, this one was quixotic. We were poorly funded, but what we lacked in money was more than made up for in brain power (mostly John's) and lots of enthusiasm. Vermont is still one of those places where you can be a credible candidate, if not a winning one, without huge cash reserves. It was a bad year to be running as a Reagan Republican. Stafford beat us in the primary and went on to win reelection in the closest Senate race in the nation that year. Had John won the primary, the Republicans would have lost that Senate seat.

Paul Jannuzzo had baptized the lecture series the "Richard J. Feldman Job Search Program." As things turned out, he wasn't far off the mark.

With John McClaughry as my political rabbi, Bernie Wunder was pleased to offer me a Schedule C appointment as his special assistant when I graduated in 1982. Young Mr. Feldman went to Washington.

●   ●   ●

Two years later, I looked up from my D.C. bar exam study notes. Not even noon yet. The dim hallway outside my little fourth-floor office was hardly a corridor of power. But I was stuck here until I passed the bar.

The phone rang.

"Richie, are you sitting down?" It was my law school classmate, Larr Kelly. He'd taken a job with a K Street legal factory.

"You bet, Larr, chained to my damn desk."

"Good. Listen to this; it's from the *Washington Legal Times*," I heard a newspaper flutter. "'The State and Local Division of the National Rifle Association is seeking three individuals to run political and legislative programs across the country.' Sounds like a job custom-made for you, Richie."

I was literally gripping the phone with white knuckles. *Holy shit.* "Ah, read it again, Larr, slowly."

I had to be hallucinating.

Larr read the ad once more. "So, whatd'ya think, Richie?"

I normally had a *bon mot* or at least a glib opinion on every subject, but this time I was almost mute.

"The NRA . . . political and legislative programs . . ." I stammered, reading from my scribbled notes. "It's almost too good to be true, Larr. It sounds like, well, like a *dream* job."

"Like I said, custom-made for you, Rich. There's a number to call, and an address."

My thoughts were zinging, planning strategy and tactics, mentally building a hierarchy of heavy-hitter references . . . John McClaughry, of course, Bill Bennett . . . Bernie Wunder. I'd have to update my résumé, tailor it to highlight my political experience on the state and local level.

I'm not going to let this opportunity slip away.

The NRA, politics, *and* guns. This really would be a dream come true.

When I thanked Larr and gingerly replaced the phone, my hand flew to my Rolodex. Gardiner . . . There it was. Richard Gardiner, Assistant General Counsel, National Rifle Association. Good old distinguished lecture series.

As I punched in Gardiner's number, my mind was reeling. *Do I really stand a chance? Do I?*

3

THE ASSOCIATION

NRA Headquarters, June 1984: The Red Top cab swung around Scott Circle in the rush-hour traffic and stopped at the 16th Street entrance of NRA headquarters.

"Dere you go, mon," the Jamaican driver said. "Sixteen Hun'dret Rhode Island Avenue."

I was right on time for my 4:15 appointment with Richard Gardiner. I tipped the dreadlocked driver a buck, and was glad I'd taken a taxi rather than walking the seven blocks from Commerce in the June humidity.

As the cab pulled away, I scanned the building occupying the southwest side of the circle. An eight-story cube, the facade was a grid of white marble and glass, functional mid-1950s architecture, solid and conservative.

Etched in the dark stone lintel above the entrance was the pivotal phrase from the Second Amendment: "the right of the people to keep and bear Arms shall not be infringed."

I couldn't help but notice that the association had chosen *not* to inscribe the full text of the brief amendment: "A well regulated Militia, being necessary to the security of a free State, the right of the people to keep and bear Arms, shall not be infringed."

I had no problem with abridging the amendment. The National Rifle Association was a membership organization, supported by almost 3 million dues-paying individuals in 1984. And protection of these *individual* citizens' inalienable constitutional right to own, transport, and use firearms lawfully was fundamental to the NRA's doctrine. Indeed, the association's principle mission was safeguarding this unique American freedom. So in the twentieth century, the militia preface was confusing at best and a red herring at worst.

But I also knew that the authors of the Bill of Rights, which of course included the Second Amendment, had intended all healthy white men in their prime adult years to be members of their states' militias. The Militia Act of 1792 (enacted just three years after the Bill of Rights was adopted) *required* all able-bodied male citizens eighteen to forty-four years old to enroll in state militias—and, equally important, compelled each militiaman to "provide himself with a good musket or flintlock" and the other accoutrements of an eighteenth-century foot soldier.

In other words, America's Founding Fathers not only permitted every freeborn man to "keep and bear Arms," they made firearms ownership a civic obligation. Therefore, the arguments of gun control advocates two hundred years later that the Second Amendment applied exclusively to military formations and not individual armed citizens were specious. And it was the fundamental Second Amendment freedom of American citizenship that the NRA was dedicated to defending.

Or so I believed on that warm June afternoon more than twenty years ago.

Entering the lobby, my eye caught the huge seal of the association dominating the far wall, the familiar American eagle clutching rifles in its talons. A bronze-framed scroll with the names of thousands of Endowment, Patron, and Benefactor Members was mounted near the guard desk.

As I approached the middle-aged guard at the desk, a weird anxiety seized me. Suddenly I remembered the hateful postcard I'd mailed to this very building in November 1963, two days after the assassination of President Kennedy. I'd just been a kid of eleven, but news reports that Lee Harvey Oswald had bought the cheap

Mannlicher Carcano rifle he'd used to shoot JFK from a mail-order ad in the NRA's *American Rifleman* had outraged me. The association reputedly kept unusually complete records of both friends and enemies. Would I lose this job because of the ill-advised words I'd written as a boy?

Nerves. Ridiculous paranoia. But still . . .

"Mr. Gardiner will be right down, sir," the telephone receptionist across from the guard said.

And he was, a brief smile, a handshake, the reserved young attorney, just as I remembered him from the lecture series. He took me to the eighth-floor cafeteria, where the kitchen staff was finishing the cleanup after lunch. The air smelled of fried food and floor wax. I saw on the breakfast menu above the steam tables that employees could order the "Special"—sausage, grits, eggs, and toast—for only eighty-five cents.

"Cheaper than McDonald's," I joked, hoping to break the ice as we sat down with our Styrofoam cups of coffee.

"Better, too," Richard Gardiner added pleasantly. "So, what can I do for you?"

I'd been rehearsing my spiel and tried to speak slowly, in a logical, persuasive sequence, beginning with the Institute for Legislative Action recruiting ad.

". . . and I really think my particular skills, experience, and my dedication to the cause of the Second Amendment make me uniquely qualified for the job, Richard," I concluded a few minutes later.

Gardiner had been jotting on a yellow legal pad. "You sure do have a lot more campaign and legislative experience than I'd expected," he said, standing. "One of the openings is for the northeast district, a region you seem to know quite well. I'll talk to Mr. Lashbrook. He's director of state and local in ILA, but I've got to tell you that he might have already picked out his new staff."

This news stung like a slap, but I tried to appear calm. On the way out, Gardiner gave me the name of Susan Snyder Johnston in personnel, suggesting I write her immediately. "There've been a lot of applicants, and ILA only has these three openings."

●   ●   ●

Near midnight, sitting at my desk in my small rental house on North
22nd Street in suburban Arlington, a half-eaten slice of pizza near my
elbow, I hunched over my Smith-Corona portable electric typewriter, knocking out the final draft of the letter to Ms. Johnston that
I had planned to hand carry to the NRA's headquarters in the
morning. The crumpled sheets of earlier drafts were proof that I'd
agonized over the seemingly straightforward message announcing my
interest in the job.

Wanting to lead with my strongest suits, I planned to enclose
the résumé I'd prepared that spring job-hunting on Capitol Hill.
It was a persuasive document, revealing my legislative and political
campaign experience in the state of New York and New England,
the heart of the NRA's northeast district. But there was a potentially
serious problem with this job history. Two years earlier, before my
Commerce job had been approved, New York Republican senator
Alphonse D'Amato's chief legislative aide, Tanya Metaksa, had
interviewed me for a staff position.

Prior to our meeting, I'd heard that she was an abrasive, generally
unpleasant former lobbyist in the NRA's Institute for Legislative
Action. According to John McClaughry, the word on the street was
that Ms. Metaksa was also a "Second Amendment fundamentalist."
She proved to be all of that and more. Within thirty seconds of
scanning my résumé, she'd focused on my 1977 job as personal aide
to Sheriff John Buckley during his Massachusetts gubernatorial
campaign.

A dour, stout, middle-aged woman, she tossed my résumé on her
desk and glared at me. "You worked for *him*?"

The interview went downhill from there. Even though I'd
explained my lowly job as Buckley's advance man was only after
his failed People vs. Handguns referendum battle, Metaksa had
obviously seen me as an enemy. We'd exchanged thinly veiled insults
before I'd left D'Amato's offices.

Now, seven hours after meeting Richard Gardiner, I was still
sitting at my typewriter, worried about the résumé. Metaksa and her
former ILA boss, the take-no-prisoners Second Amendment fire-
brand, Neal Knox, reputedly still had many allies inside the NRA and
a few on its board of directors. After that acrimonious interview,

could she have slipped a back channel blackball to the association, warning them about me?

I gnawed some cold pepperoni and cheese. That was dumber paranoia than my anxiety about the 1963 postcard. But the people who did the hiring and firing at the NRA's Institute for Legislative Action *would* certainly recognize the name of Sheriff John Buckley. Catch 22: if I made no mention of him, it might seem I had something to hide. But would raising his name give undue importance to that job? I decided to grab the dilemma by both horns and turn the Buckley issue in my favor.

I directed Ms. Johnston's attention to my job with Buckley, "a known advocate of gun control," during his abortive race for governor, pointing out that I'd held a low-level position and also that I had not yet given "serious thought to the Second Amendment and related firearms issues." But I added that, as an auxiliary police officer in Cambridge, I began developing a "cogent framework of ideas" on the gun issue. I further noted that as "a multiple gun owner" and member of the NRA, I'd become known for my "adamant support" of the association's position. To cap this argument, I emphasized my close association with John McClaughry, one of the founders of Gun Owners of America, and a senior Reagan White House adviser who was a leading pro-gun intellectual.

Next I stressed my "intimate understanding of northeast politics" and hands-on experience organizing coalitions. "Simply put," I immodestly concluded, "I believe I am the person for the job!"

Before leaving for the metro into the District the next morning, I called John McClaughry, knowing he was an early riser, and read him a copy of the letter.

"You did the right thing, Richie," he assured me. "But you've got to get yourself read up on the NRA. I'll send you a packet of background material by express mail."

"I've been reading back issues of *American Rifleman*, John," I said. "I think I'm familiar with the basics."

"Do yourself a favor, Richie. Read *everything* I send."

As always, John was right. The material he sent—as well as the back issues of *American Rifleman* and *Gun Week* that Paul Mollica delivered—provided insights to facets of the National Rifle

Association of which I, as a loyal, dues-paying member, had been woefully ignorant.

For the next three days, I ignored the grant applications at Commerce while I followed John's advice and studied the newsletters, photocopied columns and articles from the gun press, position papers, memoranda, and manifestos tracing the turbulent history of the NRA. By the time of my formal job interview with ILA's State and Local Division director, Michael Lashbrook, later that week, I knew a lot more about the National Rifle Association than I had four days before.

And what I learned was fascinating.

●   ●   ●

Like most venerable institutions, the NRA had woven a creation legend that had never been seriously challenged, even though the association itself had bent and shaped the history of its origins to match evolving politics.

Under the NRA's traditional doctrine, the association was organized at the 7th Regiment Armory in Manhattan in 1871—just six years after the Civil War—when two northern veterans, Colonel William C. Church and Captain George W. Wingate, addressed the challenge of the Union Army's overall poor marksmanship during the bloody conflict. Allegedly, most Yankee soldiers were city boys who had never hunted or fired rifles and had been literally outgunned by the hardscrabble Johnny Rebs of the Confederate Army who'd learned to shoot squirrels, rabbits, and deer in the woods and hollows of the overwhelmingly rural South.

This myth contained elements of truth, but was also deceptive. No doubt, there were tens of thousands of mill hands and urban laborers in the Union ranks, especially after conscription was enacted midway through the war. But the North, like the Confederacy, was still primarily agricultural. The majority of Union troops, like their southern counterparts, were farmers. Some of the most successful—and straight-shooting—northern regiments came from farming towns in New England, the Midwest, and from the open plains of Iowa and Nebraska. It was no accident that the Union "Iron Brigade," comprised of soldiers from the

Midwest, fought with such distinction at historic battles such as Gettysburg.

But in 1871, Colonel Church and Captain Wingate were able to tap into an undercurrent of frustration and anxiety over the poor performance of Union soldiers drafted in the slums of the industrial North, troops who included large numbers of Irish immigrants who had in fact no experience with guns.

In any event, the New York State legislature supported the nascent NRA with grants for its first nine years. But the association did not attract a national membership and almost dissolved several times in the final decades of the 1800s. The NRA's fortunes revived, however, after the Spanish-American War when state militias gave way to National Guard units.

Soon, the NRA received government surplus rifles and ammunition to distribute to its members and went on to establish marksmanship programs under the aegis of state affiliates. Congress even voted for taxpayers' money to subsidize the association's programs. The NRA now had a dependable patron in the federal government. And the basic structure of the organization had evolved: state and local shooting clubs that functioned independently but under the guidance of the association in Washington.

But political policy eventually became intertwined with the shooting sports. As the NRA became more politically active, its true position on local, state, and national firearms issues was not easy to track. For example, in 1934—according to the association's official history—it established the Legislative Affairs Division, "in response to repeated attacks on the Second Amendment rights." One of these attacks was apparently congressional passage of the National Firearms Act of 1934, which followed the assassination attempt on President Franklin D. Roosevelt the year before. This law taxed and regulated the sale of machine guns and outlawed sawed-off shotguns—weapons that Prohibition-era criminal gangs had often used against their rivals—the 1934 Act also banned silencers on pistols. The NRA did not lobby individual members of Congress until years later, but instead tried to educate its members on the issues and encouraged them to contact Congress directly.

Again, according to official NRA history, the organization supported the Federal Firearms Act of 1938, which gave the government the power to license gun and ammunition makers, dealers, and importers, and to regulate interstate firearms sales. The 1938 Act also barred known felons from legally buying guns of any type—this last provision being an important goal of the association. In supporting these laws, the association staked out a basic philosophical position: although criminals might use firearms like sawed-off shotguns, machine guns, and silenced pistols to commit violence, guns were not inherently evil and law-abiding citizens had a constitutional right to own and use guns legally. Over the years, this argument evolved into the unofficial mantra of the NRA's most dedicated supporters, "Guns don't kill people, people do." The 1938 Act passed, and the NRA found itself a de facto ally of the U.S. government. Reading this history in my windowless cubicle at Commerce, I realized the relationship was ironic, given the group's later vilification of big government and its gun controllers.

But it was clear that promoting firearms training and marksmanship at the state and local levels were the NRA's primary interests until after World War II when hunting emerged as an issue. Up until the 1950s, hunting and wildlife legislative issues had largely been the purview of the states. But increasingly complex federal regulations—establishing sanctuaries and determining the dates of hunting seasons for migratory birds—coincided with a postwar renaissance in hunting.

The association fostered the idea that the millions of servicemen returning from overseas duty liked to shoot and tromp around the woods and marshes, hence the rising popularity of postwar hunting. It also realized that the guaranteed forty-hour workweek, paid vacations—and rapidly expanding car ownership—helped make hunting popular.

Whatever the cause, almost three hundred thousand people joined the NRA in the postwar years, nearly doubling its membership. Beyond the promotion of hunting as a wholesome pastime, the NRA retained its interest in such shooting sports as skeet and trap, where the dead pigeons shed broken chunks of clay, not blood and feathers.

In the 1950s—and for several years after—the NRA enjoyed slow but steady membership growth, while remaining a relatively minor participant on the Washington political stage. The association had fewer than two hundred employees when it moved into its new Scott Circle national headquarters in 1957. There were few national hot-button political issues to arouse members. And lobbying was low-keyed, focused primarily on wildlife conservation, hunting and the shooting sports, and firearms safety.

Although the 16th Street entrance of the headquarters' building displayed the association's emerging political face through the Second Amendment inscription, the words etched above the Rhode Island Avenue doorway—leading to the NRA's popular museum read: "Firearms Safety Education," "Marksmanship Training," and "Shooting for Recreation."

But in the 1960s, violence engulfed the country, with the decade witnessing a wave of assassinations, urban riots, and street crime—all involving guns. For several years, it seemed like the fabric of society had been shredded. Ghettos in Los Angeles, Newark, and Detroit erupted. To pacify the areas the federal government dispatched Army and National Guard soldiers with rifles and automatic weapons to shoot snipers, looters, and an unknown number of citizens simply breaking curfew. Senator Thomas J. Dodd, a Connecticut Democrat, and chairman of the Subcommittee on Juvenile Delinquency, sponsored legislation beginning in 1963 to end all firearms sales to minors. The NRA supported Dodd. But in March 1965, the association broke ranks when Dodd expanded his bill to prevent all interstate gun sales except to dealers with a federal firearms license (FFL). The bill was defeated.

By this point the NRA had evolved a structure similar to that of other large membership organizations. A seventy-five-member board of directors—a third of which was elected at each annual convention—shaped the association's overall policy goals and advised on allocation of finances through specialized committees. The board also elected a president for a one-year term, which could be extended by a year, and it annually appointed the executive vice president, who shaped policy and oversaw daily operations.

In the mid-1960s, the NRA shifted more dramatically toward supporting state and federal regulations meant to keep guns out of the hands of felons, the mentally unstable, and minors.

Reverend Martin Luther King Jr. was assassinated in Memphis in April 1968 while standing on the balcony of the Lorraine Motel.

And only two months later, Senator Robert F. Kennedy was killed in the kitchen of a Los Angeles hotel after a presidential primary election victory celebration. The 30–06 Remington deer rifle used to kill King and the .22 caliber target pistol used to kill Kennedy were both legal, easily purchased weapons. But the sale of the 30–06 rifle to an escaped convict and fugitive like James Earl Ray was clearly illegal.

It seemed as if guns were destroying the United States. Under pressure from outraged voters, Congress took decisive steps to end the five-year debate over the availability, distribution, sale, and ownership of most types of firearms. The result was the Gun Control Act (GCA) of 1968, which the House and the Senate wrote in near-record time and President Lyndon B. Johnson signed into law in the fall.

Like most major federal legislation, the Act was a latticework of compromises and had been influenced by lobbyists, including the NRA.

But the federal government had become more closely involved in the regulation of gun manufacturing and commerce than ever before. The GCA banned the mail-order sale of firearms—like the Italian Mannlicher Carcano rifle Lee Harvey Oswald had ordered from an ad in the NRA's *American Rifleman.* In fact, modern foreign military surplus firearms could no longer be legally imported. The GCA also established a national age standard for firearms purchases from dealers: twenty-one for handguns, eighteen for rifles and shotguns.

The NRA was slightly less concerned about the requirement that newly made guns have a serial number than it was about the provision that interstate transfer of firearms between individuals. And the Act mandated that these licensed dealers now had to record the details of each gun transaction on the new Form 4473 (the "yellow sheet", named for its paper color). These records were open to inspection by officials of the Treasury Department—whose alcohol and tax division soon evolved into the Bureau of Alcohol, Tobacco, and Firearms (BATF). This was not gun registration per se, but the provision was nearing that slippery slope in the eyes of many Second Amendment purists.

Based on the NRA's public position, one of the few favorable aspects of this section of the law was that by signing Form 4473, a gun buyer attested that he or she wasn't among the "prohibited categories of persons" barred from gun ownership. This included those who were mentally unbalanced, convicted felons, fugitives, illegal drug users, illegal aliens, and those dishonorably discharged from the military. In theory, the association had finally achieved its goal of keeping guns out of the hands of criminals but not of law-abiding citizens. These restrictions, however, also confirmed the suspicion among a growing number of influential NRA officials that the government was expanding its gun control efforts, as exemplified by the creation of a whole new caste of bureaucrats, the BATF.

Enactment of the Gun Control Act and the BATF's becoming a permanent feature of the federal government energized the Second Amendment–activist branch of the National Rifle Association. Among these activists were board members and officials, and thousands of average members like my buddy Paul Mollica, who were less interested in the traditional shooting sports than in safeguarding Americans' rights to gun ownership, which they now saw as increasingly threatened.

My research revealed that the NRA's first major schism over what policy direction it should follow erupted in the mid-1970s. Should the organization devote its limited staff and financial resources to firearms safety, competitive shooting, and hunting— as many wished—or focus more intently on the bare-knuckle arena of Washington and statehouse lobbying?

The traditionalists found the increasingly raw belligerence of the gun debate distasteful. Some board members, executives, and rank-and-file members wanted to withdraw from the political fray and return to the wholesome, uncomplicated world of the shooting sports and firearms education. This branch, the "old NRA," called the Old Guard under retired major general Maxwell Rich, then executive vice president, worked toward a goal that would have radically transformed the association in the 1970s. They planned to sell the marble fortress of its national headquarters in Washington, and relocate to the cleaner and "nonpolitical" atmosphere of Colorado Springs, Colorado. There, the association would focus on conservation and environmental issues. It also hoped to establish a sprawling National Shooting Center in nearby northern New Mexico. Under Rich and the Old Guard, the NRA was going "green" and abandoning any political activism of protecting the "threatened" Second Amendment.

But as this fundamental policy shift gathered support among some NRA leaders, influential members of the board's twenty-member executive committee had other plans. The ink was still damp on confidential studies to uproot the NRA from Washington to the Rockies—when, in 1975, Michigan Democratic congressman John Dingell, a board member and Second Amendment activist, convinced his colleagues they needed dedicated, full-time professional lobbyists to counter the antigun rights groundswell that was emerging in the states and in Washington following passage of the 1968 Gun Control Act.

The board acquiesced and established a formal lobbying arm called the Institute for Legislative Action (ILA). The board, however, placed severe restrictions on the ILA. It could not draw on the association's operating budget to meet its payroll and was even obliged to pay commercial rates for advertising in NRA publications. As if to dramatize its orphan status, the ILA had to rent office space at a hotel next door to NRA headquarters. However, since it was officially a not-for-profit organization, the ILA could raise funds from members' contributions—solicited through ads in *American Rifleman* and through direct mailing appeals, a technique then in its infancy.

●   ●   ●

The ILA soon became the most active and visible branch of the National Rifle Association.

This transformation was due almost exclusively to the character and charismatic presence of the ILA's first executive director, long-time association board member Harlon Bronson Carter. People who knew Carter well spoke of his intelligence, which he often hid beneath a folksy South Texas persona, his political savvy, and his unswerving dedication to Second Amendment rights.

Harlon Carter had spent a long career in federal law enforcement, rising from the Border Patrol to become the Southwest Regional Commissioner of the Immigration and Naturalization Service. Parallel to this career, he'd served decades on the board of the

NRA. More than sixty years old in the 1970s, he was still a physically imposing figure, tall, with a hefty torso and bulldog jowls. He shaved the sparse gray stubble from his head, giving him the appearance that some described as a "cross between Mr. Clean and a .45 caliber slug."

Carter grew up in the Rio Grande border town of Laredo, Texas, just opposite the dustier and more hardscrabble sister city of Nuevo Laredo on the Mexican side of the river. As I came to know Carter and his wife, Maryann, I learned that much of his character had been formed during his childhood and adolescence in the Rio Grande Valley. These were Dust Bowl, depression years. Times were hard, and both Anglos and Mexican Americans used guns for hunting to put food on the table, and for protecting their homes and themselves against violent assailants. Venison, quail, and rabbit shot either in or out of the official hunting season were undoubtedly common dishes in the Carter family kitchen.

But Harlon Carter's boyhood was not an endless Huck Finn idyll. As a teenager in March 1931, he was involved in a violent dispute with a Mexican American youth named Ramon Casiano, who Carter suspected of stealing their family's car. Casiano pulled a pocketknife, and Carter fired a shotgun, instantly killing him. Despite his plea of self-defense, Carter was convicted of second-degree murder and sentenced to three years in prison. After a protracted appeal, the conviction was overturned.

This episode resonated in many of Carter's fundamental positions on the inevitable erosion of the rights to gun ownership, self-defense, and property protection. Years later, he would speak about the government's ceaseless quest to disarm law-abiding citizens and leave them vulnerable to violent criminals.

It was clear that Harlon Carter harbored a deep-seated and sincere distrust of government's motives in gun control. After Harlon died in 1991, I was given a copy of a letter that he wrote to his boyhood friend, Charles "Skeeter" Skelton after the two had spent the first weekend of 1969 on the banks of the Rio Grande, "goat-eating, beer-drinking, and pistol-shooting." Carter told Skelton, "If we do not do something about the Gun Control Act of 1968, the time will come when our children will not be able to enjoy the shooting sports which we ourselves have so thoroughly and completely enjoyed." He compared the growing gun control movement to the confiscatory actions of Nazi Germany that permitted only a privileged few like Hermann Goering to own firearms and to hunt.

Carter saw the "damnable" Gun Control Act of 1968 as "another drop in the water torture provided for good people by big government without a particle of effect upon bad people." Carter also predicted that the Act was only the first step of a campaign to deprive citizens of their Second Amendment rights. He cited the provision prohibiting interstate arms sales except between FFL holders as an illegal "trade barrier." After passage of the Act, he wrote, gun owners were "compartmentalized and identified as citizens apart." Big government, he predicted, had the ultimate strategy of turning the "vast resources" of law enforcement against honest citizens, including licensed gun dealers, and harassing them until both the numbers of individual gun owners and dealers were decimated.

●   ●   ●

As Harlon Carter scrambled to build the fledgling ILA—he and his staff had to buy used office furniture from the NRA next door— Executive Vice President Maxwell Rich and his allies proceeded steadily with their largely confidential plans to disengage the association from politics and reestablish the organization out west. But even if the Washington headquarters building sold for a decent profit, the NRA would still need sizable private or foundation funding to complete the transformation.

While Maxwell Rich and his allies on the board's executive committee worked toward this radical transformation, they took time for some housecleaning in Washington. The "weekend massacre" in early November 1976 cut the NRA staff by eighty officials, including any who might have effectively blocked the move to Colorado and New Mexico. The association's senior executives, who under the organization's bylaws answered to the board, not the membership, felt almost invulnerable.

Harlon Carter understood bureaucratic infighting well from his years in government service and had his own sources of information at the NRA's headquarters. He escaped the indignity of being fired by resigning just days before the massacre. Ostensibly returning to his retirement home in the Arizona Sunbelt, Carter slipped beneath the surveillance of the association's leaders and began to help orchestrate a clandestine rebellion that drew its strength and dedication from a disparate but sizable bloc of the NRA's life members.

These members ranged from obsessive far-right conspiracy buffs to blue-collar union men to constitutional scholars. Many were active in their local gun clubs or NRA-affiliated sportsmen's associations. For others, the association was the only organized body to which they belonged. What they had in common was the fear that their Second Amendment rights were in jeopardy and that the current NRA leadership could no longer be trusted to protect those rights.

But because they were so disparate, the rebels stood little chance of reversing the course Maxwell Rich and his allies had chosen. The NRA's bylaws were inflexible: only one third of the seventy-five-member board was elected every year prior to the annual meeting, and it was the board, not the members, that selected senior executives who made the crucial policy decisions.

But in the winter of 1976–1977, the growing body of rebellious members began to organize in a serious manner for what would be in effect a parliamentary coup d'etat at the annual members meeting in Cincinnati over the weekend of May 21–22, 1977. Small, often shifting coalitions of discontented members had waxed and waned in several states since the early seventies. Most of the state groups had just one or two specific local grievances but lacked national coherence.

As dissatisfaction spread among members, however, effective leadership rose from the ranks. Several smaller cells of the burgeoning insurgency coalesced under an umbrella organization, the Federation for the NRA. The group planned its tactics to operate from the floor of the convention hall, exploit chinks in the ostensibly solid wall of the bylaws, change those bylaws, and to gain control of the association.

Although Harlon Carter was careful never to be seen taking a direct part in these seditious planning sessions, he watched closely and gave advice. The most visible leader of the grassroots members' revolt was a brilliant and often fiery Second Amendment zealot from the Red River Valley of north Texas named Neal Knox. In his early forties as the federation's uprising took form, Knox was complex and driven. With his long, neatly trimmed sideburns and searching blue eyes, he evoked a self-reliant pioneer, the wagon master headed west—or maybe an evangelist at a come-to-Jesus camp meeting. He'd been fascinated by guns since childhood.

After attending Abilene Christian College, Knox took jobs as a small-town newspaper reporter. This experience gave him the confidence to become the founding editor of *Gun Week* at age thirty. He later became the editor of *Handloader* (a magazine for gun buffs who liked to custom-load cartridges) and guided the creation of *Rifle* magazine. From the pages of these specialized publications, Knox hammered continually at those he saw as threats to Americans' unique constitutional right to keep and bear arms. The word compromise didn't exist in Knox's vocabulary. Not only did he want to stop the encroachment of gun rights, he sought to roll back existing gun control laws, including regulation of fully automatic machine guns.

●   ●   ●

The tactical plan for the Cincinnati revolt was elegantly simple, but it required good communications and careful coordination on the convention floor among the majority of the approximately two thousand voting life members who'd been secretly enlisted by the Federation for the NRA.

On the night of Saturday, May 21, the federation's activists, wearing blaze-orange hunting caps and carrying little two-way CB radios, posted themselves at the doors of the hall as an overflow crowd filed in. The activists distributed neatly printed summaries of the proposed changes to the association's bylaws that the federation hoped members would support.

The move caught the Old Guard leaders from Washington headquarters totally unprepared. "They were like deer in the headlights," members who were there would later tell me. Because the association's regulations required convention officers to open the floor to members' motions during the new business portion of annual meetings, they could stall but not stop the federation's well-orchestrated siege. Activists wearing orange badges or caps were lined up twenty deep at the three microphones on the floor, patiently wearing down the Old Guard's attempts to halt debate or bury it in extraneous side issues. The heat and humidity in the hall were uncomfortable, and many on the floor grumbled that the "big wheels" from Washington had bribed the convention hall staff to shut down the air conditioning and end the debate in that under-handed manner.

The routine meeting that had been scheduled to last from 7 to 10 p.m. dragged on past midnight, and still the debate was unre-solved. Then Neal Knox took a floor microphone. The holdouts at the stage rostrum could stall no longer. Knox methodically read from the printed "package" of fifteen bylaw changes that the federation offered for acceptance or rejection by voting members. These new bylaws were the essence of the federation's campaign. Some were truly revolutionary: the election of the executive vice president by an annual vote of the *members* (not by the board), abolishing the board's management committee that had overseen the "Weekend Massacre" six months earlier, a moratorium on the planned National Sports Center, and a commitment to keep the NRA's headquarters in Washington with the Institute for Legislative Action fully engaged in protecting Second Amendment rights.

By 3:30 a.m. on Sunday, May 22, Maxwell Rich and his cronies had been voted out of office. Harlon Carter had been elected as the new executive vice president. After several minutes of cheers, hoot-ing, and echoing applause, he took the rostrum.

To renewed waves of applause, Carter spoke with his trademark rhetorical flourish.

"Beginning in this place and at this hour, this period in NRA history is finished. There will be no more civil war in the National Rifle Association. You, the membership, are entitled to have an NRA that is responsible to *your* wishes. . . . You're America's greatest people, my friends. Don't ever forget that you are."

Again, the crowd exploded with joyful pride.

● ● ●

"Please have a seat, Richard," Mike Lashbrook, head of the ILA's State and Local Division, said a few days after my first contact with

Gardiner. Lashbrook had my application folder open on the desk of his seventh-floor office and a yellow legal pad of notes beside it.

He was about my age, but there seemed something out of place about him. His sandy hair, wide-set blue eyes, and slow manner of speaking gave Lashbrook what I initially saw as a country bumpkin persona. I couldn't imagine how an organization like the NRA relied upon a guy who came across as a plodding hayseed to run an important division of the Institute for Legislative Action.

I soon found out.

What I'd initially seen as slow-witted disguised a probing thoroughness that I had rarely encountered. I'd been expecting a standard thirty-minute job interview. Mike was still steadily and patiently working through his list of detailed questions two hours later.

We had started at the beginning, way back when I was a kid running my high school Nixon-Agnew chapter in 1968. I hadn't listed my stint licking envelopes for William Buckley in 1965, or I'm sure Mike would have wanted to ask about that.

As I'd expected, he focused on my job with Sheriff John Buckley in 1978.

I grinned, trying to lighten the moment, but Lashbrook kept a poker face. "Buckley's antigun crusade was already dead by the time I took the job with him," I explained. "Besides, I was agnostic about the issue then. It wasn't until I was a city constable in Cambridge that I began to realize how important our Second Amendment rights really are."

Lashbrook made a note and moved to his next question, concerning my relationship with John McClaughry, one of the founders of Gunowners of America. "I consider John a close friend and a mentor," I said. Not only was this true, but it should be a counterweight to the negative point of having worked for Sheriff Buckley—or so I hoped.

"What guns do *you* own?" Lashbrook asked.

That was a softball question. "Smith & Wesson .38 Model 15 snub nose. Ruger .22 bull barrel. A Raven .25, and an S&W .357 Highway Patrolman, which is my main home defense weapon."

If Lashbrook was impressed he didn't show it. So far, I'd gotten very little out of him, other than the fact that he was no farm boy but had been raised in Rochester and was well versed in the nuances of Upstate Albany politics.

Lashbrook switched track again: "This job would keep you on the road about two weeks each month. But you'd have a very fair travel and expense account because you'd be expected to entertain the leaders of local affiliates. Would you have any problem with that?"

Please don't throw me in the briar patch, I thought, picturing martinis and steaks in Albany and lobster in Maine. "No," I managed with a straight face. "That would be fine."

Lashbrook's office was rather utilitarian, with a metal desk, a veneer bookcase, and wire racks of the NRA's "Fact Packs": *Ten Myths on Gun Control*.

The most dramatic of these brochures, *A Question of Self-Defense*, featured a quote on its cover from a "Boston rape victim":

"Tell them what rape is. Be graphic. Be disgusting. Be obscene. Make them sick. If they throw up, then they have the tiniest idea of what it is like."

The text presented a well-researched, well-reasoned argument for citizens arming themselves against violent criminals. A spooky picture of a middle-class neighborhood at night, looking vulnerable to intruders, illustrated the story of the young Boston victim raped in her home. Another picture showed an American family at home. The mother was an attractive blonde. The daughter and son favored her, while the father-protector appeared calm but resolute. This photo ran above the section titled, "A Matter of Choice," which argued that all Americans should be able to choose what form of self-defense best suited their needs. From my days on the National Moot Court Team, I appreciated such persuasive rhetoric.

The Institute for Legislative Action had produced all this convincing material, and there were millions of copies being distributed across the county. The ILA was the big leagues. In 1976, a year after ILA's formation, the National Rifle Association started its own political action committee, the Political Victory Fund (PVF), which made campaign contributions to candidates the association favored.

Both the ILA and the PVF became major players on Capitol Hill and in statehouses nationwide after Harlon Carter took over as the NRA's executive vice president in 1977. The ILA had also proven to be a fund-raising dynamo and had helped Carter push membership up toward 3 million.

In the process, Second Amendment orthodoxy had begun its slide behind building institutional power inside the Beltway as the NRA's main priority. In 1980, Carter had fired ILA's deputy director, the abrasive "Toxic" Tanya Metaksa, for using flame-thrower lobbying tactics on Capitol Hill and shunted her off to a sidetrack job in the Reagan campaign.

I later learned from John Aquilino, then ILA's public affairs director, that Metaksa's coarse style had made her persona non grata in Congress. A staffer of Alaska senator Ted Stevens, a longtime NRA supporter, called Aquilino and announced, "If you don't keep Tanya off the Hill and out of our office, the senator is going to vote with the gun control crowd." Tanya had to go.

Then, in 1982, Carter dismissed Neal Knox from his position as ILA director. Ostensibly the reason was because of Knox's own ideological inflexibility and habit of antagonizing congressional leaders with whom the NRA needed to maintain cordial relations. I'd heard that some insiders saw this as a case of the revolution eating its young, and John McClaughry explained that Neal Knox himself had also been involved in various intrigues among his own supporters to unseat Carter and seize control of the association.

John had also said that Harlon Carter preferred more nuanced lobbying and he had advised me to speak my mind honestly on the Second Amendment during the job interviews, but to avoid any hint of Knox's doctrinaire rigidity.

So in this interview, I stressed my skills and experience in meshing politics and policy. Mike Lashbrook made it clear that the position would be a blend of both. As he described the job, I suddenly thought, *this is exactly what I want to do with my life right now.*

I knew it was important to convince him that I was both practical and dedicated to the cause. "Ten years ago," I said, "if you'd have asked me where I stood on the gun issue, I'd have said I was for gun control. But I was a college student who didn't understand the issue. I do now. And you know there's nobody more dedicated to a cause than a convert."

Mike made more notes in his slow, precise manner.

"Michael," I blurted out, "I shouldn't be saying this, but you'd be doing yourself a great favor by hiring me. I'm the *perfect* person for the job."

He made another note.

At the end of the interview—which had lasted two hours and forty minutes—Mike saw me out.

Again, I couldn't refrain from speaking. This job was too important to lose without a fight. "So," I said, "given what you know about me now, what can you tell me about my chances?"

"Well, you're in the running."

"Okay," I persisted, "I'm in the running. Would you say I'm toward the top of the list?"

"Let's just say you're in the running and leave it like that." There was no way to break that poker face.

The next day I got a call from the NRA announcing that Warren Cassidy, Mike Lashbrook's boss, and the director of the Institute for Legislative Action, wanted to interview me as soon as possible. *I guess I am in the running.*

Cassidy would never be accused of having a rural persona. A Dartmouth graduate, he epitomized the urbane establishment East, and had that easy confidence that comes from money. In his case, it rested on the solid foundation of a family-owned insurance business in Lynn, Massachusetts.

If Mike Lashbrook's office down the hall was utilitarian, Cassidy's suite on the northeast corner of the building was furnished and decorated for an executive. His wide desk was positioned to provide a good view of Scott Circle. The conference table was solid wood, not veneer. A glass-fronted gun case with several expensive shotguns locked inside made the statement that Cassidy was in fact an outdoorsman, despite his well-tailored, tropical-weight woolen suit and his precise New England manner.

Cassidy's secretary, Jackie Mongold, showed me to the comfortable Queen Anne chair in front of his desk, and as soon as I sat down, I led with my best rhetorical shot: "Congratulations on beating Sheriff John Buckley seven years ago. I worked for him, but had no understanding of the gun issue then."

Cassidy—who had led the Massachusetts fight against Buckley's anti-handgun crusade—smiled and offered a slight, nonverbal "touché" nod. And then his face became expressionless.

"How do you think the election is going to play out in the northeast?"

The director of the ILA was asking *me*?

"Well," I began, "as concerns guns . . ."

"Excuse me, Richard. We'll get to guns in a moment. Now I'm more interested in hearing your analysis of the overall political dynamics in what would be your region of responsibility, should you join us."

For the next ten minutes, I offered my take on politics from New Jersey to Maine. The city hall and statehouse races were usually complex, I said, feeling self-conscious doing so to the middle-aged man who had been the mayor of Lynn, Massachusetts. "Reagan Democrats are still a major factor in New Jersey and New England," I concluded. "They'll provide the swing vote in a lot of constituencies."

From reading the *American Rifleman*, I was well aware that Ronald Reagan was a valued NRA ally, and that the loyalty was longstanding and mutual. Republicans had told me that the NRA's endorsement of Reagan in North Carolina in the 1976 Republican primary—an unexpected win—kept his presidential ambitions alive during Jimmy Carter's single term.

That key Reagan primary victory had obviously influenced Carter in the 1976 debates with Jerry Ford. He told moderator Barbara Walters, "I have been a hunter all my life and happen to own both shotguns, rifles, and a handgun." He went on to echo the NRA's credo that law-abiding citizens should be allowed to own guns.

And the Democrats' 1976 campaign platform affirmed "the right of sportsmen to possess guns for pure hunting and target-shooting purposes." But their 1984 platform shifted to the left, focusing on the manufacture, transport, and shipment of "snub-nosed handguns, which have no legitimate sporting use and are used in a high proportion of violent crimes." The plank ignored the fact that millions of Americans depended on such handguns for home defense. So, by choosing this approach, the Democrats probably drove a significant number of blue-collar handgun owners into Reagan's camp—and probably toward joining the NRA.

Sensing an opportunity, the Republican Party used their next two national platforms to curry favor with gun-owning voters. The 1980 gun rights plank proclaimed: "We believe the right to keep and bear arms must be preserved. Accordingly, we oppose federal registration of firearms." The platform urged mandatory sentences for convicted armed felons and for reversal of the more onerous provisions of the Gun Control Act of 1968. The gun rights plank in 1984 echoed this language, and both could have been crafted at the NRA's headquarters.

Not so coincidentally, in the 1980 presidential campaign, the ILA targeted critical swing states like West Virginia with almost 1 million postcards endorsing Ronald Reagan. After Reagan won, then ILA director Neal Knox had let the Republicans know that they'd been the beneficiaries of this campaign, which had happened beneath the radar of most traditional political pundits.

Bill Clinton was one politician who came to recognize the electoral clout of the NRA. Running for a second term as Arkansas governor in 1982, Clinton had submitted an NRA political preference chart questionnaire of the type that the special interest organizations routinely ask candidates to complete to assess their views on key issues. The ILA called Clinton to announce that his questionnaire did not pass muster. Clinton immediately changed it, telling Cassidy directly, "I am in support of the NRA position on gun control." The NRA gave him an "A" rating.

In 1983, Reagan had been the keynote speaker at the organization's annual meeting in Phoenix, an appearance that had come just two years after he had been severely wounded in an assassination attempt.

He told the overflow crowd in the convention center: "No group does more to promote gun safety and respect for the laws of the land than the NRA." Reagan proceeded to detail how his administration was cracking down on "career criminals," noting that, "locking them up and throwing away the key is the best gun control law we could ever have." The crowd cheered wildly. There was no doubt that the president was with us.

I finished my political review of the northeast region with a quick summary of districts where local pro–gun rights candidates were running.

"That was a very well-reasoned, practical description," Cassidy said.

"Well," I answered, "I see politics as the art of the practical."

"Good, Richard," Cassidy said. "Because we prefer hiring people without a lot of ideological baggage or rigid opinions. It's a given that we're all dedicated to the cause of the Second Amendment, but in politics, a sound grasp of both strategy and tactics is essential."

He did not have to mention Neal Knox, his predecessor, but the unspoken name hung in the air. We might have been discussing the theological difference between High Church Protestants and Pentecostal fundamentalists. In this regard, Warren Cassidy was a Second Amendment Presbyterian elder, and Neal Knox was Elmer Gantry.

"Richard," Cassidy added, "you'll probably hear the expression, 'Never give an inch,' around here concerning our position on the Second Amendment. But just remember this: never be afraid to give an apple for the orchard."

I got the message. Clearly, Knox and his allies would rather see the orchard burned to the ground than even consider a tactical compromise.

We chatted a while about Republican politicians and officials of mutual acquaintance. He seemed impressed that I'd known Andrew Card in Boston, long before his White House days.

"Mr. Cassidy," I said, shaking his hand at the end of the interview, "I really am the best candidate for the job."

He didn't seem taken aback by my bold show of confidence.

By that night, I'd solicited letters of recommendation from John McClaughry, Andy Card, and Senator Robert Stafford of Vermont.

Two days passed with no word, the weekend came, and by Wednesday of the next week I was dejected, sure that Richard Gardiner's prediction had been accurate: The ILA already had filled the job openings before I had interviewed.

I was sitting in my hutch back at Commerce that morning when Mike Lashbrook called. "We'd like to offer you the job, Richard. Can you come in to talk about it?"

A wave of relief and excitement rose inside me. Then I suddenly thought of practical matters. "Of course," I managed in an even tone.

"But I have to prepare for the D.C. bar exam next month, so I won't be ready to report for duty until early August."

"That's no problem," he assured me.

As soon as Lashbrook hung up I called Paul Mollica. "Paulie, you will not fuckin' *believe* this. I got the job. I'm going to work for the NRA!"

●　　●　　●

Although I was enthusiastic about the actual job, I found the title, "State Liaison, Institute for Legislative Action," a little on the blah side. From my experience, liaison people tended to be paper-pushers, like the faceless ranks of middle management "coordinators." I intended to be out front, to become personally involved with the NRA's activist members in my states. When they thought of the association, I wanted them to picture me.

The salary offered was my other problem. The total compensation package came to just under $30,000. I was already making that much at Commerce, and I expected a better salary in the private sector. But Mike Lashbrook pointed out the travel benefits that included a generous per diem allowance and virtually endless frequent flyer miles. The only restraint on airlines, he added, was that "we don't fly People Express." Because that airline would not allow passengers to send unloaded firearms in their checked luggage, which was permitted under federal "red tag" regulations, it was an enemy of the NRA.

Mike also subtly alluded to the NRA's ethos of dedicated service to the cause of the Second Amendment rather than motivation grounded mainly on salary. "You can make a lot more money as a K-Street lobbyist," he said, pointing to the south. "In this building, nobody's getting rich, from the eighth floor down. But you'll never have as much . . . *influence* elsewhere."

I was pretty sure he'd intended to say "power," but had chosen a milder word because I was still an unknown.

Once more, we shook hands. "I look forward to coming to work."

That night, I called my parents in Long Island to tell them about my new job. "It's a real opportunity," I said.

"Oh, Richard," my mother answered. "Why leave a good position with the government to go to work for *them*?"

It was as if she couldn't bring herself to say the words National Rifle Association, as if I'd just announced I was going to work as a lobbyist for the Ku Klux Klan.

• • •

The ILA had never simultaneously hired three new state and local reps, so Mike Lashbrook decided to put us through our orientation and training together. The "Three Musketeers," as we inevitably were called, were all about the same age. And we were all Gung Ho.

Rick Manning was responsible for much of the South, from the Carolinas to Texas. He had a cum laude degree in political science from the University of Southern California. Manning came to the NRA with considerable experience mobilizing volunteers for candidates and for legislation in his native California. He had been the deputy campaign manager with George Young & Associates, the political consultants hired by the NRA to run its successful battle against California's Proposition 15 referendum in 1982.

Defeating Proposition 15 had been among the NRA's most important recent victories. Then San Francisco mayor Feinstein had been one of the major proponents of a handgun "freeze" referendum, which would have blocked the sale of new weapons while allowing owners to keep the guns they had. The key to the referendum winning was to convince voters that this was a freeze and not a ban that would lead to confiscation. The NRA sought to undercut this interpretation.

The association, Rick Manning told me, had "thrown all its resources" into the fight because, if they lost in California, the freeze movement would spread nationwide. Manning and his colleagues, following the George Young/NRA party line, shaped the debate on an emotional issue: the law-abiding citizen's right to self-defense against ruthless criminals.

One particularly effective George Young & Associates television commercial showed an elderly woman cringing in bed to the sound of breaking glass. Her 911 call is met with a busy signal. The ad ends with a close-up of her bedroom doorknob turning. The NRA managed to bulldoze through the complex provisions of the referendum and play on people's most basic emotion—fear. The sheriffs of every county except Los Angeles were united behind the NRA position.

On Election Day 1982, California voters rejected Proposition 15 by a margin of 63 percent to 37 percent. Harlon Carter joined gun activists at a celebration that night in Los Angeles. "We haven't talked them out of it," he proclaimed, "but if they try, we'll beat them. This is the kind of message that legislators all over the United States will understand because the people have spoken."

Indeed they had. Rick Manning told me that the NRA had registered more than three hundred thousand new voters at California gun stores alone. They all voted "no" on Proposition 15—and many also became NRA members. And the message spread beyond California in the next two years—no other state had attempted such ambitious gun control legislation since 1982.

Chuck Cunningham's background also qualified him to represent the NRA territory from the mid-Atlantic states to the Midwest. He was a hefty guy, with a neatly trimmed beard and a soft Virginia accent, proud of his Southern heritage. Chuck had become what we then called a Movement conservative while a student at James Madison University and had assumed leadership of Virginia's Young Americans for Freedom after graduation. That had led to lobbyist positions with several right-to-work organizations opposed to closed union shops.

I was the only lawyer in the group and had more diverse political campaign and legislative experience in my region than the other two did. I was also a couple years older than they were and felt at least as qualified as them. But that optimism wasn't shared universally on the seventh floor. Mike Lashbrook had introduced me to Paul Blackman, Ph.D. Blackman was an analytical genius with crime data, and ILA staffers fondly nicknamed him "Doctor Death." He was responsible for cherry-picking gun-ownership and criminal-violence statistics, which made our Fact Pack brochures so convincing. Like me, Blackman was Jewish. But he was dour and solitary, whereas I was outgoing and sociable, or so I liked to think.

After we shook hands, Blackman appraised me coldly. "You're from New York. You're a lawyer. And you're Jewish . . . That's three strikes to start with," he said, then turned and walked away.

But the rest of my colleagues weren't so negative about my background or profession—although Chuck Cunningham liked to tease me about my *Noo Yow-akk* accent: "Hey, Richie, How R *ya?*"

I learned that my territory, especially New Jersey, New York, and Massachusetts, was considered a lost cause, a political wasteland that the gun control zealots had captured years earlier and held ever since. Lashbrook and Cassidy hoped that my personal experience in the region's bare-knuckle politics would help the association regain at least some ground. I knew I could do better than that.

Our first training sessions were with the ILA's Public Education Division. This office published a bimonthly informational tabloid, the *Monitor*, a free publication for members interested in state, local, and national gun issues.

The division also coordinated press releases and acted as the media fire brigade whenever an emergency arose, such as the shooting of any celebrity like John Lennon or the pope.

"We've carefully worked out our positions on *all* these issues," said division director Johnny Aquilino, passing around sample news releases.

We began our formal media classes, starting with basic structural analyses of newspapers, radio, and television outlets in our areas. Then we moved on to these media's past record on the gun control issue and where they might be headed in the future.

"You're not going to make a dent in the *New York Times*," Johnny told me. "But the *Post* will run a pro-gun story if you pitch it right."

I made a note of that.

I also noted that Johnny's shop were masters at pitching our gun rights message. They had orchestrated the highly effective "I'm the NRA" print media advertising campaign that had been running for more than a year. Each ad featured an appealing, mainstream man or woman association member, confidently facing the camera with their firearm prominently in view. More than 200 million Americans had seen these ads. There was a black Revolutionary War reenactor holding a replica musket, a young marksmanship champion, a rock-steady state trooper, several hunters . . . and my favorite: Diane Goldstein, a sexy Missouri police officer in a well-cut uniform.

"Jewish, beautiful, *and* she likes guns," I joked, studying the page. "Where was she the last time I got pulled over for speeding?"

Next, we moved into practical media training. Although I was fascinated by the professional approach the NRA took to this important aspect of our work, Rick and Chuck found the lessons somewhat boring—irrelevant to their work as lobbyists. They assumed there'd always be professional make-up artists at any television studio where they'd speak, so why bother? But I realized a positive TV image was never an accident.

"Always think about your clothes," Johnny told us. "No wavy lines or check patterns. They strobe out the camera and distract from your message. Pastel shirts, not flat white. Solid color ties."

Using a tripod-mounted minicam, Johnny taught us how to look through the glaring lights into the lens without squinting. "Move your whole head slowly," he said, "not just your eyes. That makes you look shifty."

I took more notes. And that night, dressed in my best navy blue suit, a light blue button-collar broadcloth shirt, and a solid red tie, I stared into my bedroom mirror. "Good evening," I said confidently. "My name is Richard Feldman and I represent the National Rifle Association."

● ● ●

One important aspect of our ILA training that Mike Lashbrook shared with Johnny Aquilino was instructing us on the "preemption" issue. For several years, the NRA had been pushing legislation at the state level meant to override draconian municipal laws that virtually stripped law-abiding citizens of their Second Amendment rights. The most notorious municipal case was in the Chicago suburb of Morton Grove, which in 1981 had passed an ordinance banning the sale of handguns and their ownership by private citizens. The NRA had lost court battles against the ordinance but had distributed tens of thousands of "Morton Grove—Never Again!" bumper stickers, lapel badges, and caps. The *Monitor* and the *American Rifleman* ran repeated articles demonstrating that these gun bans, no matter how well intentioned—and which also existed in such crime-ridden communities as New York City and Washington, D.C.—did nothing to prevent violence and actually encouraged it. As ILA's representatives, we would lobby elected officials in the state capitals to enact preemption bills.

At the same time, we would help those officials move through their legislatures amendments to their states' constitutions reinforcing citizens' gun rights. To date, eight states had passed such amendments, and Mike Lashbrook had made it clear that we were expected to keep chipping away every time we met with a state senator or assembly member.

"A lot of people in Washington, especially in the media, picture Capitol Hill lobbyists when they think about the National Rifle Association," Mike told us. "That's a mistake. It's in the statehouses from Annapolis to Sacramento, from Boston to Baton Rouge, where a lot of gun laws and most administrative regulations are made, where our members' fight is won or lost. You guys are the grunts."

"Don't forget Trenton or Albany," I said. "I think I'll have to order a helmet and a flak jacket when I launch my first recon patrol up there."

●   ●   ●

Our training moved into the Information and Member Services Division, which produced a large variety and volume of material tailored for our activist membership, collectively known as "the rank and file" NRA.

One of the popular brochures that the division's director, Mary Corrigan, showed us was ILA's *The Myth of the "Saturday Night Special."* The association's position was straightforward on a pending congressional bill sponsored by Massachusetts senator Edward Kennedy and New Jersey congressman Peter Rodino calling for a national ban on handguns that were "cheap, easily concealable, unsafe, readily obtainable, nonsporting, and preferred by criminals"—not exactly a precise definition. The persuasive Fact Pack brochure presented sound academic data (thanks to Doctor Death) indicating that handguns made by well-known manufacturers were "as likely to be used in felonies such as murder and robbery as are handguns bearing less familiar brand names and selling for less than $60." Further, the ILA argued that a handgun's price and size were not related to its effectiveness as a self-defense weapon and that depriving poor people of guns to protect their homes would also deny them a constitutional right and lead to more crimes not fewer. "The majority of the 50-million handguns now held by individual Americans," the brochure stated, "are owned for the purpose of self-defense."

Almost seamlessly, the brochure led to the familiar NRA argument: banning small, cheap handguns would lead to the eventual confiscation of *every* handgun in the United States—including those owned by law-abiding citizens of all economic classes.

The last page presented an appeal to solve gun violence not "by embracing the single siren song" of bans leading to confiscation but rather by strict enforcement of existing laws and a sharp reversal of the national trend toward "revolving door" justice. "Rehabilitation," the ILA warned, "should be tempered with the realization that not all can be rehabilitated."

Here, the ILA made its direct appeal for support: "Donate to us. Work with us. We need your help."

That's a well-reasoned appeal, I thought. I would be proud to deliver this type of literature to the activists in my region.

Mary Corrigan, a skilled communications professional, was clearly devoted to the cause. "The other side calls what we do propaganda," she said. "But they've never caught us in a factual error. Out in the regions, you and your activists can count on us to back you up."

And her division's materials were in great demand. So far that year, Mary's shop had distributed multiple thousands of Fact Packs that members had requested. With the gun issue heating up as the November elections approached, the pace of the demand for reliable information was also rising.

"Here's a perennial favorite," she said, holding up a fold-over, wallet-size "NRA Firearms Fact Card." Both sides of the card were jammed with text and numbers, and at first glance, I wondered what made it so popular. Then, looking closer, I realized the fact card was a trove of information assembled in a very small space.

"Some of the state reps call it the bar card," Mary said. "Because there's enough data there to settle almost any argument about guns while having a beer with your buddies."

She was right. The first of the accordion-fold pages quoted the full Second Amendment and explained in detail that courts had repeatedly upheld the individual right to keep and bear arms.

I was fascinated by the next pages on statistical analyses of firearms ownership in the United States, their relationship to crime, and the answers citizens gave when questioned about the purposes to which they put their guns.

"One caveat," Mary said. "No one really knows the exact number of guns out there in America because nobody started even estimating their numbers until around 1930. We do know that there have been gun collectors going back to the founding of the Republic, so what we're left with is an estimate, a pretty good one, but an estimate nonetheless."

Through a combination of law-enforcement data and academic research, the NRA determined that there was a total of between 180 and 200 million firearms in the United States, with 55 to 60 million being handguns. Gun owners numbered around 60 million, with as many as 40 million of them owning at least one handgun. Between 11 and 13 percent of gun owners annually used firearms for self-defense. But annual "criminal misuse of firearms" was less than 0.2 percent of all firearms, which included 0.4 percent of handguns.

One of the most persuasive pieces of data on the card read:

> Over 99.8% of U.S. firearms and 99.6% of U.S. handguns will *not* be involved in criminal activity in any given year. Survey research suggests that about 600,000 Americans every year use handguns for protection from burglars, robbers, rapists, assailants, and would-be murderers.

The NRA had done its homework, and I knew that the association would backstop me out in the field.

"*These* are something you're going to see a lot this fall," Mary Corrigan continued, handing out red-white-and-blue bumper stickers. Inside a box near the left edge the profile of a vigilant eagle guarded the words, "I'm the NRA." Beside the box to the right, the bumper sticker proclaimed in bold letters, "and I Vote." The eagle's profile was scarlet, as was a decisive check mark beneath the word "Vote."

In closing her presentation, Mary added that member services could fill requests for NRA speakers that might arise in our regions.

Bingo! I thought. It had been Mary who'd sent Richard Gardiner up to speak in my lecture series at Vermont Law School. That had led, indirectly at least, to my sitting here in Mary's conference room, getting paid to do what I loved.

• • •

As Mike Lashbrook had noted, to many people in Washington, ILA's Governmental Affairs Division (known to us at headquarters as simply "Federal") was the big leagues, while we state and local reps played on the farm teams. I knew this wasn't true, but I also recognized most people working inside the Beltway had distorted views of their own self-importance.

The director of Federal was Wayne LaPierre. He was about my age and had come to the division from being state and local's northeast liaison (my new job) where he'd worked under Tanya Metaksa. Wayne's office was in the middle of the seventh floor corridor and had a window overlooking 16th Street.

The room was cluttered with heaps of dog-eared yellow pads, thick black binders of draft legislation, political reference books, and campaign literature. Near his desk, Wayne had a small conference table where Cunningham, Manning, and I sat to hear his briefing on Federal affairs.

My first impression of him was not favorable. His handshake was weak. He avoided our eyes, and his expression was almost furtive. Wayne clutched a stack of manila folders to the chest of his rumpled blue pinstripe suit as if for protection. He evoked the image of a harassed and absent-minded political science graduate assistant— who had 289 projects in the works, and none ever completed. This impression was not far off the mark: Wayne had been a doctoral candidate who had never finished his degree before finally leaving academia and working as a statehouse staffer in Richmond, Virginia.

From there, he'd joined the NRA, a move that was due more to his fascination with politics than any passion for guns. I'd heard that some people had qualms about him because he was not a bona fide "gunny," a person who hunted, collected firearms, or was a competitive marksman.

Ten minutes after the meeting, I couldn't remember any answer he provided to our questions about Federal's operations. He would start to speak, pause, then consult another folder, only to glance away, almost mumbling, and shift to a new subject.

This guy just doesn't have what the human resources gurus call "people skills," I thought. Which was ironic as hell, considering that I'd always been taught that successful lobbying required someone who could communicate.

Although Wayne and Mike Lashbrook were equals on the association's wiring diagram, Wayne gave the impression that he was far above minor city hall politics or statehouse hardball over preemption bills, he was preoccupied with more substantive issues.

(I later learned that Wayne was—at this stage of his professional evolution—quite shy, much more comfortable discussing obscure aspects of legislation than managing employees. He and I would soon spend amicable hours talking political minutia. It was during those relaxed bull sessions after business hours that I realized Wayne LaPierre was, like me, a true politics junkie.)

As much as Wayne was detached and seemingly unfocused, his colleague in Federal, James Jay Baker, seemed to be the quintessential hot-button Washington lobbyist. With his wavy hair and full mustache, Jim Baker fit the persona of a gentleman big game hunter, maybe Robert Redford on safari. In fact, hunting large mammals was one of the passions that had drawn him from a successful career as a prosecutor in Missouri to the office of the general counsel at the NRA: invitations to hunt on exclusive property were one of his job's perks.

But he was more interested in being a lobbyist than sifting the legal gibberish that the association's lawyers dealt with daily. I could appreciate that. And working in Federal also gave Jim Baker visibility, bolstering his image. From my days as a bouncer at Lucifer's disco in Boston, I could recognize a party animal. A bachelor, Jim wore well-cut suits and favored the bright suspenders—braces, he called them—then in fashion. He chain-smoked at his desk and avoided lunch in the noisy Formica gym of the eighth-floor cafeteria. Instead, Jim often ate down the block at the Jefferson Hotel.

He had an air of authority that I'd found lacking in Wayne LaPierre. Jim was savvy, good-looking, and confident as hell.

He was friendly and seemed sincerely interested in hearing about the work I'd be doing.

One afternoon, I asked Jim for a more-focused briefing on Federal's priorities than what Wayne had given us in our initial meeting.

"You're going to be hearing the words 'Volkmer-McClure' until you get sick of them," he said with an insider's assurance. "We've bet a lot of chips on those cards."

I was confused. I'd followed the Capitol Hill seesaw over a bill known as the "McClure-Volkmer Firearms Owners' Protection Act" that been pending in Congress for five years. But, once more, the NRA had its own nomenclature. Instead of following tradition and calling the legislation by its Senate sponsor, Idaho Republican James A. McClure, the association always first cited House sponsor, Representative Harold L. Volkmer, the Democrat from central Missouri who'd introduced the bill in the House.

Jim explained why. Anticipating a tough reelection race in 1980, Volkmer had sought the help of the NRA in identifying an issue he could use in the campaign to win the support of the many people in his district interested in maintaining their constitutional gun rights— and in regaining many of those lost in the ambitious "reforms" embodied in the Gun Control Act of 1968.

"The '68 GCA is filled with onerous, duplicative, and sweeping provisions, Rich," Jim Baker said. "It does nothing to keep guns out of the hands of criminals while it simultaneously tramples the Second Amendment rights of law-abiding citizens—including our members."

Jim laid out the latest incarnation of the NRA's position paper on Volkmer-McClure. He'd highlighted points with a blue ballpoint. "Here's what the new legislation does."

The paper's introduction presented a well-reasoned argument that tolerating the quashing of one civil liberty—the right to buy, sell, and transport arms—had inevitably led to the erosion of other rights—not just in the United States, but also abroad, especially in Nazi Germany and the Soviet Union.

And the Gun Control Act of 1968 certainly did limit several basic aspects of gun ownership and use. But the language of the act was so vague in places that state and local law enforcement was obliged to form its own interpretation of federal law.

This often led to abuses. As Harlon Carter had commented on the "damnable" 1968 law, it restricted interstate sale of firearms except between FFL holders. The GCA also had ill-defined sections regulating persons "engaged in the business" of buying and selling firearms and was muddled about private firearms sales involving what we called "kitchen table" dealers and the quasi-professionals who supplemented their regular incomes by selling at gun shows. Under the GCA, private dealers had had their homes ransacked by the BATF's agents or local law enforcement searching for contraband. Often, valuable gun collections never intended for sale had been confiscated and retained as "evidence."

"Transporting your firearms is also a big problem, Rich," Jim said. "I'm a hunter, and I'm a lawyer, *and* I work in this building, and even so, I sometimes get mixed up."

He explained that driving with your shotgun—unloaded and locked in the trunk of your car—across state lines could lead to a warrantless police search, your arrest, confiscation of your gun, and possible jail time. "New Jersey troopers on the turnpike are notorious for stopping and searching cars during the hunting season. Guys headed for the Maryland Eastern Shore to shoot geese, deer hunters on their way to Pennsylvania. It's getting like the Gestapo up there, especially for people with NRA decals on their windows."

"Jeeze," I cracked, "I *knew* there was a reason I preferred shooting clay pigeons in Virginia."

I studied the paper. Once more, the NRA's talking points were convincing. Volkmer-McClure would redress real inequities.

Each of several staccato paragraphs began: "A fair firearms law will . . ."

Among the most important sections in Volkmer-McClure was the call for mandatory prison sentences for those who used firearms in criminal acts, balanced by a stringent "proof of criminal intent" before prosecuting a person who inadvertently violated one of the myriads, overlapping provisions of the 1968 GCA.

"Well," I said. "*I'm* convinced."

"The key to winning this fight is going to be convincing enough members of Congress to pass the bill," Jim said. "That hasn't happened yet. The Democrats control both houses and have got all the key committees locked down. When Volkmer and McClure reintroduce their bill each session, they get unofficial word from the committee staff to save their collective breath."

●   ●   ●

We moved on from ILA divisions to other branches of the NRA. One of the more important was the Field Services Division, which supported the association's traditional marksmanship, firearms safety, and law-enforcement training programs. Field Services was run by Dick Cox, a big, gruff former California undercover narcotics officer who had infiltrated and ridden with the Hell's Angels. Behind his back ILA staffers who didn't like Cox called him "Penis-Penis" as much for his manner as for his unfortunate name. He made it clear from the beginning that he had to tolerate us but he didn't have to like us. To him we were the punk kids at ILA who got more money to spend than he did.

Cox's deputy, Tony Madda, had been a Marine sergeant major ("You're never a 'former' Marine," he made a point of telling us). He also said that it would be best if we steered clear of his field services reps in our regions while we were out there "jerking off the politicians." Although he didn't go into detail, it was well known that his reps were often in competition with state and local reps. Much of the problem stemmed from field service representatives poaching on our turf, getting involved in politics themselves—despite Dick Cox's scorn for lobbyists. Rick Manning had already had a run-in with the field services guy in Austin, Herb Chambers, a former Texas Ranger, who figured he understood politics in the Lone Star state better than this kid from Southern California. I was lucky in this regard, especially in New York and New Jersey. My New York field services rep was Dick Sorrentino, a former Glen Cove, Long Island cop who knew more about New York rough-and-tumble politics than

I could ever learn. He promised to advise me when I needed it, but never to interfere. And he kept his promise. My New England rep was Bob Pemberton, who had been the Nassau County Police range officer while I was growing up. Bob was equally supportive but disliked politics almost as much as I loved it. He was all too happy to leave me alone on lobbying expeditions unless I needed him.

But the tension between ILA's State and Local Division and Field Services wasn't just about money and turf. The ILA represented the emerging "new" NRA that was much more concerned with political victory and accruing the power that accompanied it than it was about traditional marksmanship and law-enforcement training. I got the feeling that Cox and Madda would have been happy if the NRA *had* moved out of Washington in the 1970s and set up shop in Colorado and New Mexico.

● ● ●

Meeting Harlon Carter in his comfortable corner office on the eighth floor was the highlight of our welcome to the NRA. It was a muggy August morning, but the room was well air-conditioned, and the view down 16th Street to the White House spectacular.

Carter came out from behind his solid oak desk, striding in an upright posture, broad shoulders, big-domed head shaved to his trademark gray bristle, his muscular hand extended to shake. My first impression was of a tough Southwest cop, maybe an Arizona sheriff or a captain in the Texas Rangers. But his twinkling blue eyes softened his otherwise gruff features.

As we took our seats on the comfortable chairs and sofa, I noted near the door a gleaming silver trophy that Carter had won as the U.S. Border Patrol champion decades earlier. The stylized officer atop the trophy held his revolver, right arm fully extended, legs locked, which seemed a little quaint when compared to the looser, two-handed "combat stance" that contemporary marksmen had adopted.

He observed my interest—very little, I would learn, escaped his scrutiny—and smiled. "I imagine you were taught to shoot a handgun differently," he said.

"Yes, sir," I said, returning his smile. "But I never won a championship."

His laugh was mellow, paternal.

This is where the power of the NRA emanates, I thought. *From this room, from this man.*

And no one could doubt Harlon Carter's power. After becoming executive vice president in 1977, he had quashed the ambitious and wrong-headed scheme to move NRA headquarters to Colorado Springs and to establish the nearby "Outdoor Center." Instead, the association's headquarters had stayed here, and Carter had put his own stamp on the New Mexico facility. A 1980 *Rifleman* article I'd read described the center under development near Raton, New Mexico, as "the NRA's shooting and training site," and detailed the rich hunting available on the land. There was not a single mention of "conservation" in the article.

If anyone needed tangible proof that the revolt in Cincinnati had been successful, it was all right there in that *Rifleman* article.

An even more striking demonstration of Carter's vision and influence was the dramatic increase in members since 1977. When he'd taken power, membership had been just under 1 million. Today, it hovered near 3 million.

Chuck and Rick were quiet, reluctant to join in the repartee between Lashbrook and Harlon Carter, two of the architects of the new NRA. But, again, reticence had never been my strong point and I jumped right in.

With a slight nod of his blunt chin, Carter ended the small talk and looked at us each, a slow contemplative scan of our eyes. When he spoke again, his tone was formal, commanding.

"The role that you will play in the National Rifle Association is much more important than you probably now realize." He let those words linger. "The role that you will play is *vital* to this organization. You will be the link between NRA headquarters and our grassroots members, especially the activists on whom so much depends. Indeed, on whose shoulders the future of this country's Second Amendment rights depend."

I realized Carter had given this pep talk many times before, but the three of us were transfixed by his words. In this regard, Harlon Carter was like General George Patton inspiring his troops for combat—and victory. Or at least George C. Scott playing Patton so convincingly.

"You must be *inflexible* in the protection and furtherance of our fundamental right as citizens to keep and bear arms." Again, he swept us with his wise, sparkling eyes. "But you must not confuse inflexibility with rigidity. We're in this battle for the long haul. And we are in it to win."

4

VICTORIES

nterstate 95 Northbound, August 1984: Mike Lashbrook drove the Avis Chevy just above the speed limit in the right lane, letting the faster traffic pass us. When we crossed the Delaware Memorial Bridge and entered New Jersey, he slowed to a steady fifty-five. He probably wanted to use all of the three hours of our drive up from Washington to attend the Coalition of New Jersey Sportsmen to continue briefing me on the activists with whom I'd be working—and on the issues of mutual importance to the NRA and its members.

"Jersey's a fascinating state, Richard," he said. "You've got some of the most rabid anti- and staunchest pro–gun rights people in the country. The more the antigun crowd pile on the restrictive laws and ordinances, the harder the activists fight back."

He explained that gun laws in New Jersey were a patchwork of overlapping federal, state, county, and even township regulations. For example, a licensed hunter could get arrested for having hollow point shotgun slugs purchased legally in New Jersey if he stopped for coffee and wasn't therefore going "to or from" the range or field and his home. Just as Jim Baker had told me earlier, this meant marksmen traveling to competitions risked arrest and confiscation of their valuable firearms if they didn't obtain a complicated set of official documents, even though their guns were unloaded and locked in cases inside the locked trunks of their cars. Sporting clay and skeet shooters often faced the same hurdles.

"New Jersey," Mike said, "is not friendly to gun owners."

This was why preemption legislation in Trenton would be vital. This antigun climate also meant that the state's marksmen and hunters—and average citizens wanting a firearm for home defense—would benefit from the overall loosening of the more restrictive provisions of the Gun Control Act of 1968.

"Getting Volkmer-McClure passed on the Hill is a priority for our members in Jersey," Lashbrook said. "But we've got a couple of big hurdles in Washington. One is named Peter Rodino and the other William Hughes." They represented New Jersey districts in Congress.

Rodino was one of the most senior Democratic members of the House, and chairman of the Judiciary Committee that had voted to impeach Richard Nixon. Hughes had been elected in the 1974 "Watergate Class" and was also moving up the seniority ladder. He chaired the House Judiciary crime subcommittee. Both congressmen adamantly opposed Volkmer-McClure. Further, any changes to the 1968 GCA would have to pass through their committees to reach the House floor for a vote. And, because Democrats controlled the House in 1984, Rodino and Hughes were in the position to serve out an impressive amount of pork in their districts.

"But congressmen listen to voters," I said. "Especially well-organized constituents who get their message out."

"Well, Richard," Lashbrook said in his slow, methodical manner, "that's going to be part of your job."

"Yeah, I forgot about that part, Mike."

"The message, Richard," he continued. "That's the key. 'I'm the NRA and I Vote!' We've got to convince our activist members to spread that message, at their town hall meetings, American Legion posts, and local sports leagues . . . the full gamut. There's a reason we call this grassroots activism. The most important task is keeping up the pressure on their congressmen and senators: letters. We provide sample formats and text, they take over from there. Effective lobbying isn't all martini lunches and steaks. Elected officials *do* read their mail."

I watched the traffic flow by in the left two lanes, the long semitrailers roaring past us. "I assume that the text we provide is the official association line on a particular issue," I said.

"The position and language we offer members has been carefully vetted in ILA."

"That's good to know."

"But," Lashbrook added, "you'll have to watch out for extremist tendencies among some members."

I waited for Michael to continue.

"You might have already heard the term 'Knoxer,'" he said. "That's going to take some explaining because the issue is not as simple as it might seem."

"I've heard the expression, Mike. And I think I understand it."

"Well, let me give you my take."

The tutorial Mike Lashbrook now provided on the NRA's internecine conflicts confirmed a lot of the information I'd already garnered from Rick Manning. After his success helping defeat the Proposition 15 handgun freeze in California, the NRA hired Rick in 1983 as a consultant in a much less-publicized confrontation: the struggle between Harlon Carter and Neal Knox for control of the association.

Carter had been fending off opponents from the Old Guard sportsmen-conservationists on the left and Neal Knox's fire-eaters on the right for several years. At the annual members' meeting in Denver in 1979, the Old Guard, still rankled over losing the fight in Cincinnati—and even more bitter at the political direction Carter had taken the NRA since then—had tried to change the bylaws again so that the board, not the voting membership, once more elected the executive vice president. They also threatened to make public Carter's old Texas negligent homicide conviction. Carter fought back with a threat of his own. If the bylaws weren't immediately modified to allow him to serve a five-year term, he would quit then and there, leaving the old fogies holding the bag.

Carter won. He got his five years as executive vice president. The Old Guard lost more power.

But after Carter fired Neal Knox in 1982—both for his overly aggressive lobbying tactics and his shallowly submerged intrigues to gain more control of the association—Knox tried to muster enough grassroots loyalists at the 1983 Denver members' convention to regain a position of power at the NRA's headquarters. Rick Manning had worked the Harlon Carter side of that struggle for the hearts and minds of the voting members. Once more, Carter's side prevailed. Knox did not return to the eighth floor of head-quarters, but he'd assembled sufficient supporters to win a seat on the board.

Knox could not restrain his zealous absolutism, however. In the 1983–1984 congressional sessions, the NRA backed a version of Volkmer-McClure that Knox viewed as a "compromise." Even though Neal Knox was probably the best-known member of the NRA's board of directors, he adopted the guise of a concerned private citizen and went to the Hill to lobby against the bill. This was too much for Carter and Cassidy. At the January 1984 board meeting, Knox's fellow members voted to expel him, the first time this harsh measure had been found necessary.

Warren Cassidy had commented that Knox had "sown dissention, confusion and distrust among friends and allies."

"The eighth floor figured it was time to fight fire with fire," Rick Manning had explained.

"Maybe," I'd replied. "But you know what they say about old Abdul the Camel Driver. It's better to have him inside the tent, pissing out than outside the tent, pissing in."

●   ●   ●

As we moved up the Jersey Turnpike, I finished telling Mike what I'd learned so far about the power struggles involving Neal Knox. I added that Warren Cassidy had advised me to be prepared to give up an apple to save the orchard—and that I figured Knox would rather see the orchard a heap of smoldering ashes than compromise.

"You're getting the picture, Richard."

"How does all this play in my region?"

"State and local need grassroots unity on all the important battles," he said. "If our activists are at each other's throats, word gets out to elected officials: governors, state assemblymen, mayors, city council members, and eventually congressmen . . . they'll see us as divided and ineffective. We need tangible victory—like passage of

Volkmer-McClure and success on other issues—so that the politicians continue to take the association seriously."

"And the Knoxers don't get the message?"

"Remember Warren's burning orchard, Richard. And be very careful of the Knoxers in your region. They'll shake your hand and then reach over your shoulder to stab you in the back."

"Can't tell the players without a program, Mike," I said.

"Okay," he began. "Here in New Jersey, Rodger Iverson, chairman of the coalition, a really good guy, a natural leader, a strong supporter of Harlon and Cassidy. You can trust him." Mike added several other Jersey activists to the "good guy" roster. And then he got to Bob MacKinnon, the coalition treasurer. "Watch him. He's a Knoxer."

●   ●   ●

That fall after visiting all my region's activists, I told Rick Manning and Chuck Cunningham about the situation I'd found. "It's what I've started calling 'Byzanknox,'" I said. "Or maybe this whole deal is happening in 'Knoxantium.'" We got a laugh out of these lame witticisms.

But we also recognized that a bitter struggle was under way. And I would soon understand just how much of a challenge to the strategic goals of the association's leaders the zealotry of Knox and his disciples represented. To a large degree, Harlon Carter had solidified his and the NRA's national power by steadily increasing membership—recruited mainly from the moderate middle classes. But when fire-eaters like Knox and his brethren spoke about the absolute right of every citizen to buy and sell full-auto machine guns—one of their favorite topics—potential dues-paying members were scared off.

It wasn't so much the lost dues that mattered; by now the association had accumulated a nice cash flow. And contrary to the conventional news media view of the NRA's role in American politics, I would soon understand that grassroots activism either in support of or opposition to candidates was more important to politicians than the direct campaign contributions from the association's legendary "war chest" (the Political Victory Fund PAC).

The NRA needed to talk the Second Amendment talk to pacify its own right wing. But the association also had to walk the walk of responsible firearms ownership to continue attracting new members from the untapped veins of suburbia.

• • •

As the turnpike traffic thickened approaching northern New Jersey, Mike discussed other recent problems—several still unresolved—that the NRA had worked on with the activists.

"We continue to catch all kinds of hell in the media over the phony 'Cop-Killer Bullet' issue," he said. "Frankly, the ILA hasn't handled things very well." He paused. "And we're in danger of losing our traditional allies in law enforcement if we don't watch it. This is all confidential, of course, and you didn't hear any criticism of my colleagues from me. But you've got to know the score to function well."

In other words, don't speak your mind unless you know and trust the person to whom you're speaking. I would soon learn an important insider axiom: "At the NRA, we all have Second Amendment—but very limited First Amendment—rights."

The entire matter was poorly understood but extremely emotional, Mike explained.

In January 1982, NBC broadcast a prime-time news special provocatively titled "Cop-Killer Bullets." The show presented a sensationalized account of a new type of handgun ammunition that easily penetrated law-enforcement officers' "bulletproof" vests. These bullets were made of ultrahard metals and were "Teflon-coated," ostensibly to separate and slide through the densely woven Kevlar fibers of body armor that conventional soft lead slugs could not pierce. And many viewers came away from the show with the strong impression that this bizarre ammunition had been specifically engineered to kill cops.

A public outcry arose to outlaw the bullets. As the media bandwagon began to roll, several influential members of Congress hopped on board. They included Representative Mario Biaggi, a New York Democrat and highly decorated NYPD veteran—and former ally of the NRA—who'd been twice wounded on the streets. He began to work on a sweeping bill to ban the "cop-killer" ammunition. New Jersey representative William Hughes joined Biaggi as a co-sponsor.

But public understanding of the issue was muddled. The bullets were officially called KTW handgun ammunition and had been developed in the 1970s by an Ohio coroner, Dr. Paul Kopsch; police sergeant Daniel Turcos; and Kopsch's special investigator, Donald Ward—the acronym being based on their last names. They were searching for handgun bullets that would penetrate "hard" targets such as the safety glass of windshields and doors of criminals' vehicles. It took a decade of experimentation, but by 1981 they had produced a solid bullet of hardened brass alloy. In standard police handgun calibers, KTW bullets pierced safety glass and metal. But the projectiles were so hard that they quickly wore out handgun barrels. The Teflon coating solved that problem, but, despite media hype, had absolutely no effect on the bullet's penetration qualities. Under rigorous control, KTW bullets were sold to the military and law enforcement beginning in 1981.

One fact was true, however: a KTW version of a .380, .38, 9 mm, or .45 ACP bullet typical of most handgun calibers *could* penetrate almost all standard soft body armor vests.

"But of course that was only half the story," Mike said. "What about rifles?"

Virtually *any* of the literally thousands of calibers and shapes of perfectly legal rifle bullets—from a .223 to a .375 Winchester—that marksmen and hunters fired, moved at much higher velocities than handgun bullets, and could rip through police vests.

But the bill that Biaggi had introduced in the House, written by antigun staffers with little knowledge of firearms, focused on the penetration performance of the projectile. It would ban all bullets capable of being fired from five-inch handgun barrels that could pierce "18 layers" of the Kevlar fabric found in the most common police vests. The language of the bill was technically inaccurate and legally vague, which meant the proposed ban could also be applied to most rifle ammunition.

"And probably to some BB guns as well," Mike quipped.

Firearms experts from almost every federal law-enforcement agency—including the FBI and the BATF—testified that the Biaggi bill would be impossible to enforce. The NRA's position "seemed" straightforward, Mike explained. The association recognized the technical flaws in the Biaggi bill. But rather than "compromise" by working to correct the bill's faults and focus it instead on keeping KTW bullets away from civilians (and the criminal black market), and at the same time protecting the rights of millions of rifle-owning hunters and marksmen, the NRA rejected the entire bill in its draft stage.

This approach exacerbated the legislation's flaws. The association capitalized on this, through repeated scornful ILA updates to the membership that mocked the technical incompetence of the bill's drafters while warning that the KTW ban was yet another attempt to deprive citizens of their Second Amendment rights and by "grabbing" their hunting and target-shooting ammunition. One alarming message to members—which doubled as a fund-raising appeal— called the "'cop-killer' bullet issue a Trojan Horse waiting outside gun owners' doors. If the antigunners have their way, this highly publicized and emotionalized issue will be used to enact a backdoor, national gun control scheme."

The campaign against the Biaggi bill began while Neal Knox was still executive director of the ILA, and the issue seemed ready-made for his burn-the-orchard political tactics. The NRA wasn't going to cooperate with Biaggi and Hughes to salvage their unsound legislation.

Instead, the association began working with veteran Texas Democratic congressman Jack Brooks (a longtime NRA friend from Beaumont) on a bill that carefully defined the exact characteristics of armor-piercing handgun projectiles as opposed to legitimate target shooting or hunting ammunition—and banned the sale of actual KTW-type bullets to civilians. The "Brooks substitute" bill quickly gained two hundred sponsors on both sides of the House aisle and was supported by the NRA, many law-enforcement groups, and the Reagan administration.

But reacting to media pressure, state and local governments had quickly drafted and enacted simplistic legislation banning the sale of virtually any bullet capable of piercing police vests—including target and hunting ammunition. The NRA worked at the state and local level, trying to redefine "armor piercing" ammunition while simultaneously helping craft language for federal legislation to prevent the criminal abuse of these bullets. This bread-and-butter lobbying had proven effective in fourteen states—including California, Illinois, and New Jersey—and was pending introduction in state legislatures throughout the rest of the country. But while the NRA was winning the "inside baseball" legislative battles, it was losing the perception war in the media and among the average uninformed middle-of-the-road public.

In Washington, the dueling Biaggi and Brooks bills slowly made their way through the House. And rather than work with the media to explain our position, we "took our hits" and kept the membership abreast of the antigunners' dirty tactics. The NRA's plan, Mike said, was to emerge as the champion of both its traditional supporters in law enforcement and the hunters and marksmen members.

But with the Biaggi and Brooks substitute bills stalled in committee, Biaggi managed to accrue increasing support among urban police organizations, particularly the chiefs and commissioners—the political appointees of the mayors.

"Nobody figured on the cops jumping ship," Mike said. After all, Biaggi was a former officer who long stood at the side of the NRA. "Heck," Mike said. "We used to support him—ask Jerry Preiser."

Gerald Preiser was the president of the Federation of New York State Rifle and Pistol Clubs, a true pro-gun insider in Manhattan.

But the ILA apparently had ignored the fact that it had been the New York police union that had urged their ex-colleague Biaggi to introduce the bill. Predictably, headlines such as "NRA Opposes Cop Killer Bullet Ban" soon appeared nationwide. And even while the association was working behind the scenes to fine-tune the Brooks substitute legislation, the message wasn't getting out, and police—especially senior officials—across the country were souring on the NRA over this issue.

"And nobody on the top two floors at headquarters seems to be paying enough attention to this problem," Lashbrook said.

"It's complicated," I replied. "It seems that we—the association—have to strike the proper balance in a situation like this."

"Almost *every* situation we're facing is complex and requires a sophisticated approach, Richard," he said. "ILA is less than ten years old and we haven't had that much organized resistance so far. But all that's changing, and we're going to have to mature or the antigun crowd will start eating our lunch."

I must have looked skeptical because Mike elaborated. "Up until now, the antigun councils and coalitions have been weak, short of members, and poorly organized. But the situation won't stay static." He thought for a moment. "And we can't give them freebie issues like cop-killer bullets to gain traction in the media and in Congress."

Mike described the two national antigun rights organizations that had the most potential to hurt us, *if* we didn't pay more attention to them. They were Handgun Control, Inc., and the National Coalition to Ban Handguns. Both groups had some permanent national structure, as well as shifting ad hoc alliances with like-minded state affiliates.

Handgun Control, Inc. (HCI), began as the National Council to Control Handguns in 1974, launched by a victim of criminal gun violence, Dr. Mark Borinsky. He had been mugged as a university student in Chicago, and then came to Washington to found the council. In 1975, the group's leadership passed to a DuPont corporate executive named Nelson "Pete" Shields III, whose oldest son had been shot to death in 1974 during the notorious black-extremist Zebra murder spree in San Francisco. Pete Shields was a very compelling and increasingly media-savvy antigun advocate. He retired from DuPont and in 1980 changed the organization's name to Handgun Control, Inc. In 1983, the group created a tax-exempt educational outreach affiliate, the Center to Prevent Handgun Violence. Sarah Brady, wife of Ronald Reagan's press secretary, Jim Brady, who was maimed in the assassination attempt on the president, was becoming more visibly involved with HCI.

"This cop-killer bullet myth is an issue HCI can take to the bank," Mike said. "Literally."

Although their dues-paying membership was only a few hundred thousand, HCI's out-front media prominence, which defied the NRA on such an emotional issue, bolstered their support from liberal groups and left-wing foundations.

Individual philanthropic and foundation support also provided the daily sustenance of the NRA's other major nemesis in the mid-1980s, the National Coalition to Ban Handguns (NCBH). Its roots also in left-wing politics ran deeper than HCI's. The coalition's driving force was an ex-congressional staffer named Michael K. Beard who had cut his activist teeth during the radical turbulence of the 1960s and 1970s. (His coalition bio sheet noted that he'd worked with World Federalist Youth–USA but did not cite his leadership of New Right Watch, which had evolved into the coalition.)

The organization's official goal was "banning the importation, manufacture, sale, transfer, ownership and possession of handguns." Obviously, achieving these policy objectives would entail draconian enforcement measures: nationwide handgun registration and licensing leading ultimately to confiscation. All this was anathema to the NRA, and probably to millions of other nonmember handgun owners who saw their weapons as the principal tool of home defense.

But Beard's organization went further by attacking the basic legal foundation of the Second Amendment. Like others before him, Beard had testified that the amendment established a collective, not an individual right to "keep and bear arms." This was more than anathema to the NRA. It was sacrilege.

But until the mid-1980s, such extremist positions, visibly connected to left-liberal groups of the 1970s, was useful to the association. The very name National Coalition to *Ban* Handguns probably helped keep up the NRA's membership. After all, if celebrity left-wingers like Judy Collins and assorted Christian and Jewish social-activist organizations were sponsoring Beard's coalition, it would probably not find many backers among middle-class political moderates.

"But they *are* slowly growing," Mike Lashbrook said. "And we can't let them grab onto an issue like 'cop-killer' bullets and run with it."

That was not the only highly charged issue that the two large antigun organizations were gnawing at with some success in the media, in Congress, and in many statehouses. The case for and against waiting periods for buying handguns from a licensed dealer had a long history. Under the Gun Control Act of 1968, dealers had to require all buyers to complete a BATF Form 4473 that certified they weren't convicted felons or hadn't been adjudged insane. In many states—as in Vermont where I bought my Model 15 .38 revolver in the Snowsville General Store in East Randolph—this simple procedure was all that was required.

But several other states had laws establishing waiting periods that lasted anywhere from five to fifteen days, between the payment for the handgun, completion of the Form 4473, and when the buyer could legally take possession. Supposedly, such "cooling-off" periods reduced handgun violence by stopping people from buying a firearm when their anger rendered them irrational or when, on the spur of the moment, they planned an armed assault. California, Mike said, had the most stringent waiting periods in America. In 1923, the California Legislature imposed a one-day waiting period, which was increased to three days in 1955, five days in 1965—when 1960s gun-crime paranoia erupted—and to fifteen days in 1975.

But these waiting periods had no significant impact on gun violence, including murder rates. Like the rest of the country, California's murder statistics waxed and waned, but certainly had never declined significantly in proportion to the increasing length of waiting periods.

"So much for 'getting guns off the street,'" Mike said. "Our members know that criminals don't buy guns from licensed dealers. *We* know this, too. But the antigunners are beginning to body-punch us in the media, claiming we ignore crime by opposing waiting periods."

The ILA's official position was that waiting periods infringed on Second Amendment rights, did not reduce crime, and were an insidious step toward gun registration and eventual confiscation.

Permits to carry handguns were another contentious subject. Cities like New York, Boston, Chicago, and San Francisco had very strict "carry" permit regulations. In theory, law-abiding citizens (like the Portuguese immigrant shopkeeper on my Cambridge beat) had the right to apply for a handgun license. The same right existed in principle for Hassidic diamond dealers in Brooklyn or California pawnshop owners—all of whom needed handguns for self-defense against armed predators. But, like the Cambridge shopkeeper, few permits were ever issued to these people.

In New York City, for example, a wealthy and politically influential figure like former mayor John Lindsay could readily obtain a handgun carry permit. But for the average person seeking a permit allowing him to carry a gun in his home or on the street was almost futile. The permit office was only open for limited, inconvenient hours and the red tape required for the process was Kafkaesque. This system kept guns out of the hands of the law-abiding but did nothing to prevent criminals from getting the weapons they sought.

"But the handgun control crowd is telling the media that the NRA wants to abolish carry permits and turn the streets into war zones," Mike said. "This is another one we're going to have to watch."

•   •   •

The coalition dinner meeting that evening was held at the Coach and Four Restaurant in Hightstown. Before the formal gathering, Mike and I conferred with Rodger Iverson and other coalition officers.

Iverson was more than just the "good guy" that Mike had described. Tall and husky with a trimmed mustache, he had a solid, unflappable presence. *This man's a real leader*, I thought. I knew that Iverson was well off, a self-made, self-educated owner of a successful construction business—who also liked to hunt and firmly believed that the NRA protected all Americans' Second Amendment rights.

That evening we discussed Volkmer-McClure and increasingly restrictive New Jersey gun control laws pending in Trenton—the subject of NRA preemption law lobbying—and the prospects for state political campaigns.

"Rodino and Hughes are probably shoe-ins," I said.

"Certainly *this year*," Iverson said. "But Rodino's getting old, and Hughes could be vulnerable by '86." He then proceeded to give an insightful summary of the New Jersey political landscape. Iverson could have been a poli-sci professor at Princeton. Instead, he was a rough-hewn businessman with a passion for gun rights.

I hope I've got more people like this elsewhere in my region.

•   •   •

The 1984 campaign heated up that September. At "1600" (NRA headquarters named for our address on Rhode Island Avenue), the Three Musketeers, Lashbrook, and Wayne LaPierre had several long sessions that completed the political preference charts for each congressional, governor's, or statehouse race in our regions. These meetings doubled as practical mentoring. Most of the candidates had completed detailed questionnaires, which well-paid consultants and gut logic told us would reveal the politician's true feelings about Second Amendment rights, Volkmer-McClure, and the other priority issues we faced that year.

We fledgling state reps were taught that very few politicians ignored the NRA's campaign questionnaires.

"It's not just that we've got money in the Political Victory Fund to back the opposition candidate," Mike said as we sat around the seventh-floor conference table with our paperwork spread around us. "Our local activists can get out the vote, depending on who we endorse. Politicians know this."

Wayne LaPierre, sitting at the head of the table, explained the key dynamics. "In a good election year, you might get 50 percent of registered voters to the polls. But if you motivate *a hundred* percent of NRA members to vote following our lead, we can make a real difference in races." He paused and looked toward me. "Richie, we've got over seventy thousand members in New Jersey. They read *American Rifleman* or *American Hunter* and know the issues. Every member will receive a political preference chart in the mail, listing all the races and the grades we've given the candidates. Local activists take it from there."

The charts would be mailed to members in October in envelopes emblazoned with a wide burgundy band: "ELECTION ALERT . . . Please open immediately." Several states would receive a "Special Insert" on key congressional and Senate races. The chart I received as a Virginia member, for example, backed incumbent Republican senator John Warner as a staunch Second Amendment defender.

In the New Jersey races, Rodger Iverson and I had already discussed where to concentrate our members' energy. And I was on the road at least four days a week, connecting to the NRA's activist leaders to plan similar campaign efforts. I was determined to show that the northeast region was not in fact the lost cause that many people in the building considered it to be.

When it came time to discuss my region, we looked at Vermont as an example of a small state that had a strong gun rights record, which both Republicans and Democrats supported. Each NRA chart's standard first page defined the report card–style grading system, with A on top and F at the bottom; "?," "letter," or "refused" indicated that a candidate's gun rights position was unknown, he or she had not completed the NRA's questionnaire but instead responded with a letter explaining his or her position, or the candidate had refused to take part.

A candidate we graded A was "Solidly pro-gun, pro-sportsman, opposed to any more controls on firearms or legislation restricting hunting."

The grades fell as candidates' gun rights positions weakened. A politician graded B was "Basically on our side, but might vote for some form of additional restrictions." Candidates rated C "would probably vote in favor of more restrictive controls such as registration and/or licensing but *not* in favor of banning the private possession of handguns."

A politician who drew a D would "definitely" vote for restrictive gun control and against hunters' rights. The lowest letter grade, F, went to candidates who favored the most restrictive "prohibitive legislation or would vote for *banning* handguns, all firearms or hunting, and/or accepted a campaign contribution from Handgun Control, Inc."

In Vermont, the state's single incumbent congressman, Republican Jim Jeffords, received a question mark ("?") grade but also a symbol denoting that Handgun Control, Inc., had contributed to his campaign. Overall, in the state senate those candidates who had completed the NRA's questionnaire mostly received high grades, but a significant minority of both Republicans and Democrats were rated F.

After the senior ILA staff had tutored Rick Cunningham, Chuck Manning, and me in the subtleties of assigning grades based on the questionnaires that the candidates had submitted, we got down to the drudgery of working up our political preference charts for Mike Lashbrook and, eventually, for Warren Cassidy to review.

●　　●　　●

The next seven weeks were hectic. It seemed as if I spent more time behind the wheel of rental cars or slumped in narrow Eastern Airlines seats flying from my district to Washington and back out again than I did in my office or house. But I felt that I was part of a dedicated and hardworking team.

Nobody at 1600 doubted that Ronald Reagan would defeat Walter Mondale on November 6. We were also confident that the Republicans could hold onto the Senate and maybe even gain control of the House. As always, though, the ILA was careful not to make any partisan political judgments—at least not on the record. And in fact antigun Republicans failed their preference chart report cards as readily as pro-gun Democrats who were rated A.

I went to an election night party on Tuesday, November 6, at the NRA's headquarters. We hadn't really gotten into the drinks and hors d'oeuvres when the early returns made it obvious we'd soon be uncorking champagne. Ronald Reagan was winning by the largest landslide in American history. By the end of the night he had won 525 electoral votes to Mondale's 13 and carried every state except Minnesota and the District of Columbia.

In my own region, the candidates I'd worked with had done surprisingly well. There were some odds-on favorites in the traditionally pro-gun districts of New Hampshire, Vermont, Maine, and upstate New York. But I had also won a couple of victories for the association in state assembly districts that the antigun community had long considered safe.

New York City and its bedroom suburbs gave me the chance to show that "lost cause" territory could be recouped. A case in point was the campaign of Democratic assemblyman Tommy Catapano, a state assemblyman from Brooklyn. He had held his seat for several years while running without significant opposition. But in 1984, Catapano got nervous, and my local field rep, Dick Sorrentino, told me, "He needs our support." After Catapano completed his questionnaire to the ILA's satisfaction, he got his endorsement letters and that support, as well as a small contribution from the Political Victory Fund PAC. More important than money was the backing of the NRA's grassroots activists in his district. They read their political preference charts and got out the vote.

The state senate race in New York's 9th Senatorial District (my old neighborhood of southwest Nassau County on Long Island) was more interesting—and challenging. The incumbent was Democrat Carol Berman, an antigun crusader who had earned consistent "F"'s on the ILA's political preference charts. Her opponent was former assemblyman Dean G. Skelos, a moderate-to-conservative

Republican. Although Skelos rated high with the ILA, the guardians of the Political Victory Fund weren't convinced when I requested we back his campaign with the maximum $1,000 contribution. "Don't throw money away," I was told. "He's going to lose."

"I don't think so," I said. "And I'd take a side bet if it were ethical."

I knew something the people in Washington did not. Ultra-Orthodox Jews were moving out of New York City following the path of the Long Island Rail Road to buy homes in the Five Towns of the South Shore where I'd grown up. These people were devoutly religious, but they weren't pacifists. Many were gun owners and NRA members. One of the pro-gun leaders they looked up to was Dr. David Caplan, a prominent New York patent lawyer and staunch advocate of Second Amendment rights. He had done pioneering legal research on the connection between the right to self-protection enumerated in the Torah and the individual right to keep and bear arms and their use for self-defense guaranteed in the Second Amendment. For the Orthodox Jews moving to Long Island, the post-Holocaust credo, "Never Again," encompassed protecting their homes and families with firearms. It didn't matter a bit that Carol Berman was a secular Jew. It mattered that the NRA promised to help them legally keep their guns.

To back up Dean Skelos's "A" grade, I managed to get the ILA to sign off on several special endorsement letters to the local membership. In 1984, it was state-of-the-art information technology to target mailings by zip code, which made these endorsements much better focused than in the past. There were 2,200 NRA members in Berman's senate district. They all received multiple letter mailings, in which I had pointed out that Carol Berman had supported *every* gun control bill that was ever proposed in Albany. Once more the activists were encouraged to boost the endorsed candidate among their friends and acquaintances. Our endorsement letters were often posted at local gun clubs and shooting ranges. On November 6, the ILA in Washington and Republican leaders in Albany were still convinced the Carol Berman would capture a "comfortable" majority of the 9th District vote.

The turnout was large for a state race, almost seventy thousand. By the end of the night, Carol Berman conceded defeat. Dean Skelos had won by a margin of slightly more than two thousand votes, despite the fact that all of Berman's traditional liberal-left supporters had voted for her.

"Our members made the difference," I told Dick Sorrentino when I called him late that night from Washington.

The respectable tally of victories in my region was part of an overall favorable trend. The association had backed candidates in 1,128 federal and state races. By morning, 956 of them had won—an amazing 85 percent pro-gun victory. The NRA was riding high.

• • •

But I didn't have time to kick back and rest. On Friday, November 9, I escorted Maryann and Harlon Carter to New York aboard the Amtrak Metroliner. He would be the featured speaker at the annual formal dinner of the Federation of Greater New York Rifle and Pistol Clubs held in the historic red brick 7th Regiment Armory where the National Rifle Association assembled soon after its creation in the 1870s.

The ride up in the train's well-appointed club car was comfortable, and we quickly established a warm rapport. Predictably, we discussed Tuesday's election.

"You did well, Richard," Harlon said, "very well."

"He doesn't say that to everyone," Maryann interjected.

After three months in the NRA, I felt I'd found a home.

Outside the speeding train, the fall colors streamed by. Soon, the rust-orange leaves gave way to the spreading Rust Belt of northern New Jersey and then we entered the city.

After seeing the Carters to their hotel in midtown, I checked in with Jerry Preiser and Dick Sorrentino to make sure everything was ready at the Armory. Preiser owned an indoor shooting range on the West Side and was one of the NRA's best organizers anywhere.

I then took the Long Island Rail Road to Lawrence and picked up my parents, whom Harlon and Maryann had graciously invited to their table at the Armory banquet. My folks appreciated the invitation but were apprehensive about the nature of the event. The old Armory was an impressive structure, occupying a full city block of prime Upper East Side real estate between 66th and 67th streets and Park and Lexington avenues. But my parents remained convinced that I'd gone over to the dark side in joining the NRA, and probably expected to find the dining room thronging with storm troopers tuning up for a rousing chorus of the *Horst Wessel Song*—or at least beer-gut bubbas who hadn't bathed in a few days.

Instead, they encountered well-dressed, well-spoken people, many of whom were doctors and lawyers. My father was particularly impressed when he recognized Dr. Richard Drooz, who had been my father's supervisor when he was in training at Hillside Psychiatric Center in the Bronx in the 1950s. Drooz was well known in pro–Second Amendment circles: he had used his handgun twice to defend himself against violent assailants.

Harlon and Maryann Carter couldn't have been more welcoming to my parents. "Dr. Feldman," Harlon said, "it's an honor to meet you. Your son is a fine young man."

His manner was that of a Texas gentleman. He addressed my mother as "Ma'am." They were even more impressed. The dinner conversation was sophisticated, and once more concerned the Reagan landslide.

When Carter delivered his remarks, he reverted to his deep bass rhetorical voice, summarizing the recent successes in assuring our Second Amendment rights while also emphasizing the "long road" that lay ahead to ultimately securing these rights for all Americans.

On the way back to Lawrence, my mother commented, "What lovely people. I never would have expected it."

(About a year later, my father asked me to help him select a shotgun "to have around the house." We chose a short-barreled 12 gauge side-by-side, simple and safe when no round was chambered, but devastating against intruders. "This certainly *does* give you a sense of authority," he said, hefting the gun in his office.)

●   ●   ●

The next Monday morning, I learned, Carter asked Warren Cassidy, "Who *is* this guy Richard Feldman you hired? We can use more like him."

5

DEFEATS

NRA Headquarters, December 1984: Near sunset on Saturday, December 22, I was half dozing as I watched local television news on a couch in my parents' Long Island living room. The NRA was shut down until after the New Year, and I took the opportunity to enjoy some of my mother's traditional Chanukah cooking. I was still working off the effects of my holiday eating at lunch when the local ABC-TV news was interrupted by a breaking story.

"Subway gunman shoots four young men," the slide behind the anchor announced.

That snapped me awake. Anybody shooting someone in New York was by definition my business.

Over the next hour and during all three network news broadcasts, more details emerged. The four young men were African American. The shooter was white. The incident had occurred on the IRT downtown express train near the City Hall station. From confused witness accounts it seemed that the four young blacks had surrounded the thin, frail-looking white man and demanded money. One witness told a reporter the black kids had said, "Give us five dollars for video games."

Instead, the man had pulled a shiny short-barreled revolver from a holster inside his jacket and had methodically shot three of them in quick sequence. When one, Darrell Cabey, who was unwounded, slid down the bench, trying to pretend that he wasn't part of the four-some, the shooter leaned over and reportedly said, "You don't look too bad. Here's another." He then shot the would-be mugger at close range.

The man slid his revolver back inside his jacket. "They were trying to rip me off," he said calmly, and then climbed down from the platform between the cars and disappeared into the dim tunnel.

The police and paramedics who arrived found three screwdrivers sharpened to stiletto points on the boys. Darrell Cabey, the last to be hit, was paralyzed from the waist down. A .38 bullet had severed his spinal cord.

As the story swept through the New York media, I called Johnny Aquilino. "John, I'm sorry to call you at home during the holidays, but there's something *big* happening up here."

Indeed, by the 11 p.m. news, every station was comparing the "subway vigilante" shooting to the tough-guy actor Charles Bronson's one-man judge, jury, and executioner in the wildly popular *Death Wish* movies of the 1970s.

The next day's New York tabloids and radio shows were loaded with more detailed accounts of the shootings and reactions from the community and its leaders. When the police established a hotline for tips on the gunman, hundreds of people called to applaud his action. "It's about time somebody had the guts to do this." "Those punks got what they deserved, and the guy that did it should get a medal."

Mayor Ed Koch and Governor Mario Cuomo, not surprisingly, held the opposite view. "Animal behavior," Mayor Koch declared. "Undoubtedly, those who called the police hotline saw their fantasies lived out." This was completely wrong, he stressed, and would erode the difference between a "civilized society and the wild West."

Mario Cuomo described the shooting as "attempted execution."

The intensity of the New York citizens' fervor was impressive. On the filthy, graffiti-covered subways, people felt victimized, powerless prey that the police—their legally authorized guardians—could not protect. In less than a minute on one winter afternoon that imbalance had been slightly redressed.

I knew there was an opportunity here for the NRA to capitalize on the intense public interest and upwelling of emotions. For several years, the association had been unsuccessfully lobbying New York state senators and assemblymen to pass legislation eliminating the unfair discrepancy between handgun possession and carry permits issued in the city and the rest of the state. Under existing law, anyone with a New York City carry permit could take his weapon upstate or to Long Island, for example. But people from all these other counties would be arrested if they tried to carry their legally licensed handgun into the city. So just possibly, we could use this subway shooting as a public-awareness tool in our lobbying campaign.

But I also recognized that the association would have to be careful: if we jumped out front in defense of the gunman, and he proved to be a psychopath, the situation would backfire. But the man remained a mystery; he was still at large, nameless, just that spectral image on the police sketch, crowned with a growing number of felt-pen halos.

Despite the holiday, I conferred with the ILA closely over the next several days. Johnny Aquilino was cautiously enthusiastic. Michael Lashbrook seemed neutral, as did several others. If there was a potential home run in the offing, they wanted to take part of the credit. But they would stay the hell away from any embarrassing media disaster. ILA executive director Warren Cassidy told me to keep my finger on the pulse, but to avoid committing the association to any irreversible position. Meanwhile more witness accounts confirmed that the four young men had clearly been menacing the slightly built gunman.

As this information came out, it was Roy Innis, chairman of the Congress of Racial Equality (CORE) who jumped ahead. On Thursday, December 27, Innis announced that CORE would pay the gunman's legal expenses if he turned himself in. The next Saturday, a police tip identified the subway vigilante as Bernard Goetz, a soft-spoken, electronics expert, age thirty-seven. Within days, Goetz surrendered to police in Concord, New Hampshire, and allowed extradition proceedings to begin while he assembled a legal defense team who initially took his case pro bono.

Roy Innis, I thought, reading the front page of the *Daily News*. If the NRA could get him on board a joint campaign for the right of all citizens' to self-protection, we'd make waves nationwide. But I doubted anyone at 1600 believed such an alliance was feasible.

Meanwhile, the Reverend Al Sharpton entered the fray, not surprisingly defending the wounded young black men against the white vigilante. Nationwide, the media coverage grew hot. *This Week With David Brinkley* devoted a long segment. Members of *The McLaughlin Group* shouted and postured pro and con. The tabloids continued front-page coverage, but even when Goetz was extradited to New York and quickly released on $50,000 bail, the *New York Times* avoided the story.

But I was becoming increasingly eager for the NRA to get involved. Goetz had no criminal record. He was a productive citizen who paid his taxes and voted. Three times in the past he had been the victim of muggers, one of whom had beaten him brutally. Goetz had applied for a legal handgun carry permit, based in part on the fact that he transported valuable electronic components and had a special "nuclear clearance" from the federal government, but he had been denied. New York City's pistol license regulations, extensions of the original Sullivan Act of 1911, gave exclusive—and arbitrary—authority to the police in granting a pistol carry license.

"John," I told Aquilino, "this guy's a poster boy for the 'Armed Citizen,' and we can get media coverage out of him that reaches far beyond the *Rifleman* or *Hunter* columns."

Aquilino agreed. "You'd better talk to Mike Lashbrook and Warren Cassidy."

• • •

On Tuesday, January 8, I took a taxi from the Eastern Shuttle terminal at LaGuardia to CORE's headquarters, 237 West 116th Street in Harlem. The grimy brick building just off Amsterdam Avenue didn't look very impressive. But, as I got out of the cab I noticed that its walls were free of the gaudy graffiti that defaced so much of the neighborhood.

Growing up, I'd been steeped in the myth that a lone white man in an expensive business suit, carrying a briefcase would be a snowball sliding down the chute to hell by standing on a street corner up here. I wondered what the young bloods nearby would think or do if they knew I was an official of the NRA about to meet the legendary leader of the civil rights struggle, Roy Innis, to plan a public relations strategy to defend Bernard Goetz—the vigilante who'd shot down four of their peers.

But my business up here was important. After talking to Jerry Preiser, I was convinced that the NRA and CORE could in fact collaborate to turn the Goetz case to our mutual advantages. I had obtained tentative approval—and a good deal of freedom—from ILA to explore this collaboration.

Innis's secretary, a dignified woman named Angie gestured to a chair. "Mr. Innis will be with you in a moment, Mr. Feldman."

When he came out, his tall, muscular frame filled the door. His smile was broad, his handshake strong. Innis grew up in the Virgin Islands and had been an amateur boxer.

"Richard, please come in and sit down." There was still some Caribbean lilt in his voice.

The office was modest, clean but a little threadbare. On the walls hung a collection of plaques commemorating civil rights victories— on the streets and in the courts. From the second floor, I could see that the graffiti-free walls extended up and down the street.

"We own this whole block," Innis explained. "Economic self-determination. And we don't allow our property to be defaced . . . or the criminal abuse of our people."

He explained that CORE had a "flying squad" of tough young men trained in the martial arts and who sometimes carried guns who protected this block. "There's no crime around here, Richard. We'd never tolerate hoodlums like those who attacked Bernard Goetz."

We planned the details of a joint CORE-NRA news conference scheduled for Thursday, January 10, at the Omni Park Central Hotel. Innis would be the featured speaker, addressing the issue of the fundamental "civil rights" of all citizens, including law-abiding people of all races and social classes in New York City, to be granted handgun permits. With me representing the NRA, two local Republican leaders, Brooklyn state senator Chris Mega and assemblyman Douglas Prescott, would outline their plans to reintroduce legislation in Albany that would prevent municipalities from enacting gun regulations more restrictive than those in the state penal code.

When we'd finished reviewing arrangements, Innis explained that his assistant, Cyril Boynes, would be my point of contact. I was a little nervous because Roy hadn't provided any detailed indication of what his remarks would be at the press conference. But then I realized that he was a persuasive, charismatic speaker who had faced television cameras and microphones literally thousands of times since the early 1960s. It was *I* who was the novice, having never before faced the media. And right now, this was one of the hottest stories in the country.

As Roy Innis rose to shake my hand, he offered me that confident smile. "Richard," he said, "it's wonderful that the NRA is finally recognizing us."

Cyril Boynes drove me down to the Omni Park Hotel, where we inspected the room on the mezzanine level that we'd booked for the Thursday news conference. The room seemed vast, and I wondered if we'd be able to even fill a part of it with TV crews and reporters. What if only ten or fifteen people showed up and the media mocked us with pictures of a scant turnout?

Before returning to Washington, I spoke with Jerry Preiser, the NRA's unofficial ambassador to New York. He knew the local media well and would help draw up the media advisory and mailing list for the press conference that would go out that afternoon.

Jerry rattled off an impressive roster of television and "pencil press" reporters he was confident would attend.

"But what if they *don't*, Jerry?"

"Don't worry. They will."

Jerry and I then held a conference call with Johnny Aquilino to discuss the content of the quarter-page ad sponsored by the NRA, CORE, the Coalition of New York Sportsmen, and Sue W. Caplan, who, like her husband, David, was a successful attorney and Second Amendment advocate.

The ad headline read "Self-Protection Is Your Right."

The text stated that self-protection was a "basic right held sacred by all law-abiding citizens." The second paragraph noted that "millions of New Yorkers" were concerned about self-protection because local courts had ruled the city had no absolute duty to protect individual citizens. This left people with a "personal decision: whether or not to protect yourself."

"The National Rifle Association believes it is your right and your choice to own a firearm for self-protection.

"The National Rifle Association offers training in safe and responsible use of firearms.

"Don't let anyone take away your rights, your life, or your livelihood."

The ad was blunt and provocative. But it did not mention the name Bernard Goetz. That was totally unnecessary in January 1985.

Warren Cassidy, Roy Innis, Jerry Preiser, and Sue Caplan would sign the final draft.

"This ought to shake up the media," Jerry said. "It's the first time CORE and the NRA have cooperated. That's bound to draw a bunch of curious reporters."

While Jerry coordinated with the two local politicians who would appear with us, I took an evening shuttle back to Washington. The next morning as I rode the elevator to the seventh floor, people seemed to be looking at me differently. I noted a few stifled smiles and recognized what they were thinking: Feldman's bit off far more than he can chew. A news conference in New York. Huh? The NRA had never dared such a brazen act, nor had they ever allied themselves with a black civil rights group. *Well*, my associates were thinking, *good luck. The New York press is going to eat you for lunch and spit out the seeds.*

I nodded politely to acquaintances. They hadn't shaken my confidence. New York City was *my* hometown. And I knew that Roy Innis had already been all over the media, defending Goetz. So I really wasn't dragging the association out onto thin ice.

Still, friends were concerned. "I hope you know what you're doing," Rick Manning said before I'd even taken off my coat in the office. "You're making a career move for better or worse with this press conference. Are you *sure* you know what's at stake?"

"I sure do, Rick," I said. But suddenly my voice sounded brittle.

Any way I cut it, one fact remained: I had never faced a big-league TV camera. And the only time I'd been on radio was a brief local talk show segment in Hanover, New Hampshire.

I called Aquilino. "John, I'm going to need a little more training for this thing."

"Good idea, Rich. Come on down the hall and we'll see what we can do."

For the rest of the day, Johnny Aquilino and Jack Adkins, the Public Education Division's deputy director, peppered me with hardball questions and guided my answers.

"Did the NRA advocate *Death Wish*–style vigilantism?"

"No. The NRA believes in the *lawful* right of individuals to protect themselves and their families."

"What would happen to public safety if *everyone* was licensed to carry firearms?"

"There is strong evidence that the states with the least restrictive gun regulations also have the lowest level of violent crime."

Johnny and Jack grilled me. They reminded me to keep my shoulders square and to move my whole head, not just my eyes. I'd had less stressful root canals than this marathon training session. But my confidence was growing.

"Remember," Johnny said, "do *not* talk about Bernie Goetz. But if you have to, use the incident to support what we want to achieve in Albany."

"Goetz had tried to obtain a carry license," Jack added. "But they denied him. This whole thing is not about Goetz, it's about breaking legal ground in New York City."

I felt wrung out, but we still had a crucial element of this preparation to complete.

"Rich," Johnny said, "what's your fundamental *core* message? What do you want everyone to take away from the press conference?"

"Ah . . . well . . ."

"Tilt," Johnny said. "The pinball game is over. And you just lost."

In the end, it was Johnny who crystallized our message. "Try this on," he said, reading from his yellow pad. "A government that cannot protect its citizens has no right to deny them the means to protect themselves."

"Homerun," Jack said.

"Grand slam," I echoed.

●　●　●

Wednesday afternoon I got a hotel room at the Sheraton New Yorker, which became the NRA's unofficial command center for the press conference. Because fax machines were still relatively new and e-mail didn't exist, Jerry Preiser used his local activists as a messenger crew to hand deliver press conference invitations to the media outlets.

But I was still worried no one would show up at the Omni in the morning. And I had to fight my lingering fear that I'd screw up on network TV.

That night I was physically exhausted but torn between the dread that the press *would* show up in large numbers, and the fear that we would be ignored.

Then I watched President Ronald Reagan's 8 p.m. televised press conference from the East Room of the White House. ABC's correspondent Sam Donaldson asked a stentorian question about the President's views on the Goetz case. If Reagan damned Goetz, I was damned as well. But the Great Communicator worked his magic, speaking in a well-paced reasonable tone.

"In general," he began, "I think we can all understand the frustration of people who are constantly threatened by crime and feel that law and order is not protecting them."

The ILA could have written that line for the President.

"On the other hand," Reagan continued, "we all realize that it is a breakdown of civilization if people began taking the law into their own hands."

He was a careful political leader but under the conventions of rhetoric his first statement carried the most persuasive impact. Score a big one for the NRA.

I was still apprehensive about our press conference in the morning, but managed to sleep several hours. After bolting down a breakfast of pastrami and eggs and rye toast at the Carnegie Deli, I walked up the crowded sidewalks to the Omni, again picturing a room crowded with nasty antigun reporters or filled with empty seats.

The conference room was ready. There was a clean copy of our press release on each chair. The hotel had set up a plug-in connector for the TV and radio audio feeds. I found a perfect place for the NRA flag between two door frames behind the rostrum. At 10:50, Senator Chris Mega and Assemblyman Doug Prescott appeared. Two minutes later, my mother and my old law school buddy Merrill Gugerty showed up to lend moral support. But the undisputed star of the show, Roy Innis, was late.

"Not to worry," Cyril Boynes assured me. "He *will* be here."

At 10:55, there was not a single reporter in the room. Innis had still not appeared. I felt a little dizzy. This was like one of those law school nightmares in which I'd show up for an important exam only to discover an empty classroom and learn that the test had been given the day before.

At 10:59, Murray Kempton, the liberal columnist from *Newsday*, appeared. Thirty seconds later, Roy Innis sauntered calmly into the room, shook our hands and stood beside me on the rostrum. About fifteen seconds before 11, the elevator opened out in the corridor and a jostling scrum of TV crews strode down to the front and positioned their light-and-camera rigs. I recognized the logos of PBS, the local Fox station, three other New York channels, and even the BBC and Spanish Broadcasting. Radio technicians were hooking into the connector, elbowing one another as they did so. Looking up I saw a throng of print reporters pushing toward the front chairs.

In about three or four minutes, the conference room had gone from empty to standing room only. The din fell quiet. I swallowed and stepped forward to the microphone. "Good morning," I said through dry lips. "You all have a copy of our press release. If not, we have more. Our first speaker will be Roy Innis, executive director of the Congress of Racial Equality."

I remembered to move my entire head toward Roy as he leaned into the microphone and beamed at the assembled press.

"I believe those of you who've been following recent events know my position about the right of the people to defend themselves."

His voice was melodious, the cadences practiced. He knew when to smile and gesture with his open hands, and when to lower his head while discussing the somber reality of crime on the city's streets.

"The strict gun laws we now have are making decent citizens prey for criminals," Roy Innis intoned. "The greatest supporters of gun control are criminals."

Experienced public speaker that he was, he paused to allow print reporters to capture his words in their notebooks.

"Never before have I seen white people and black people so together on one issue, and that issue is crime," he said. "We've got to find some way to bring some kind of fear into a criminal. We have to make the streets *un*safe for criminals."

In his best civil rights stem-winder style, Roy sternly announced that CORE intended to sue both the city and state of New York for "discriminatory practices against minority people" for consistently denying their law-abiding members firearms permits.

Senator Mega and Assemblyman Prescott discussed their plans to reintroduce legislation in Albany that would prevent New York City's boroughs from preserving handgun regulations more restrictive than the rest of the state's counties.

Jerry Preiser spoke next. "The mayor and the governor have made it virtually impossible to get a pistol carry permit," he said. Like Roy, Jerry knew when to pause and when to speak. "We're going to push hard for legislation," he continued. "As long as this city government fails in its most elementary obligation to protect citizens, then people will arm themselves for self-preservation, and for self-defense."

Now I was up. My nervousness had dissolved. I had practiced my brief statement so often that I didn't even have to refer to my block-printed remarks. After reviewing the NRA's position on the basic right to self-protection, I focused on New York.

"When will Mayor Ed Koch provide the people the same level of protection that he enjoys riding in his armored limousine guarded by a phalanx of *armed* New York City police officers? The police cannot *possibly* catch all the criminals, and the courts cannot or *will* not punish those who are caught."

The TV lights were hot and glaring, but I saw the print reporters writing fast. "The National Rifle Association does not encourage citizens to go out and purchase guns for self-protection. What we *are* saying is that you have the right to self-protection and the right to choose for yourself." I let the note-takers catch up. "The National Rifle Association in general supports the right of citizens to obtain firearms lawfully. We support the rule of law. And you folks in the media have an opportunity here to get a message out to criminals that armed citizens prevent crime."

I ended my comments with the rhetorical gem Johnny Aquilino had created. "A government that cannot or will not protect its citizens has no right to deny them the means to protect themselves."

We had reached the planned thirty-minute cutoff time and opened the floor to reporters' questions. Not surprisingly, the repor-ters tried to draw all of us out on the record to support Goetz and his vigilante action. Roy skillfully deflected the most hostile questions, alternating between smiling charm and unyielding demeanor. I prefaced most of my comments with, "It is the position of the National Rifle Association that . . ."

A little after noon, the conference broke up. Most of the reporters left with our press release and with ILA's Fact Pack on self-defense, which cited New York City legal precedent that the police were under no legal obligation to protect individual citizens.

The only journalist who remained was Murray Kempton. He was leafing through our printed handouts with a skeptical sneer. Jerry Preiser took it on himself to educate Kempton, assuring him that all the facts and statistics in our material would stand up to scrutiny. Left unsaid was the role of "Doctor Death," Paul Blackman, who kept the NRA facts honest.

Before Kempton had a real chance to respond, my mother descended on him to voice her support for Bernie Goetz. "Why shouldn't that young man have the right to defend himself?" she said sternly. Kempton, a journalist with deep liberal roots, found no way to argue with a Jewish mother and former social worker who'd worn out lots of shoe leather on the streets of Brooklyn.

Back home in Lawrence, Long Island, that night, I had the odd sensation of watching myself on television for the first time since my college years. Every network affiliate in greater New York ran a segment on the news conference, each of them focusing on my statement, "A government that cannot protect its citizens . . ." The *MacNeil/Lehrer NewsHour* introduced a long segment that highlighted my comment at the news conference that criminals made an effort to avoid armed citizens. "The greatest single deterrent to crime is an armed citizenry."

That was a videotaped setup for a live studio debate between Warren Cassidy and Michael Beard, president of the National Coalition to Ban Handguns. Each threw some good punches and absorbed some body blows. But Warren (again with Paul Blackman's unseen assistance) presented a convincing array of statistics to show that most violent crime went unpunished, and that states that had the highest concentration of firearms ownership had the lowest per capita crime rates.

I slept well that night in my old bed.

• • •

The next afternoon when I got back to NRA headquarters and rode the elevator to the seventh floor, people slapped my shoulder, shook my hand, and even gave me a couple of high fives. *Success has a thousand fathers*, I thought.

An hour later, I was in Warren Cassidy's conference room with Mike Lashbrook and Wayne, discussing our lobbying push for less restrictive firearm permit legislation in Albany at the next legislative session.

"Getting those bills through the New York senate and assembly will be the brass ring," I said.

I thought that Wayne LaPierre had a slightly pained expression. On the one hand, he was sincerely pleased that we were doing well in enemy territory. But we all recognized that this success had stemmed from *my* initiative and willingness to risk failure, two attributes that Wayne lacked.

• • •

While Manhattan district attorney Robert Morgenthau brought attempted murder and firearms violations against Goetz to a grand jury, the media kept the debate simmering, and bumper stickers began to appear—on cars, mailboxes, and walls: "Bernard Goetz— American Hero," was one. Another was even harder hitting: "Ride with Bernie—He Goetz 'Em." These stickers were funded and distributed by pro-gun groups far to the right of the association, but the NRA did nothing to condemn their appearance on the street.

With the Manhattan grand jury hearing evidence, I took Roy Innis down to Washington to meet Warren Cassidy and other senior NRA officials. After the amiable discussions on joint strategy and tactics, it was clear at the NRA's headquarters that we'd acquired an impressive ally in Roy. The concept of tapping into large numbers of potential members among urban blue-collar and middle-class blacks was very appealing to the association.

• • •

On January 25, 1985, the first grand jury refused to indict Goetz. Morgenthau took the unusual step of presenting a second "indict-ment" of felony charges of attempted murder, assault, and criminal possession of a weapon to another grand jury, which finally indicted Goetz on March 12, 1985.

Three years later, when Goetz was convicted, the jury found him not guilty of the serious felonies and guilty on a single firearms charge. He served eight months in jail and paid a $5,000 fine. After Darrell Cabey won a multimillion-dollar civil suit, Goetz filed for bankruptcy and disappeared from public attention.

●   ●   ●

In the winter of 1985, Harlon Carter stunned the National Rifle Association—outside the eighth-floor heavy hitters—by announcing that he intended to resign as executive vice president, effective at the annual members' meeting in Seattle that April. At age seventy-two, Carter planned to retire to the home he and Maryann had built in Green Valley, Arizona, ten years before. Almost as surprising as this announcement was his choice of successor. Carter had gone outside the association and anointed G. Ray Arnett, an experienced Washington administrator, and apparently also an ideological neutral in the NRA's internecine struggles between the Second Amendment fundamentalists and the team of aggressively pragmatic lobbyists that Warren Cassidy had assembled.

Ray Arnett had impressive credentials. He was a tall, broad-shouldered Marine veteran who'd won a battlefield commission in the Pacific in World War II and had been recalled to active duty during the Korean War. A passionate hunter and also a conserva-tionist and wildlife manager, Arnett served seven years as California's Director of Fish and Game under Governor Ronald Reagan. When Reagan became president, Arnett was named Assistant Secretary of the Interior for Fish and Wildlife, a position that he used to open increasingly wider tracts of government land to hunting and other recreation. It also didn't hurt that Arnett was a close friend and hunting buddy of outgoing NRA president Howard Pollack, a former Alaska congressman.

Arnett hadn't served on the NRA's board, nor had he left any distinctive record of his position on the association's future political agenda—other than stating in his initial public interview, "On the legislative front my first priority is to keep the NRA on the offensive in protection and projection of our right to keep and bear arms."

That platitude didn't give much of a clue as to where Arnett would stand on controversial issues, I thought. When—not *if*—Neal Knox and his followers regrouped and tried to regain control of the association after Carter formally relinquished power Arnett would need a solid team behind him. It was well known that Knox still had friends on the board, but not among those on the "power curve."

The word among insiders at 1600 Rhode Island Avenue was that Arnett's choice had been Carter's compromise, a leader who would straddle the middle ground. Arnett would be the steadying keel, Carter the guiding rudder. Arnett's credentials as a dedicated hunter and as a pro-gun senior civil servant in the Reagan administration—as well as his cachet as a decorated Marine—established Arnett as a potential leader of great promise.

Many people at 1600 were surprised—and a few displeased— that Harlon Carter hadn't thrown holy water on Warren Cassidy, but had instead gone outside the association to choose his replacement through an executive placement agency. Warren certainly could be counted among those who were displeased. He felt that he deserved the top executive position. After all, he had fought beside Harlon Carter for years against Neal Knox's zealotry. But Arnett came from central California oil country, which was culturally much more like Carter's native Texas than Warren Cassidy's New England home turf. I also began to hear murmurs that the earlier alliance between Cassidy and Carter was one of the reasons Carter had tapped Arnett and not Cassidy. Choosing Cassidy while Knox was still confident that the membership would elect him executive vice president in Seattle would have simply ignited more internal strife at the NRA.

In the three months before the members' meeting, Carter held the fort in Washington while Arnett traveled the country, soliciting support for his candidacy from various blocks and alliances among the voting membership. Harlon had chosen my state and local colleague, Rick Manning, to be Arnett's campaign manager. I didn't envy Rick: if Arnett defeated Knox in Seattle, the successful campaign manager would make some enemies among the Knoxers. If Knox won, Arnett's manager might be blamed. I was learning to watch my back in the association.

●   ●   ●

I spent a lot of that spring in my most active states, New York and New Jersey. Most of my effort was in Albany because Warren Cassidy and Mike Lashbrook had given me the green light to lobby hard to reform the state's restrictive firearms laws. Our allies in this campaign included Roy Innis and several state assemblymen and senators. Beyond traditional visits to senior elected officials' offices in the nineteenth-century limestone wedding cake of the capitol building modeled on the Hotel de Ville in Paris, we kept up our drumbeat of media events and advertising.

But Mayor Ed Koch and Manhattan "District Attorney for Life," as some called the long-serving prosecutor, Robert Morgenthau, were badly stung by the reversals they'd suffered in the Goetz case. In early June, they showed us their intentions. The city council voted 33–0 to double the annual pistol license fee from $50 to $100.

"Some guy elbows your eye in a playground basketball game," Roy told me, "you'd best elbow him right back."

That's what we did.

The next day, several city papers ran the quarter-page ad we'd written with Democratic assemblyman Dov Hikind, who represented the largest Orthodox Jewish community in the United States. Hikind's picture in the ad was of a charismatic and handsome mensch with a well-trimmed beard and alert dark eyes.

"Peace, Safety, Health . . . In our streets, our shops, our homes, the criminal robs us of each!"

"To revere life and to follow The Law," the ad continued, making a direct reference to Torah, "is to preserve life: The lives of ourselves and our loved ones."

The heart of the message was *our* elbow-in-the-eye to city hall. "Today, New York law stops most law-abiding citizens from legally having the means to repel a criminal assault. That law must be changed!"

In the coming weeks, these ads ran in thirty-eight newspapers in the state, reaching millions of readers.

"The mayor and the DA are going to be *very* displeased," Roy Innis said with a baritone chuckle. "As well they should be." He lifted his strong right fist. "On the one hand, they see a recognized black leader, me. . . . On the other, a popular Jewish city Democrat and a suburban Westchester Republican—Peter Sullivan—with a middle-class suburban following. The liberal mind just can't *process* that kind of information."

"They'd better get used to it," I said.

"Maybe they will," he said. "Stranger things have happened. Did I ever tell you about our guns and all those cracker sheriffs going belly-up during the Freedom Rides and voter registration in the sixties?"

"No, sir. You definitely did not. I'd have remembered *that.*"

Roy laughed loudly. "Well, after the first couple of times those crackers roughed our people up, we let them know that 'We Shall Overcome' and nonviolent resistance were all well and good, but henceforth they'd be dealing with Mr. Smith and Mr. Wesson. We had armed men call 'deacons' on each bus and at each polling station. Tough young guys, many of them veterans, who knew how to shoot and weren't afraid of some fat white boy with a nightstick. Those deputies were cowards. They didn't like the idea of colored folks from up north pulling a gun on them."

"Maybe that's what's got Ed Koch worried," I said.

"Maybe so," Roy said.

●   ●   ●

But there was an even more irritating issue for Democratic politicians in New York State at that time. Governor Mario Cuomo, their putative presidential candidate for 1988, had committed one of the most grievous faux pas in recent memory and then proceeded to compound the problem, all to the glee of the National Rifle Association.

In early April 1985, during an otherwise routine interview with the *Los Angeles Times*, Cuomo stumbled badly and ended up with his foot and leg up to his gonads firmly in his mouth. The issue began innocently enough. The governor had just signed the nation's first mandatory seat belt law for motorists. Almost immediately, thousands of letters poured in attacking his action. In this interview, Cuomo apparently tried to deflect criticism by claiming that the most vehement letter writers were "NRA hunters who drink beer, don't vote, and lie to their wives about where they were all weekend."

When the story was reprinted in several upstate New York papers on April 8, Jerry Preiser called me in Washington. "Richie," he said. "We've got something even bigger than Goetz."

I realized that Cuomo's implications were both nasty and inaccurate: NRA hunters took pride in firearms safety; they rarely mixed alcohol and cordite. And it was well known that the association's members voted in far higher numbers than other citizens. The smear about lying to their wives contained a gratuitous sexual innuendo that was sure to outrage the NRA's members *and* their families. Cuomo might just as well have thrown a Molotov cocktail into a barn full of hay, given the mood of the association's members in the state. As soon as Jerry hung up, I said, "Gotcha!" and ran down the corridor to Warren Cassidy's office to tell him about Cuomo's snafu.

"Oh, Richie," Cassidy said, "that's great. Put it in the file to use against Cuomo in his reelection campaign."

But before we could act, Cuomo attempted to defuse the growing controversy and only enflamed it. During his monthly *Ask the Governor* radio call-in show on April 18, he tried to dodge responsibility for his comments. It had, he said, been "a small thing," adding, "I was quoted somewhere as disparaging, if you will, National Rifle Association members." He admitted only a vague recollection of the notorious quote and claimed, "Now, I regret very much that if anybody took that to mean a condemnation of all NRA members because I certainly don't mean that." His mere "bantering quote," Cuomo insisted, had been "heard out of context." Those few words, he concluded, were "perhaps not so artfully said."

"What the hell does that mean?" Johnny Aquilino asked, reading the transcript of the broadcast.

"Well," I commented with a straight face, "maybe it would have been more *artful* to have said, 'NRA hunters overimbibe, neglect their civic duties, and are mendacious toward their wives concerning their extramarital activities.'"

"The guy's a sleaze ball," Johnny said.

But he was *our* sleazeball, and we intended to use him. I was beginning to appreciate just how gruesome a blood sport politics could be.

But before we launched our campaign against Cuomo, there was serious internal NRA business to complete.

●   ●   ●

The 1985 members' meeting in Seattle was meant to be Harlon Carter's triumphant departure from the limelight and Ray Arnett's inauguration. But it became a dramatic confrontation between Carter's side and the Knoxers, who fought for control of the association for most of that week.

Carter had made sure that all the life members on the Washington staff were flown out to Seattle because he anticipated a tight vote on the floor and every vote for Arnett would count.

Seattle seemed like an intriguing, misty city, reputedly the home of some of America's great restaurants. But I didn't have time to linger over Dungeness crabs or Coho salmon. This was my first convention, and I was impressed by the exhibits, the thronging crowds—comprised mostly of nonvoting "tire-kickers"—and by the ritual "will life members born before 1905 please stand to be recognized." Klieg lights, patriotic music, chant "NRA . . . N . . . R . . . A!"

We loyal staffers had other business, however. We were all working our tails off on Arnett's campaign and had come equipped for a proper political convention: with badges (STAY TOUGH WITH ARNETT), hats, and stickers. With more than two thousand voting members on hand, this was the largest such assembly in the NRA's history.

As soon as I arrived, Tony Madda and Dick Cox handed me a map and the keys to a rental car. "It's already loaded with brochures and bumper stickers. I've marked the location of all the gun shops. It's going to take you awhile, Rich."

It took me almost ten hours to convince the owners to distribute our pro-Arnett, anti-Knox material.

Probably our most dramatic message was a bumper sticker that we slapped up on key locations of the conventioneers' hotels: "If

Knox Wins . . ." was printed in blue on the left side. "You <u>Lose</u>!" was emblazoned in much bolder scarlet type on the right. The credibility of the sticker was enhanced by the tagline at the bottom: BY AUTHORITY OF THE NRA POLITICAL VICTORY FUND.

What few people realized, however, was that the NRA had originally commissioned the message for an election in Tennessee. The Knox in question was no relation of Neal's. There were several thousand surplus stickers in Washington, and we put them to good use in Seattle.

But the message seemed clear enough: the powers that be at 1600 Rhode Island Avenue were opposed to Neal Knox. Washington headquarters exercised not only the executive leadership of the organization but also the funds that could influence elections nation-wide.

Tanya Metaksa was Neal Knox's campaign manager, which seemed like a serious tactical error on his part. She was her usual overaggressive, grating self and probably alienated more wavering voters than she won for Neal.

By the morning of the vote, Saturday, it looked like Neal's camp was in disorder and Arnett's better organized campaign would prevail. The Knoxers never lost their zeal, but they just did not have the votes. One after another their motions and maneuvers were voted down. This would not be a repeat of Cincinnati. Michigan congress-man John Dingell officially offered Ray Arnett's candidacy for executive vice president to the voting members. We handed in our ballots.

Neal Knox lost by a margin greater than two to one. G. Ray Arnett was the new leader of the National Rifle Association, elected for a five-year term.

What occurred next that night has become part of the NRA legend. Neal Knox stormed out of the convention hall and jumped up onto a big green dumpster on the sidewalk outside. He harangued a group of disciples, and then tried to attract Seattle citizens passing nearby through the drizzle.

According to witnesses, Harlon Carter was leaving the conven-tion hall at this time and stopped abruptly to take in the spectacle of Knox, his face streaming with either rain or tears, bellowing in his characteristically deep prairie-prophet's voice.

"Well," Carter told colleagues at his side, "if you want to get rid of Neal Knox, you'll have to drive a stake through his heart, cut him up in seven pieces, bury him in seven deep holes . . . and then hire seven strong men to guard all seven holes."

•   •   •

Back in Washington, Governor Mario Cuomo was still very much on the agenda.

On April 29, I sent a memo to Johnny Aquilino's shop recommending that, "We shouldn't let Cuomo off the hook so easily."

The next day Warren Cassidy called the governor's comments, "A grave insult to NRA members everywhere, particularly to the more than two hundred thousand–strong who reside in your own state."

After chiding Cuomo for perpetuating "an unfair and prejudiced stereotype," Warren noted that Cuomo had "made a critical error in your assertion that NRA members don't vote." Warren reminded the governor that he had won the election in 1982 on a pro-sportsman platform, but had proceeded since then in vetoing every piece of pro-firearms and pro-conservation legislation to reach his desk.

"Our memories are long, Governor Cuomo," Warren concluded. "Much longer than yours appears to be. We will remember your words in 1986, 1988, and beyond. You will see for yourself whether or not NRA members vote."

Within days, front-page stories featuring Warren's letter to Cuomo appeared in New York newspapers. The Associated Press version of the story was picked up across the country. Even the *New York Times* ran a four-paragraph article in its Metro section, "Rifle Group Criticizes Statement By Cuomo."

Time magazine, using one of the standard gun-related clichés reserved for the NRA, described how Cuomo was taking "heavy fire" from the association.

That June's issue of *American Rifleman* had a collage of correspondents running in Doc Garcelon's "President's Column": Cuomo's original "inartful" letter to Pollack; the transcript of the "bantering quote" remarks in the *Ask the Governor* radio show; and the full text of Garcelon's scathing reply. Heavy fire indeed.

Since the story still had legs, ILA decided to launch a combined political information and fund-raising solicitation mail campaign to all of the NRA's members in New York State. Warren Cassidy was the titular official signing the letter, but it was a joint effort of many of us in ILA.

"As you have undoubtedly read," the letter stated, "Mario Cuomo—who's off and running for the White House—falsely accused you and me of being 'NRA hunters who drink beer, don't vote, and lie to their wives about where they've been all weekend.'"

After citing Cuomo's antigun record, which included his habit of vetoing all pro-gun legislation passed by both houses in Albany, Cassidy reviewed the pending legislation we hoped this renewed "pro-gun pressure" might force Cuomo to sign. The letter contained one of our colorful, "I'm the NRA, and I Vote!" stickers.

Seamlessly, the letter slipped into the contribution appeal for "as much as you possibly can afford" from ten dollars all the way up to one hundred, needed "to launch our pro-gun offensive."

This mailing was one of the NRA's most successful, both in terms of contributions, and as a stimulus to our activists. Within days, the blue-and-red bumper stickers appeared on cars across the state, including on state troopers' and deputies' cruisers.

• • •

The ILA also drafted a letter for Ray Arnett to send to Cuomo via his press officer, Gary Fryer. This was vintage NRA take-no-prisoners rhetoric. The association rapped the governor's knuckles on his antigun record, and did so in a manner that would create more scorn for Cuomo among our members (and by extension, more support for us). We cited six pieces of pro-gun legislation that had passed both Houses in Albany, and ended each paragraph with the jackhammer phrase, "Governor Cuomo Vetoed It!"

To remind Cuomo of our power, the letter concluded that "meaningful" pro-gun and hunting legislation would be weighed in the upcoming session of the New York State legislature. "We at NRA and our 182,000 New York State members will be understandably interested in the Governor's treatment of those issues."

By mid-November Mario Cuomo was reaching out to hunters who were purchasing their licenses for the upcoming season. "Hunting in New York State is a safer recreational activity than swimming, bicycling, even basketball. . . . Hunters play an important role in the management of the state's wildlife population, contribute to tourism and environmental programs, and personally benefit from healthful recreation."

"All the while drinking beer, forgetting to vote, and lying to their wives," I told Jerry Preiser on the phone as I read the *New York Post* story on the governor's statement Preiser had sent me.

"When are we going to ease up on him?" Preiser asked.

"When he finally admits he was wrong," I said.

That day arrived on Monday, January 6, 1986. In a brief statement to the *New York Times*, Mario Cuomo admitted his comment about the NRA's hunters had been "the blunder of the universe." But he continued to imply that he had made the statement in jest.

We didn't drop the pressure. Admitting to a "blunder" was not the same as apologizing for it. When Cuomo finally understood that we were not about to ease off, and that this harassment was seriously eroding his chances for the 1988 presidential nomination—satirical references to his "inartful" dodges had appeared in the liberal mainstream media nationwide—he agreed to meet an NRA delegation in his Albany office.

That February, Mike Lashbrook, Jerry Preiser, and I crossed the snow-covered capitol grounds and met Gary Fryer, who escorted us into Cuomo's wood-paneled office. His Excellency stood smiling thoughtfully behind his desk. After shaking our hands like a Roman counsel acknowledging minor officials from the provinces, Cuomo turned his back and dropped rather heavily into his polished oak chair. A clap of flatulence worthy of a farting stallion ensued.

Grinning, Cuomo jumped back up to display the whoopee cushion that had been lurking on the chair. "Seat of Power" was printed on the now-deflated novelty device.

If he had expected that ploy to cut through the palpable tension in the room, he'd been mistaken. *Is this what he thinks we are?* I wondered. *A bunch of buffoons from the sticks?*

Everyone smiled nervously, most of all the governor. But no one spoke. Finally, Gary Fryer offered some preliminary chitchat. I mentioned the exchange of correspondence between Cuomo's office and the NRA's headquarters, as well as the outpouring of support we'd received over this issue from our members, not just in New York but nationwide.

Cuomo conceded that his office had received "quite a few" letters on the subject.

"Well," I said, "I guess we've got your attention now."

As the meeting progressed, Cuomo turned in his chair, gazed out at the snowdrifts below and spoke with his characteristic fluency, about New York's "great traditions" of outdoorsmanship as well as the "pressing need" to reduce gun violence. He could have been addressing an unseen radio audience for all the attention he paid us. Like most politicians, he liked the sound of his own voice.

I interrupted, reminding His Excellency that in his 1982 NRA candidate questionnaire, his position had been unambiguously pro gun. "For example, here's question five, sir," I said. "'Do you support additional legislation regulating firearms ownership and possession?' You answered no. 'New York already has stringent laws and they need to be enforced.'"

Cuomo's questionnaire answers had not wavered from that pro-gun rights line. That was the reason that the NRA had given him decent "report card" grades. But since entering office after his 1982 election, he had turned his back on us. The strained atmosphere in the office grew more charged.

The hell with it, I thought, boring in. New York City's Sullivan Act of 1911, I lectured him, had been enacted to "prevent immigrants of southeast European origin—*mainly Italians*—from owning guns, even though the establishment forced them to live in crime-ridden tenements."

Cuomo winced. He prided himself on his immigrant roots. But like the Portuguese shopkeeper on my Cambridge beat, his grandfather probably "hadn't been in America" long enough to have earned the right to carry a pistol to defend his family.

Soon thereafter, the meeting ended on a chill note.

As our car bumped over the black, rutted ice on the way to the airport, I had the feeling that Mario Cuomo's political career had stalled in the rococo confines of the executive chamber.

●   ●   ●

The NRA's long campaign to win passage of the Volkmer-McClure Firearms Owners Protection Act gained ground dramatically on Capitol Hill in 1985. On July 9, the legislation passed on the U.S. Senate floor by a vote of 79–15. But Representative Volkmer's version was stalled in the House Judiciary Committee. Representative Peter Rodino, the committee chairman, had scornfully announced that he considered the bill "dead on arrival" in the House.

The major gun control organizations were also working hard to make sure that the bill was crushed. Handgun Control, Inc., the most active of these groups, also took a play from the NRA's game book, to use the pending legislative struggle as a major fund-raising tool. In a hard-hitting appeal sent to its wide mailing list, HCI asked the harsh rhetorical question, "Just who the hell is running this country . . . Congress or the National Rifle Association?"

The appeal went on to cite the NRA's multimillion-dollar campaign to eviscerate gun control laws, which would result in the "mail order purchase of handguns" and "permit the sale of Teflon-coated 'cop-killer' bullets." These were grossly misleading exaggerations, of course, but apparently struck a resonant note among HCI supporters. The fund-raiser—again following the NRA template—requested donations ranging from $25 through $100 to "Other $."

HCI needed us as much as we needed them. *That's a perfect example of symbiosis*, I thought when I read the fund-raiser.

The letter also had a coupon that HCI promised to send to representatives in Congress: "You work for me. So I want you to know that I favor national legislation to keep handguns out of the wrong hands. Enough is enough. Please care."

Representative Rodino obviously cared. And he was one of the longest-serving congressmen on the Hill, where seniority was a primary attribute of leadership.

"If that bastard says it's dead in his committee," Jim Baker told me, "then it's never going to make it to a floor vote."

"Not unless we can produce a discharge petition," I responded. We'd all been studying House rules and procedures in our "spare" time. A discharge petition was a parliamentary maneuver that required a majority of House members to vote to "discharge" a pending bill that was locked up in committee and move it onto the floor where all the members could vote yea or nay.

Jim looked at me over the top of his aviator's glasses. "We've been thinking along those lines in Federal, too, Richie," Jim said with a confident smile.

Everybody got to work. The strategy was to convince members of the House that 60 million American gun owners would support the discharge petition. Conversely, we had to make congressmen aware that gun owners did indeed have long memories and did not forget those they considered enemies of Second Amendment rights. But Rodino and Hughes had strong hands to play, and we were relatively weak. That was where New Jersey came in.

New Jersey was one of the few states to hold off-year elections, which meant 1985 was a crucial year. Both Rodino and Hughes believed they could count on the back of a solidly Democratic legislature in Trenton. We had other plans. Following our successful campaign against Mario Cuomo in neighboring New York, as well as the favorable publicity Bernie Goetz was still generating, we hoped to help a slate of pro-gun Republican candidates make a strong showing that fall and maybe even gain control of the statehouse in Trenton.

Winning big in New Jersey would demonstrate the association's growing clout in the urban northeast. But there was a subtext with national implications: if NRA activists—and money—could reverse the political tide in the New Jersey legislature, this combination of resources could work in other states. State legislatures redrew congressional districts following the census every ten years. This process would begin again in 1990, less than five years ahead.

If we could pull the statehouse chair out from under the antigun Democrats in Trenton that fall, the power of the NRA would cast a shadow across the country.

"You've pretty much got carte blanche," Michael Lashbrook told me. "Warren and the eighth floor want to see some heads roll up there and some new faces in Trenton. You said you could deliver, and we're counting on you."

When will I learn to keep my mouth shut?

There were 120 seats in the legislature (80 in the assembly and 40 in the senate), and we made sure every candidate received a detailed questionnaire carefully written to ascertain his or her true opinion on the gun rights issue.

I also had $30,000 from the Political Victory Fund to back candidates we supported—five times bigger than the previous election war chest for the state.

The major issues we wanted candidates to address included unreasonably long delays in receiving firearms' permits, costly registration fees, and blatantly arbitrary foot-dragging by local police departments in approving firearms' permit applications. And then there was the ongoing law-enforcement harassment of law-abiding gun owners on the roads and highways of the state.

"Whatever it takes to defeat antigunners in this state, we will do," I told a reporter from the *Trenton Inquirer*.

There was a lot of chutzpah in that statement. So if we lost we were going to lose big.

By late October, we had distributed more than seventy-five thousand political preference charts based on the questionnaires to New Jersey members and another hundred thousand at sports shops across the state. We began to feel some optimism.

"Richie," Rodger Iverson told me, "I got a feeling something good is coming."

An understatement, indeed.

• • •

The efforts to win in New Jersey and to secure the Volkmer-McClure discharge petition became commingled. That fall, as more congressmen signed the discharge petition, Hughes decided to hold ostensibly open public hearings of his House Judiciary Subcommittee on crime around the country, to which panels of "representative citizens" would be invited to speak. The first hearing was scheduled for Monday, October 28, on my home turf, New York, and would be covered by media from the tri-state area.

We helped coordinate requests to testify from Roy Innis and CORE; Jerry Preiser representing the Federation of Greater New York State Rifle & Pistol Clubs; and State Assemblyman Dov Hikind, whose Hassidic constituents had unduly suffered from armed street criminals. After considerable prodding, Hughes's staff finally informed Roy and Hikind that there was no more room on the panels to offer testimony. Hughes's subcommittee told Jerry Preiser that he could present a "brief statement" when the last panel of the day spoke, late in the afternoon—and when the news media covering the hearing was already writing their copy and editing videotape.

"Those sons of bitches are going to bury us alive," Preiser said, almost quivering with anger.

"The hell they are," I said. Back at our offices in Washington that night, Rick Manning and I sat down and drafted a statement for Roy Innis to consider sending as a Western Union Mailgram that would hit the desk of every congressman in Washington the next morning.

"I like it," Roy said, after some rigorous telephone editing.

The mailgram noted that the subcommittee had rejected Roy's request to testify and added:

> My request was based on experience gained as the national chairman of the congress of racial equality and as a victim of numerous well publicized crimes both personally and through my family.

Roy added that "others holding a similar position to mine on the question of guns and crime" had also been denied the opportunity to testify.

Dov Hikind also sent a mailgram to congressmen. The message was clear: we recognized the devious game Hughes was playing.

In fact, it was obvious to everyone that Hughes and his staff had stacked the deck of panelists. Representatives of both Handgun Control, Inc., and the National Coalition to Ban Handguns were scheduled to speak early in the day—when the members and the media were wide awake.

"I've got an idea," Roy said. "All those liberals on the subcommittee wouldn't be too happy if we boycotted their hearing and picketed on the sidewalk outside the federal courthouse."

It was not just an idea. It was brilliant.

On the bright Indian summer morning of October 28, I joined Roy Innis, Jerry Preiser, and Barbara Ruhe of the Connecticut Sportsmen's Alliance—and a sign-waving crowd from their organizations—outside the federal courthouse in lower Manhattan.

"Boycott this hearing!" one sign read.

"Support First Amendment Rights!" read another.

Jerry Preiser's people distributed a news release that condemned the hearing as "nothing more than a media road show" and called for all House members to support the Volkmer-McClure discharge petition.

Roy Innis, by far the most recognizable figure in the group, handed out photocopied flyers.

A CALL FOR JUSTICE AND FAIR PLAY was printed in block letters across the flyer's top, followed by, "This committee is UNFAIR. This committee discriminates against the black community's right to be heard!"

The message ended by urging all who read it to "support us by boycotting these hearings."

A little before the committee's noon break, Roy Innis led the other boycotters into the courthouse, where they proceeded to give a hard-hitting press conference. Roy's statements were especially affecting. He described the anguish he'd suffered when armed criminals had gunned down his defenseless sons.

"We demand the right to protect ourselves," Roy said. "And we demand our First Amendment rights to be heard."

During the lunch break, the media buttonholed Hughes, asking why Roy Innis had been excluded from the hearing.

Within a few days, every congressman in Washington realized they would face similar demonstrations of outrage if they continued to support Rodino and Hughes.

Now it was time to demonstrate in New Jersey what the political fallout of this pent-up anger meant.

● ● ●

By the night of Tuesday, November 5, it was clear that a major electoral upset was under way. The NRA and the Coalition of New Jersey Sportsmen had endorsed forty-seven legislative candidates in the eighty assembly races. Before midnight, forty had won their races—an 85 percent victory rate. Two major wins were in the 30th District in northern New Jersey where John Kelly and Marion Crecco trounced two overconfident antigun incumbents. Our biggest success was the victory of Minority Leader Charles Hardwick, who defeated a longtime enemy of the NRA, Democrat Andrew Ruotolo Jr. This was especially significant because Republicans had gained control of the assembly and Hardwick became speaker. In that position he could further our pro–gun rights agenda—and potentially lead the congressional district reapportionment, if he could hang on in 1987 and 1989.

When I got back to Washington that Friday, I found a box of cigars on my cluttered desk.

•   •   •

But that winter I was beginning to realize that the association's prevailing image, as an invincible political juggernaut, could be problematic. A large group of ILA state and local reps were in the eighth-floor boardroom, surrounded by portraits of the association's presidents going back to 1871. Wayne LaPierre was analyzing an editorial criticizing the NRA over the pending Volkmer-McClure legislation. He had underlined with a red ballpoint several glaring inaccurate and scurrilous passages to emphasize the media's dirty tactics. We were planning to use the editorial to motivate the NRA's members in congressional districts where we thought the representatives were especially vulnerable to public opinion on this issue.

Mary Corrigan from member services sat in on the session. "Hang on, Wayne," she said. "This material might be useful in fund-raisers. Members don't like to be ridiculed, and they don't like their intelligence questioned."

Nobody had to articulate the fact that political success such as we'd had in the previous two years was great for the prestige of the organization, but not necessarily good for fund-raising or membership renewals. If supporters thought the association was doing fine without their $15 annual dues, they might drift away. There was, I began to see, a delicate balance between delivering impressive success and keeping our membership rolls growing—which depended in large part on gun-owner anxiety that Second Amendment rights were under assault.

"Well," Wayne said, handing out the offensive material, "if you can use it in a fund-raiser, so much the better. Maybe we'll get lucky and they'll keep up this underhanded nonsense."

A little lightbulb did not snap on, but I experienced something of an epiphany. We were making slow but steady progress on the Volkmer-McClure discharge petition. But it was also apparent that now we might not be in any great hurry to achieve this victory.

I suddenly pictured one of the fund-raising letters we'd been shown during our early training in the ILA. Two phrases were printed in bold capital letters across the full width of the envelope: I WAS SO ANGRY I SLAMMED DOWN THE PHONE . . . NOW IT'S UP TO YOU TO GET OUR MESSAGE ACROSS!

These fund-raisers were usually farmed out to direct-mail consultants and then carefully vetted by ILA staff to fine-tune the content for maximum impact.

"A dramatic upfront message like this encourages people to open the envelope," Mary Corrigan had told us. The outrage expressed was from a member who'd tried unsuccessfully to reason with some antigun member of the news media. I forgot now what the issue was, but I did recall that the enclosed fund-raising appeal to "get our message across!" offered a range of contribution options, $10 . . . $15 . . . $25 . . . or more." Other solicitations requested exact amounts such as: "$17.63" or "$11.84." In theory, these donations were meant to pay for the production and mailing of specific numbers of press releases, fact sheets, and brochures. I had no way of knowing how much of these contributions actually was needed to print and mail X number of press releases, but I had a suspicion there was plenty of flab involved here. So, the longer a public dispute between the NRA and the National Coalition to Ban Handguns over Volkmer-McClure, Saturday night specials or "cop-killer" bullets could be dragged out, the greater the potential for "good mailings." It was like casting a net wide and often.

One indication that this hyperbolic direct-mail technique was working was that the antigun groups were beginning to emulate it. Handgun Control, Inc., now sent out fund-raising appeals in envelopes optimistically (and inaccurately) touting their membership as "One Million Strong . . . (and growing)." HCI would also soon solicit fund options that included "$35 (the price of a Saturday Night Special)."

I realized that this "dueling banjo" pattern of confrontation between the NRA and the antigun groups could continue indefinitely to the benefit of all the organizations involved.

Certainly, extended controversies were good for increasing membership and soliciting contributions. But that was so damn cynical, I thought. Was it even possible that the NRA would rather fight than win?

The NRA wouldn't manipulate its loyal members that way, would it?

●   ●   ●

In the early spring of 1986, anger and discontent were growing among the staff at 1600 Rhode Island Avenue, particularly inside the ILA. Johnny Aquilino's Public Education Division had done yeoman service in backstopping our successes in the northeast and in creating the material behind a rising political groundswell in favor of the Volkmer-McClure legislation. But it was becoming obvious that the new executive team on the eighth floor did not appreciate him and his staff. As expected, Ray Arnett had brought in some of his own advisers when he took over from Harlon Carter. But nobody— least of all Harlon, I learned—anticipated Arnett's imperious manner and increasingly distant management style.

"This guy's another Captain Queeg," Johnny told me one afternoon as he looked up from a stack of press releases and correspondence that Arnett had defaced with blue strokes from a fountain pen. "He's got a bug up his ass about the word 'which.'"

It turned out that an increasing portion of Johnny's time was spent purging the "which's" that had crept into official NRA documents.

That was only one of Arnett's quirks. He was devoted to seven o'clock staff meetings (soon dubbed "sunrise devotionals" by the grumbling employees). And he also rejected as unfitting the perfectly adequate full-size sedan that used to drive Harlon around the District. He insisted that the association acquire a gleaming Town Car (with driver) for his personal transportation, both official and private. More seriously, Arnett had been away from Washington on

extended hunting trips from September 1985 until January 1986—
even as senior executive guidance was needed on managing the
Volkmer-McClure legislation fight on the Hill.

I began to hear rumbles that many on the board had become
impatient with Arnett. He seemed to have turned his back on them
and had decided to act without their guidance—or permission—on
matters large and small.

This was not a good time for another internal crisis at 1600
Rhode Island Avenue because we were making incremental progress
on the Volkmer-McClure discharge petition. But Wayne recognized
that the stakes were high for both him and the association if we lost.
I met with him frequently that winter as he worked with his almost
bloodless rigor ticking off members of Congress from a neatly printed
chart. "Who have we got?" he always asked. "Who *can* we get?"

Connecticut was a typical state in my region that we scrutinized.
There were three Democrats and three Republican members of
Congress with Democrat representative Barbara Kennelly the most
senior. Since the firearms industry was a large employer in the
Connecticut River Valley, we opted for a quiet but persistent grassroots lobbying effort directed to the state's representatives rather
than a blatant counterattack, such as our boycott of the Hughes
hearing.

One morning, Wayne invited me into his office. "Richie," he said,
"I'd like you to consider managing the Volkmer-McClure media
campaign."

I was taken aback. That was a damn big responsibility. But there
were other, hidden factors involved: the guy who won the fight would
be a hero—and people often grew bitterly jealous of heroic winners.
The guy who "lost" Volkmer-McClure could easily become a scapegoat. I thought about the offer overnight, and then said, Thanks,
but no thanks. "The northeast region is where I can be most effective,
Wayne."

Wayne had a number of these subtle political operations around
the country, and he felt the need for a stronger public relations
backup than our internal media relations operations could provide.
So, much to the displeasure of Johnny's people on the second
floor, Wayne brought in an advertising executive from Ackerman-
McQueen, the Oklahoma City agency that had done the creative

work on the successful "I'm the NRA" campaign. Her name was Debbie Nauser. But her apparent inability to take advice soon earned her the cruel epithet "Debbie Schnauzer" among Johnny's staff.

Those staff members had spent cumulative decades honing the NRA's image. None of them wanted a seemingly inept outsider ruining the trust and relationships they had built on Capitol Hill and among the Washington media by firing off an endless stream of press releases filled with what Johnny told me were "total false-hoods." The mood was not good.

●   ●   ●

Despite the tensions inside headquarters, we continued to make progress on the discharge petition—helped by the knowledge that Ronald Reagan, one of the most popular presidents in decades, was prepared to sign the eventual bill into law. Of course, it didn't hurt that ILA's Political Victory Fund had contributed $1.4 million to our Volkmer-McClure supporters in Congress in 1984. The message was clear: stay on our side, and you can count on us again in 1986. But if you are a fence-sitter who refuses to commit, the NRA will turn its money and, more importantly, its activists against you.

Nevertheless, there was adequate political cover available for fainthearted members torn between the power of the House's senior leadership and the NRA. The identity of those who signed the document only became public if the petition gained a majority. And, feeling intolerable pressure from either side, a House member was free to withdraw support right up to the final tally. It was a nerve-wracking business.

By late January 1986, 158 members of Congress had endorsed the petition. We needed only 60 more to reach our "Bingo!" number: 218. This would be a historic achievement. Since 1960, only six discharge petitions had succeeded in freeing stalled legislation from committees.

But Rodino and Hughes were astute politicians—many said "devious"—and had a countermove planned if the petition passed. On March 6, Hughes introduced to his subcommittee smoke screen legislation that might *appear* a reasonable compromise, but was in fact a toothless version of the Volkmer's bill. Rodino and Hughes planned to preempt Volkmer by having their own bill on the House floor before the week of March 10, where they planned to push through a vote before the discharge petition succeeded.

House members wavering on the issue were uncertain about their best course. It was the NRA's job to win them over.

We soldiered on. Photocopy machines in small New England towns and even some vintage mimeographs in hunting clubs in upstate New York and Vermont churned out letters to uncommitted congressmen for members to sign and mail. Tens of thousands of "I'm the NRA and I Vote!" bumper stickers appeared in shop windows and walls facing congress members' district offices. Our activists manned telephone banks, urging their representatives to sign the petition. Many drove from across the country to Washington to do the same.

"Frankly," Congressman William Hughes told the *Washington Post*, "I'm not sure I've ever seen anything like it."

"I think we've got his attention," I quipped to Johnny Aquilino. "Just like we got Cuomo's."

On the morning of March 7, we had 203 signatures and commitments from eight members to sign. An editorial cartoon appeared on bulletin boards around the Capitol: a grinning congressman with his arm around the shoulder of a sleek gentleman labeled "Gun Lobby." The congressman proclaimed, "I'm the NRA's 219th best friend," in other words, the politician who had risked nothing by staying out of the fight, now wanted a seat on the bandwagon.

The Rodino-Hughes bill reached the House floor on Wednesday, March 12, and members were preparing for a vote on it the next day. The ILA spent more than a million dollars to send members mailgrams alerting them to the danger that lurked on the House floor, where Rodino and Hughes were maneuvering their bill for an up-or-down vote.

By the afternoon of Thursday, March 13, we were near the magic number of 218. Small tactical teams were dispersed throughout ILA offices on the seventh floor at the NRA's headquarters, poring over rosters of House members from our regional districts. The lists were divided into those who were pro- and antigun, as well as those who had already signed the petition, those who openly opposed it, and those who were sitting on the fence.

I had a total of eighty-nine House members in my seven states. Thirty-nine were already on board the petition, forty opposed it, and ten were undecided. Reviewing my vote roster once again, I called our activists in Massachusetts and upstate New York. Then, ILA staff met in the conference room to compare our numbers. It felt like we'd been pushing this rock uphill forever.

The phone rang and Jim Land, the NRA's membership director, took the call. He was a big tough guy, who as a Marine in the 1960s had started the Corps' sniper school at Quantico, Virginia. The phone receiver looked like a toy in his thick fist. "Okay," he said. "All right . . . that's good. Thanks for calling."

He turned to face us. And then he grinned. "We just went over the top on the petition. Two hundred and eighteen votes."

The cheering was long and loud.

That night as a bunch of us sat down to eat huge T-bones at the Palm steak house, Jim Land gave me a bear hug that practically rearranged my backbone. By the end of the petition campaign, I had delivered a significant chunk of the House members in the northeast region, the territory the NRA had considered a political desert for decades.

• • •

On Friday, April 10, 1986, after days of messy and confusing debate involving barrages of competing amendments, an up-or-down vote on Representative Harold Volkmer's version of the bill loomed on the House floor—seven years after the original legislation had been introduced.

Hughes and Rodino had arranged their own brand of powerful lobbying: as members arrived at the House chamber to vote, they had to pass between silent ranks of senior police officers in their dress uniforms—ostensibly proof that America's law-enforcement professionals were against the Volkmer bill. But most House members knew the chiefs and assorted association heads represented the Democratic leaders of their communities, not the rank-and-file patrol officer on the street. The day before, Sarah Brady, whose husband, Jim, was maimed in the 1981 assassination attempt on Ronald Reagan and now a Handgun Control, Inc., board member, spoke out in favor of the Rodino-Hughes bill. *USA Today* called the swelling debate "as furious as those that accompany abortion, prayer in schools, and other emotion-charged issues."

The dueling amendments continued on the House floor, and our allies among Hill staffers kept ILA's clunky fax machine humming as they sent us the latest revised language. The most critical amendments from our point of view concerned loosening the restraints on interstate sales and the transport of firearms, as well as on regulation of amateur dealers—people who traded and sold guns but did not derive most of their income from this activity.

At the NRA's headquarters, we tensely watched the yea or nay roll-call vote on a jury-rigged C-SPAN hookup.

"In this game," Mike Lashbrook said as he watched the small-screen TV, "you've got to give some to get some."

Harold Volkmer and his allies—especially Michigan congressman John Dingell—knew the game well. They traded the interstate sale of handguns for language allowing the interstate transport of *all* legal firearms—including handguns—provided they were unloaded in a locked container such as a car trunk, and separate from ammunition. As a sop to their antigun colleagues, they also allowed the vote on an amendment by Hughes to make it unlawful for any civilian to own or sell a machine gun except for those weapons already lawfully owned. That amendment effectively banned the manufacture and sale of new machine guns. When the voice vote came, it was clear that the nays had it, and that the amendment had been defeated. But the Chair ruled, "The yeas have it," and refused to hear any of the plaintive objections from Republican members. I could almost hear the howls of outrage among the already paranoid Knoxers across the country.

But at the end of the afternoon, Volkmer's bill passed by a vote of 292 yeas versus 130 nays. The law made obvious good sense. Law-abiding gun owners and firearms dealers were protected from the government harassment that many had experienced since 1968. One hundred and sixty-one Republicans had been joined by 131 Democrats in supporting the bill. This was testimony to the NRA's influence. Our full-court lobbying press had split almost half the Democrat members away from their solid majority of 246 over the Republicans' 176 minority. And we had achieved this victory in the face of the skilled, determined opposition of such legendary parliamentary masters as House Speaker Tip O'Neill, Judiciary Committee chairman Peter Rodino, and Crime Subcommittee chairman William Hughes.

The National Rifle Association, I thought, *is at the peak of its power*.

•   •   •

The glow of this historic victory did not linger inside the marble cube at 1600 Rhode Island Avenue, Northwest. On the morning of Wednesday, May 7, 1986, Executive Vice President G. Ray Arnett summoned Johnny Aquilino to his office. As I would learn later, Arnett gave Johnny a smarmy explanation that, although he was doing a "great job," it was in the interest of the NRA to replace the *entire* Public Education Division with people from the Ackerman-McQueen advertising agency. This massacre was made necessary in part, Arnett claimed, because the Ackerman-McQueen operation was "computerized" and had better press contacts. Johnny had been begging the bean counters on the eighth floor for computers for years.

He stayed calm on the surface, shook Arnett's hand, and then went back to the second floor to relay Arnett's orders: the seventeen members of the staff had until noon to clear out their desks and leave the building.

When I learned of this outrage, I could not believe the news. Johnny's crew was among the association's most effective workers, and they had just helped elevate the NRA to its position of supremacy among Washington power lobbies.

"We haven't heard from the board yet," I told Mike Lashbrook. Ten days later, we did.

At a hastily called meeting of the board's executive committee on May 17, Arnett was stripped of power and Warren Cassidy was ordered to perform the duties of executive vice president. The board also called Harlon Carter back from retirement to keep his eye on the shop until the dust settled, or as I put it until "the bricks stop falling."

Arnett claimed he'd been the victim of a "kangaroo court" and threatened a lawsuit. He also said he would obtain a court order allowing him to retain his position. In the end, he did not leave the building quite as abruptly as the Public Education staff, but he did leave.

• • •

Several years later, a prominent antigun organization, the Violence Policy Center, issued a press release on Arnett's sacking:

> When G. Ray Arnett was ousted from the NRA leadership in May 1986, among the reasons cited were: 'Mr. Arnett has made personal decisions on the basis of his personal interest rather than the interests of the Association.' These charges stemmed from Arnett's relationship with NRA staffer Tracey Attlee. Attlee was a frequent travel and shooting companion. In 1986 Arnett promoted Attlee from the public education division to international shooting with an unauthorized salary increase of more than $13,000. This, coupled with Arnett's dismissal of the remaining public education staff, resulted in the NRA board's removal of both Arnett and Attlee.

The Violence Policy Center didn't often understand the hidden intrigues of the National Rifle Association. This time they did.

• • •

Under the NRA's new bylaws that had been written after the heated Seattle meeting, the board—not the membership—confirmed Warren Cassidy for a five-year term as executive vice president.

Wayne LaPierre took over as executive director of ILA. And Jim Baker now ran Federal.

Wayne had been pleased with the public relations support he'd received from the Ackerman-McQueen ad agency during the last year of the Volkmer-McClure campaign. Soon "Ack-Mac" account executives had moved into the old Public Education offices on the second floor, bringing with them their state-of-the art word processors and graphics computers that Johnny had been begging for. He never worked for the NRA again.

• • •

By the next year, Ackerman-McQueen had taken exclusive control of the NRA's advertising operations and its day-to-day public affairs work. The NRA reportedly put Ack-Mac on an $80,000 monthly retainer and also paid them a generous rate for any separate advertising work. This arrangement presented a blatant conflict of interest: the agency consulted on public affairs goals and then recommended their own firm's no-bid advertising campaigns to meet those goals.

The deal wasn't necessarily bad. But it was expensive.

By the spring of 1987, Ackerman-McQueen had convinced Wayne LaPierre in the ILA and Warren Cassidy to run the slickest, hardest-hitting print media campaign the association had ever undertaken. Its message was DEFEND YOUR RIGHT TO DEFEND YOURSELF, and it obviously drew a lot from our media blitz in New York following the Goetz case. This was ironic as hell, since Johnny Aquilino and Jack Adkins had put so much creative talent into our campaign, and now Ack-Mac was replaying our tune.

But there was no arguing that the ads were arresting and effective. A "barrage" of six ads would run in major U.S. newspapers just after Labor Day. Each ad featured a stark black-and-white photograph of a dramatized crime, focusing on the criminals or the unarmed victims, with a short block of text, and the tagline, DEFEND YOUR RIGHT set in bold type below.

One ad displayed the frightening, distorted image of a man's face, cloaked by a nylon stocking. The headline read SHOULD YOU SHOOT A RAPIST BEFORE HE CUTS YOUR THROAT? The choice of gun ownership, the ad explained, was up to each person, woman or man. "American women are realizing they must take responsibility for their own self-defense."

An ad focusing on a battered wife asked: HOW MUCH RED TAPE IS TOO MUCH WHEN HE THREATENS TO KILL YOU? Another ad showed an elderly women assaulted in broad daylight on the front stairs of her house and asked the question: IF YOU'RE ATTACKED ON YOUR PORCH, DO YOU WANT YOUR NEIGHBORS TO BE OPPOSED TO GUN OWNERSHIP OR MEMBERS OF THE NRA?

Created to attract attention—and new members—the Ackerman-McQueen ad campaign reached millions, created predictable media

controversy, and solidified the ad agency's foothold at NRA headquarters. This grip only grew stronger as Handgun Control, Inc.,
and the National Coalition to Ban Handguns—still stung by passage
of the Firearm Owners Protection Act—ran their own competing
ads.

The National Rifle Association was right back where it wanted to
be, in the thick of the battle.

•   •   •

I was no longer at the NRA, however, when the sensational ad
campaign was published. I hadn't become burned out by three
exhilarating years of political combat, but I had come to realize
my earlier suspicions that the NRA manipulated its members to
shake loose contributions—better to fight than win—were well
grounded. And Ackerman-McQueen was the ideal vehicle to conduct
this cynical policy.

In the winter of 1987, the Sporting Goods Manufacturers Association (SGMA) began to sound me out to take over as their national
director of a tort-reform campaign. Their members, who ranged from
companies that made everything from trampolines to football helmets and hockey posts, were taking a beating in the courts. Lawsuit
mania had reached the high school athletic fields and ball diamonds.
Big universities and city park systems could afford high insurance
premiums or to self-insure. Small operations could not. Someone had
to stop the bleeding.

I guess my credentials were pretty good: I was an attorney and
had racked up an impressive string of victories at the NRA. The
Sporting Goods Manufacturers Association kept courting me, raising
the salary ante. I knew if I could hold them off a few more months, the
salary would go even higher.

But in May 1987, it was time for me to leave 1600 Rhode Island
Avenue. I had boss trouble. Mike Lashbrook had gone up to the
eighth floor to become Warren Cassidy's chief of staff. Mike's
replacement at state and local was Ted Lattanzio, his deputy.
Ted was one of those geeks who left at 5 p.m. on the dot with every
pencil and paperclip perfectly arranged on his desk. We did not get
along.

Our on-again, off-again warfare culminated when the Coalition of New Jersey Sportsmen planned their annual dinner on May 16 in Woodbridge, and Rodger Iverson asked if I could get a "big name" as a speaker.

Feldman to the rescue. "I'll get you two, Rodger," I said, promising to bring Warren Cassidy and none other than Congressman Harold Volkmer. Rodger was thrilled.

But a problem arose. Rodger told me in late April that the ticket sales had been "very disappointing." In other words, we'd be inviting the executive vice president of the NRA and a U.S. congressman to address a half-empty hall at the Landmark Inn. Not on my watch. I wanted to send a special alert under Warren's signature, informing all NRA members within fifty miles of the dinner and the speakers.

Lattanzio, however, vetoed the initiative, which he said "interfered" with our field services efforts. I suspected that he didn't want another Feldman success. I went around him.

Armed with a neatly drafted members' alert, I went upstairs to shoot the breeze with Warren.

"How're ticket sales going?" he asked.

"Not good." I handed him the proposed alert, to which I'd affixed official routing slips, as though it was just waiting for Warren's approval.

Warren signed. The alert went out. We got an overflow crowd. And Ted Lattanzio had a fit. I had usurped his fragile authority. Wayne LaPierre had to back his division heads. My head had to roll. I was given the choice of resigning or being fired.

When I went in to give Wayne my resignation letter, he was very nervous, his hands trembling.

"Richie," he promised, "I'll help you in any way I can to get you a good job on the Hill."

"I'll be okay, Wayne," I said. I planned to sign my contract with the SGMA within twenty-four hours.

"You did well, Richie," he said. "We're going to miss you."

"Maybe I'll be back one day."

6

LAWYERS, MONEY, AND
BACK TO GUNS

By the summer of 1987, I was busy with the Sporting Goods Manufacturers Association. I was also enjoying my new home, the Devonshire at the PGA resort in Palm Beach Gardens—a short drive inland from the SGMA office on the South Florida Intracoastal Waterway.

The SGMA was not racked by Byzantine (or Knoxantine) intrigues. And I didn't have to please narrow-minded functionaries like Ted Lattanzio.

My buddies at the National Rifle Association kept me apprised of the still-smoldering internal political feuds, but it seemed that the new leadership at 1600 Rhode Island Avenue had quelled the worst—and most public—internecine struggles. Warren Cassidy was now the executive vice president, and Wayne LaPierre ran the Institute for Legislative Action, while Jim Baker was head of Federal. Although there was an underlying distrust among the three, particularly between Cassidy and LaPierre, everyone recognized the need to work together in the wake of the Arnett fiasco.

Neal Knox and Tanya Metaksa were in exile.

For the moment, I thought, paging through the latest *American Rifleman* that had just caught up with me in North Palm Beach, *the association's in good hands*. I could only hope that intrigue wouldn't erode the prestige and effectiveness of the organization for which I had worked so hard and in which I still had deep-seated hopes.

In Florida, one of the first orders of business that Howard Bruns, the CEO of the Manufacturers Association, asked me to address was getting myself up to speed on the burgeoning spread of tort litigation squeezing our members. We represented a diverse group of companies ranging from those that made tennis rackets or golf clubs, to those that made football helmets, water skis, and sneakers. In the association's first year of operation, we were down to the last diving board manufacturer that had been a member since the early sixties.

"That gives you an idea how bad things are getting, Richie," Howard told me that first week in the North Palm Beach office.

Naturally, I'd studied torts in law school, so I understood the relevant legal theory. Simply stated, a tort is that part of civil law involving damage or injury to one party—the plaintiff—caused by the willful act, negligence, or faulty product designed, manufactured, distributed, or merely used by the other party—the defendant. A tort lawsuit can concern anything from recouping the medical expenses of a sprained ankle suffered by slipping in a motel shower to a multiple-plaintiff lawsuit against an airline whose jet crashes.

By the late 1980s, tort lawsuits had become a huge business, with some plaintiffs' law firms comprising hundreds of attorneys. The old wisecracks about the apocryphal ambulance chasers Dewey, Cheathem & Howe were no longer funny. Neither were the burgeoning commercials on local TV stations, "If you've got a phone, you've got a lawyer, and it won't cost you anything unless we collect." In other words, Americans were being encouraged to sue early and sue often.

The impact of runaway tort lawsuits for the members of the Sporting Goods Manufacturers Association arose from the economics involved. Most of the lawsuits were filed by plaintiffs' lawyers on a contingency-fee basis: "I don't get paid unless you collect."

A hypothetical—but increasingly common—type of suit might involve a high school football player who suffers a neck or spine injury in practice. Even though the kid's parents have signed a stack of waivers allowing their son to hit the gridiron with his classmates, once the boy is hurt, Dewey, Cheathem & Howe convince mom and dad to sue. And whom do they sue? The helmet manufacturer, naturally. And the school board. And the team's coaches.

The suit is filed, and evidence is collected. It might turn out that most of the fault lies with an overly aggressive coach, who pitted a skinny 130-pound Johnny, the injured end, against a hulking 200-pound linebacker, Billy. Logically, Coach Jones is most at fault—probably 75 percent. And Jackson High School shares the responsibility—24 percent for having Jones on the payroll.

But what about the Acme Helmet Company? After depositions and experts' reports, it appears the helmet maker is only about 1 percent liable. So they're off the legal hook, right?

No, they're just as liable as the other defendants. This is due to the theory of Joint and Several Liability under which *all* the defendants found liable in a tort lawsuit—no matter what their degree of responsibility—are equally liable for payment of the entire amount won by the injured party. Under this doctrine, plaintiffs generally seek cases that involve at lease one deep-pockets defendant.

Coach Jones goes bankrupt rather than face trial; the school board has some insurance but probably not as much as Acme Helmets. So, with a trial looming, it's almost certain that the helmet company's insurance company will settle out of court for an "undisclosed amount," which includes a hefty 33 percent contingency fee (plus costs) to Dewey, Cheathem & Howe.

By the time I focused on the issue, overall tort settlements (and judgments) were skyrocketing past 50 *billion* dollars a year.

•   •   •

At speaking engagements, I opened with a simple, albeit rhetorical, question: "When was the last time you saw a diving board at a public pool?" People usually perked up and listened. By 1987, most public diving boards had gone the way of the dodo. "I expect to see diving boards in an exhibit at the Smithsonian pretty soon," I always added. "Followed by football helmets and baseball bats."

Over the next eighteen months, I became a kind of Johnny Appleseed of tort reform, speaking to coaches' groups, league officials, and civic associations around the country about the crisis facing sports in the United States. In New England and the Rockies, I zeroed in on the runaway cost of ski-lift tickets—due almost entirely to rising insurance premiums. In the Midwest, I focused on the beloved small-town sports traditions of high school football and basketball.

And everywhere I spoke, I tried to convince people that their elected politicians—often including compliant judges—were in league with local versions of Dewey, Cheathem & Howe. The result of this collusion would be the "incremental elimination of sports in America"—at least at the scholastic and amateur levels. However, there was a solution, I emphasized, a *political* solution. Meeting with the local news media, I always noted my background as a successful NRA lobbyist. That fact got reporters' attention, and they invariably dubbed me the SGMA's "Hired Gun." I wanted to put politicians in Springfield, Illinois; Des Moines; or Baton Rouge on notice that their cozy—and largely unnoticed—relationship with the trial lawyers was about to end.

Tort reform was basically a state issue. The myriad details of tort law were hammered out in the country's fifty statehouses. Moreover, assemblymen and state senators were often lawyers themselves: a sizable proportion were members of the plaintiffs' bar, and many were dues-paying members of the Association of Trial Lawyers of America (ATLA). The ATLA was politically active and generous in its campaign contributions. In fact, the trial lawyers regularly outspent the NRA in state and local elections.

I began carrying a football helmet emblazoned with SOS—"Save Our Sports"—to media events. When reporters asked about my tactical goals, I sometimes replied, "I don't believe in fighting fire with fire . . ." Meaningful pause. "I believe in fighting fire with *napalm.*"

This kind of ballsy hyperbole made the evening news and the local newspapers. But I wanted to make progress on tort reform. When Howard Bruns left the SGMA in 1988, John Riddle, the new

CEO, Maria Dennison, the COO, and I quickly renamed our public-education operation the Coalition of Americans to Protect Sports— "CAPS." This was both catchier and sounded like a united national organization.

•   •   •

In August 1988, I attended the annual meeting of the American Legislative Exchange Council, which attracted state representatives from around the country. The 1988 convention was held in Nashville, and most of the delegates stayed at the Opryland Hotel, a big ersatz antebellum plantation house.

On the second day of the effort, I ran into Bill Bennett, my old Boston University mentor who had just delivered a rousing keynote address at lunch. Now, it seemed, it was he who needed some mentoring.

"Richie," he said after a rubber chicken event, "can you come up to my room? I need to pick your brain."

I had a hunch about what he had in mind.

Still in his early forties, Bill Bennett was fast achieving political prominence. Ronald Reagan had picked him early in his first term to head the National Endowment for the Humanities, and then during his second term chose Bill as secretary of education. Bennett was smart and articulate; he had a Ph.D. in political philosophy from the University of Texas and a law degree from Harvard. He'd been brilliant as a professor and administrator at Boston University. And I knew he was ambitious.

"I need some advice," Bill said. "I plan to run for national office sometime in the next ten years. What steps do you think I should be taking to enhance my national political stature?"

National office, I thought. He was talking about the White House, not a Massachusetts senate race. Bennett had made waves in Washington as a conservative intellectual who wasn't afraid to tackle controversial topics such as the liberal bias among unionized public school teachers—and the resulting erosion of American educational standards. But we both knew that no intellectual without any background in elective office—no matter how tough minded—had become president in recent history.

A campaign for the presidency was as complex as four-dimensional chess, with the fourth dimension being timing.

"I guess you're talking about the White House," I said.

Bill nodded with a youthful, optimistic smile.

"Okay," I continued, "either George Bush or Michael Dukakis will be elected this year. So 1992 would be the earliest year you could make your bid. That means you've basically got four years to stay in the public eye while simultaneously beefing up the weak spots on your résumé."

An alpha male, Bill Bennett didn't like hearing about weak spots. But he listened.

"To me," I added, "what you're lacking is pretty obvious: a solid grounding in law enforcement and any involvement with foreign policy issues. You're probably never going to attract urban black voters, but the white suburban middle class is worried about drug crime spilling out from the inner cities. They're also confused about what the holy hell's going on with Gorbachev and *glasnost* and all that. They'll vote for somebody who can provide answers."

Bill made a neat note and handed it to a silent, button-down young aide seated to the side of our shared couch.

"You make good points, Richie," he said. "As always."

My ego stroked, I departed. I had no idea that the seeds I had planted in this hotel suite would explode in only seven months when Bill Bennett would serve as President George H. W. Bush's director of the Office of National Drug Control Policy, America's first drug czar.

•   •   •

My work at the SGMA took me back to the world of guns on several occasions. And I got a preview of an issue that would come to dominate my professional life in the late 1990s: the interface between guns and high-stakes tort litigation.

The confrontation began slowly. In the 1980s, a Texas plaintiffs' lawyer named Wendell Turley was representing individuals who claimed injury from firearms. What was unique about some of Turley's cases was that they contained no claim of defect or malfunction of the weapon itself.

Rather, the alleged tort stemmed from the spurious fact that the firearm in question was unusually or uniquely hazardous. In one case, this claim was made against a "Saturday night special," a Rohm RG-38, a small inexpensive revolver that was used to shoot a person in a Maryland grocery store during the course of a robbery. The gun worked as it was designed, firing bullets, which were, of course, life-threatening. But Turley's legal theory was that the U.S. subsidiary of the German Rohm gun maker was at fault because the pistol's low cost made it easily available to criminals.

Turley won his client's case on appeal.

A more insidious connection between guns and torts arose in 1989. A state court in Philadelphia awarded an $11.3 million damage claim to a young woman who suffered a head wound when her neighbor's handgun accidentally fired. The background of the case was revealing (and it sent a chill through the gun industry): A woman named Brenda Teagle bought an inexpensive semiautomatic pistol from Donn's Gun Room in Montgomeryville, Pennsylvania. No gun store employee showed her how to load, unload, clean the pistol, or use its safety catch. One of Brenda Teagle's neighbors loaded the weapon for her, and she stored it in a bedside drawer without the safety engaged.

Two years later, the gun fired when some kids were examining it, wounding the plaintiff, who suffered permanent brain injury. The court found that Brenda Teagle shared legal responsibility for the accident with others, including Donn's Gun Room (which had the obligation to teach her safe handling of the weapon).

The gun store was the only party insured. So, under the doctrine of Joint and Several Liability, the store's insurance carrier was liable for 100 percent of the damages (up to the policy limits) awarded.

Bill Bridgewater, the executive director of the National Alliance of Stocking Gun Dealers, quickly voiced his members' disgust at the court decision: "A person who buys a gun is responsible for misusing it."

The "Stocking" dealers in his organization's name were the twelve thousand independent retail gun dealers nationwide who kept guns on their premises—in stock. It simply would not be practical for these gun dealers to give detailed and rigorous individual instructions to every buyer. But now the expansion of tort responsibility was pushing in that direction, threatening gun stores with prohibitively high insurance premiums.

When I was asked to comment on this new encroachment, I said the gun industry shouldn't just be sweating bullets, but rather "12-gauge shells."

●　　●　　●

During my frequent trips to Washington on the SGMA's business, I made sure to keep up my connection with the National Rifle Association. I stayed across the street at the Park Terrace Hotel and I still had plenty of friends in the organization, including Mary Corrigan, director of the Member Services Division, who always found me a spare desk at 1600 when I was in town. The guys I'd worked with, including Wayne LaPierre, also treated me to lunch so that we could discuss "tort reform" on their expense account nickels. In exchange for my information, they filled me in on the NRA's latest politically charged issues.

In 1988, Warren Cassidy and First Vice President Dick Riley appointed me to the public affairs and the urban affairs committees. I served beside Maryann Carter on public affairs and with Roy Innis on urban affairs. I was now part of the NRA's official family, which meant I would attend committee meetings in Washington twice a year in the week before the board of directors met and once before the annual convention.

I had hoped for a place on the legislative policy committee that focused on the NRA's lobbying priorities. But my old nemesis Ted Lattanzio was committee co-secretary, and I suspected he'd work behind the scenes to blackball me.

In any event, I did want to keep active in the gun issue because I had no doubt that was where my future lay. When I'd joined the NRA committees in September 1988, it was clear that there was plenty of work for me in those two assignments.

The inner-city crack cocaine wars were raging. And the antigun groups were using the rising urban homicide rate as a tool to scare the hell out of average Americans—white, suburban, middle class—for whom gun violence had never been a serious problem. That effort was just more grist for our mill, helping us to convince law-abiding members that the antigun groups were really "gun grabbers." So our public affairs campaigns were becoming increasingly central to reaching both the NRA's publicly stated and largely unobserved goals: simultaneously guarding Second Amendment rights while also attracting more members and contributions.

At the time, I understood and fully sympathized with the need to balance the NRA's public and the surreptitious agendas.

That was one reason that we were all pleased when the antigun groups and their media and Congressional allies made so many embarrassing technical errors in the protracted "plastic gun" controversy.

The handgun in question was the Glock 17 semiautomatic pistol, a truly innovative firearm. The Austrian toolmaker Gaston Glock, a pioneer in the development of light, tough polymer plastics, invented the pistol for the consideration of his country's army and police. Its unique feature was the extensive use of strong but lightweight polymer in the handgrip and frame. This allowed the grip—which held the magazine—to be larger, with a standard capacity of seventeen 9 mm bullets versus the seven or eight of conventional guns.

The firing mechanism, however—including the slide and the barrel—were made of high-grade steel. Metal made up a full 80 percent of the mass of the Glock 17. Gaston Glock never intended the gun to be either invisible or hard to detect when examined by airport or building security X-rays. Indeed, most types of dense plastic—camera bodies, hairbrushes, *and* the dense polymer portions of the Glock 17—were relatively easy to identify on checkpoint screens. And given the amount of steel integral to the weapon, it could also be detected at security magnetometers. Of course, the bullets always showed clearly on X-rays.

So stealth was not Gaston Glock's goal. The advantages of his pistol were its light weight, corrosion resistance, ammunition capacity, as well as its redundant internal safeties. The absence of external safeties appealed to police who didn't want to pull their gun in a confrontation and have to ponder, "Let me think, is the safety on or off? Hmm?"

Nevertheless, members of the news media and antigun groups campaigned relentlessly to have these *plastic* "terrorist" guns banned.

The genesis of this campaign was interesting. In January 1985, the muckraking investigative reporter Jack Anderson wrote an article titled "Qaddafi Buying Austrian Plastic Pistol," which was published in the *Washington Post* and which was reprinted widely in the United States and overseas. "Libyan dictator Muammar Qaddafi is in the process of buying more than 100 plastic handguns that would be difficult for airport security forces to detect," Anderson wrote, citing unnamed intelligence sources.

He was wrong on both counts. No Libyan intelligence officers had ever tried to buy guns from Glock, as Anderson had alleged. And he knew when he wrote the article that the weapon wasn't "frighteningly easy to smuggle past airport security." A Pentagon counterterrorism official *had* smuggled a Glock 17 through an airport checkpoint, but had also successfully sneaked an all-metal Heckler & Koch P-9 handgun through the same security control—due to lax surveillance by the bored contract operators at the X-ray machine and magnetometer.

Anderson's sensationalized, screw-the-facts approach, however, quickly created an urban legend: some evil European genius (Gaston Glock) had invented a plastic gun invisible to airport X-rays and was selling them to a terrorist state (Libya).

Billie H. Vincent, director of civil aviation security at the FAA tried to set the record straight and stop the groundswell of misinformation about the Glock flowing from antigun groups and the media. Testifying before Congress in April 1986, Vincent stated, "Contrary to the information being put out now . . . the Glock 17 is detectable on all our systems, whether it is the metal detector or the X-ray system."

But this common-sense approach did not stop the legend from spreading. When antigun groups like Handgun Control, Inc., and the National Coalition to Ban Handguns picked up the Glock controversy, a parry-and-thrust, punch-and-counterpunch struggle with the NRA began. It would drag on for years, and did more to promote the Glock "mystique" than any paid advertising campaign possibly could have.

The antigunners ostensibly wanted to see the importation and sale of these *terrorist* weapons banned—and to claim credit for the victory to their members. As with the phony "cop-killer" KTW bullet controversy, the National Rifle Association stood firmly against compromise on this new issue.

The association's position was clear and resonated well with its membership. Most were technically savvy and understood that the Glock pistol presented no more security threat than any other handgun. And the NRA drew on this understanding to spread the incipient fear that the gun grabbers were not just after the Glock 17. Once they used their bogus information to outlaw Glocks (a well-made and expensive pistol), *all* handguns—revolvers and semiautos alike—would be threatened. Emergency alerts flooded the nation from the Institute for Legislative Action, and contributions to fight this potential "unprecedented" gun grab poured back into the NRA's mailroom.

We all knew that the association could have educated the American people about the actual *plastic* content in a Glock pistol. But the National Rifle Association did not actually wish the media and politicians to come to their senses and abandon their unsound stance, which reinforced our position that America's law-abiding gun owners risked losing their Second Amendment rights.

"Rick," I told Manning, "they don't really want us to educate people on this issue. The association wants to use it as a club to beat the antigunners."

"You got that one right."

This was an insight of fundamental importance. The NRA insisted on absolute hegemony in every significant gun issue nation-wide, whether it was a municipal or county firearms license statute or major federal legislation like Volkmer-McClure. The association had no interest in compromise. It would have been relatively easy to demonstrate to the public that the Glock pistol was no more dangerous than any other weapon. But educating the public—either through elected officials or the media—was not the association's paramount goal. Its overriding aim was preserving its dominant position as protectors and guardians of the faith, a sort of Knights Templar–extraordinaire, of the Second Amendment.

At that time, I thought I understood the need for this inflexible attitude. And I supported it. If the NRA didn't hold firm on Second Amendment rights, who would?

• • •   ᐟ

One SGMA member I came to know well was an emerging leader of the firearms industry. Buddy Pilgrim, president and CEO of Ellett Brothers, sat on my CAPS board of directors. Ellett Brothers was one of the country's largest wholesalers of rifles, shotguns, and handguns, supplying thousands of licensed retail gun dealers from a huge warehouse in Chapin, South Carolina. These dealers included the twelve thousand members of Bill Bridgewater's National Association of Stocking Gun Dealers. Between their two organizations, Pilgrim and Bridgewater had a huge hand in a lot of gun sales in the United States.

In 1988, Pilgrim invited me up to South Carolina to see his operation. A kid in a candy store wasn't the half of it. I was overwhelmed by rack after rack after more racks stacked upon racks of pump and semiauto shotguns, and rifles ranging in caliber from the .22s I'd shot as a kid at Camp Mah-Kee-Nac to .375 Winchester big game guns. The handgun selection was equally enticing. I hefted Colt Model 1911's .45s, .38 Police Special revolvers, imported Heckler & Koch 9 mm semiautos, and long-barreled .44 magnums—Clint Eastwood's "Make my day" Dirty Harry pistol.

As I followed Buddy through the warehouse, my resolution to shift my professional focus back to the world of guns only intensified.

• • •

I had the chance to begin this shift that fall. Buddy Pilgrim and several of his high-level associates in the firearms business were becoming increasingly concerned with the future of their industry—and with the NRA's seeming inability to protect their interests. After a phone call with Buddy, it became clear that he viewed the National Rifle Association as a less-than-benign guardian of the gun industry.

"Richie," he told me, "I'm really worried about the future. And as far as I can tell, *nobody* is looking out for business people like me, not the NSSF, and certainly not the NRA."

The National Shooting Sports Foundation (NSSF) purportedly protected the interests of the firearms industry. But I'd heard a lot of complaints that the group was "stuck back in the 1950s" and hadn't kept up with current issues.

As for the NRA, "They've got a lot on their plate right now, and on their minds," I said.

Buddy Pilgrim was not overly sympathetic. He was preoccupied with the disparate, but interrelated, interests of firearms importers, ammunition and accessory manufacturers, wholesalers, distributors, and retailers. Each of these groups had legislative, regulatory, and legal issues at the local, state, national, and international levels.

"I've been talking to some of my counterparts," he explained, "wholesalers, importers, and manufacturers. We think we'd be better served forming our own association than hoping the NRA will ride up on their white horse and rescue us."

The NRA's not going to like that. After all, hegemony was the ethos of the association. But the NRA had slipped in the estimation of the insightful firearms industry professionals like Buddy Pilgrim. Its membership, and subsequently its dues revenue, had dropped alarmingly from a record high of more than 3 million members during the heyday of the Volkmer-McClure legislative campaign. Equally alarming were the reports of mismanagement and fiscal incompetence (an ill-advised five-dollar dues increase, lost magazine advertising revenue, etc.) that were leaking out of 1600 Rhode Island Avenue.

Although Jim Baker, Wayne LaPierre, and Warren Cassidy had formed a solid public front, trying to burnish the association's image, reports of internal strife were becoming persistent. Many rumors concerned an ongoing effort by Baker and LaPierre to topple Cassidy—with each of the putative rebels secretly lining up support on the board of directors. Meanwhile, Neal Knox was plotting with his own supporters, who hoped to change the NRA's bylaws back to the original procedure under which the membership, not the board, chose the executive vice president.

By itself, this inevitable internal friction would not seem especially alarming. But reports of this squabbling were not isolated. The reports had to be viewed in conjunction with the loss of more than 340,000 members, the post-Volkmer-McClure resurgence of Handgun Control, Inc., and by mounting opposition among senior urban police officials following the association's no-compromise KTW Bullet and "plastic gun" campaigns. By the fall of 1988, NRA headquarters at 1600 Rhode Island Avenue hardly seemed the monolithic fortress it had appeared to be only eighteen months earlier.

Given the NRA's situation, it was beginning to dawn on Buddy Pilgrim and many in the industry that if they were looking for support on a variety of issues, they'd probably be better off drawing on their own resources than on the NRA's. So in October 1988, Buddy asked me to join his colleagues in Atlanta to attend an organizational meeting of the American Shooting Sports Coalition (ASSC), the industry's new trade association being formed to represent them.

The one-day meeting was held at the Atlanta Airport Marriott, in one of those windowless meeting rooms that alternated from arctic chill to tropical swelter as the air-conditioning system advanced through its cycle. Because the stated business was writing bylaws for the new association, most of those attending were lawyers—not my idea of a pleasant diversion from tort reform. You get more than a dozen lawyers in the same room—no matter the problem at hand— and they're all going to whip out their yellow pads and start parsing language. They viewed a draft bylaw almost as a contract, which required absolutely every contingency to be covered. I was glad that Buddy hadn't asked me there for my legal advice, but rather for my knowledge of gun policy.

In addition to Buddy, the main organizer of the meeting was Mike Saporito, a very bright former prosecutor and municipal court judge in Rochester, New York. He was the general counsel and partner at RSR, one of the country's largest firearms wholesalers based in Winter Park near Orlando. Buddy and Mike (Big Mike, as his closest friends called him) were both "hefty" guys who made a palpable presence in any gathering.

But they were nimble thinkers. They did not trust the NRA to further the interests of firearms importers, small manufacturers, wholesalers, and retailers, so they saw the proposed coalition as a way to unify these groups. The new organization would promote "reasonable" firearms legislation while opposing laws that unreasonably restricted the purchase, transport, and use of firearms by responsible, law-abiding civilians.

In other words, the nascent American Shooting Sports Coalition would avoid the protracted controversy and sequence of annual crises so dear to the NRA. Instead, the ASSC would be bottom-line oriented. The group would lobby for concrete results, not to achieve raw political power for power's sake.

It sounded like a good idea to me.

At the end of the day, Buddy Pilgrim took me aside. "We're looking for an executive director, Richie," he said. "Are you interested in the job?"

Of course I was interested. Going back to the gun issue to work toward winnable, *reasonable* goals was very appealing. But I hadn't been with CAPS long enough to bail out in good conscience.

So instead, I recommended Manny Kapelsohn, a Yale honors grad with a law degree from Harvard, who was probably the most knowledgeable and versatile firearms expert witness in the United States. He was a certified law-enforcement instructor in virtually every kind of weapon the new association would represent.

"I think I've got your guy, Buddy," I said.

By that winter, Manny Kapelsohn was the executive director of the new ASSC.

•   •   •

Late in 1988, the SGMA's John Riddle decided he wanted a different focus for his group. He wanted to move the association away from the difficult goal of nationwide tort reform and toward improving product reliability and thus protection from unwarranted lawsuits.

The surviving manufacturers of football equipment or bicycles, for example, not only began to overbuild their gear with inevitable tort suits in mind, they also thoroughly documented the process. And tens of thousands of pages of legal gobbledygook made their way through thousands of lawyers' word processors—the iron-clad disclaimers that the manufacturer should not be held responsible for the improper use of a basketball, football, nine iron, or tennis racket. Warnings started appearing on store displays, boxes, and on decals stuck to badminton sets. We were witnessing the equivalent of child-resistant medicine bottle caps on athletic fields and playgrounds.

John Riddle might have succeeded in armor-plating the Sporting Goods Manufacturing Association, but I recognized that I was no longer needed in the new organization. They wanted to focus on risk management and I wanted to change the economics of the tort system.

I resigned in late 1989.

7

"WEAPONS OF WAR"

O n the cool morning of Tuesday, January 17, 1989, a Chevrolet station wagon stopped outside the playground of the Cleveland Elementary School in Stockton, California, a farming center about an hour's drive south of Sacramento. Patrick Purdy, twenty-six, an unstable drifter with a long record of arrests and a history of drug abuse, climbed from the car carrying a Chinese-made Norinco AK-56S, a semiautomatic version of the Soviet 7.62 mm AK-47 Kalashnikov rifle. Purdy had fitted a bulky 75-round drum magazine to the weapon. He also carried a spare magazine and a Taurus 9 mm semiautomatic pistol.

He wore a motley combination of camouflage garb and a civilian ballistic vest. Purdy, who had attended this school until age eight when he was placed in foster care in Oregon, had come to settle scores with the demons that had tormented him most of his life. On the stock of the rifle he had carved the words "victory," "freedom," and "Hezbollah." He had printed "PLO," "Libya," and "death to the Great Satin [sic]" on his flak jacket.

Purdy was methodical. As he gazed at the children and teachers filling the playground for morning recess, Purdy inserted foam plugs into his ears to protect his hearing. The few people who knew him would later recount that Purdy had fantasies of guerrilla warfare in the streets of the United States, a struggle during which he would eliminate undesirable foreign elements, especially Asians, whom, he said, were taking every available job.

He had chosen this Tuesday to move from troubled delusion to violent reality. Many of the small children tossing balls and skipping rope were Asians—Cambodian and Vietnamese immigrants. To Patrick Purdy, who often mixed street drugs with prescription psychotropic medications, they might have looked like an enemy horde.

He walked through the gate, braced himself on the fence to steady his aim, and began shooting. The semiautomatic weapon fired one round each time Purdy pulled the trigger. Children were knocked down from the impact of the bullets. Larger kids tried unsuccessfully to scatter for safety. Purdy emptied the 75-round drum and inserted a curved 30-round magazine in the weapon. By the time he had fired his full load of ammunition a few minutes later, five children had been killed, and twenty-nine others and a teacher thrashed on the ground, wounded.

Apparently satisfied, Purdy walked back to his car, set it ablaze with gasoline, and shot himself in the head with his 9 mm pistol.

The subsequent investigation revealed that Purdy had legally purchased the semiautomatic AK-56S rifle at an Oregon sporting goods store and the pistol at a Stockton pawnshop. Although Purdy had a long criminal record, with arrests for drug and dangerous weapons possession, robbery, and assault, he had been able to plea all the felony charges down to misdemeanors. In 1984, he was diagnosed with a "substance induced personality disorder" (alcoholism and drug addiction) and began receiving Social Security disability payments. After an assault on a police officer, Purdy was given another psychiatric screening and found to be suicidal, homicidal, and "extremely dangerous." But he was never committed.

So Purdy completed the mandatory Bureau of Alcohol, Tobacco, and Firearms Form 4473 for the guns used in the playground killings honestly stating that he had never been adjudicated mentally defective or committed to a mental institution. He simply chose to lie on the question about drug abuse.

●   ●   ●

The fallout from the "Stockton massacre" came quickly and spread nationwide. Soon after the shootings, Josh Sugarmann, executive director of the Violence Policy Center (an organization of zealous gun control activists)—and former spokesman for the National Coalition to Ban Handguns—published what would become a seminal policy paper: "Assault Weapons: Analysis, New Research, and Legislation."

"Many Americans do believe that handguns are effective weapons for home-defense," Sugarmann wrote, "and the majority of Americans . . . believe the Second Amendment of the Constitution guarantees the individual right to keep and bear arms. Yet, many who support the individual's right to own a handgun have second thoughts when the issue comes down to assault weapons. Assault weapons are often viewed the same way as machine guns and 'plastic' firearms—a weapon that poses such a grave risk that it's worth compromising a perceived constitutional right."

Before Sugarmann authored this paper, only a few people had heard the ominous term "assault weapon." He seemed to have loosely translated the World War II German Army designation for the Sturmgewehr 44 ("Storm Rifle," Model 1944). Like the later Soviet Kalashnikov, the German weapon fired a smaller caliber round than standard infantry rifles. A switch on the firearm allowed it to fire in the single-shot, semiautomatic mode, or as a fully automatic machine gun. The weapons were distributed to the Wermacht in very limited numbers.

But after the Vietnam War and long years of strife in the postcolonial world, fully automatic infantry weapons such as the Kalashnikov AK-47 and the American M-16 became a staple of television news—and a favorite of Hollywood. Images of drug gangs and Special Ops commandos blazing away with their weapons on "full auto" had supplanted the Tommy guns of Bonnie and Clyde and the pursuing G-men of earlier years. People thought they knew a machine gun when they saw one. If it looks like a duck . . .

Sugarmann was banking on this misunderstanding. And the Stockton shootings made his job easier.

"The [assault] weapons' menacing looks," Sugarmann wrote in the paper, "coupled with the public's confusion over fully-automatic machine guns versus semi-automatic assault weapons—anything that looks like a machine gun is assumed to be a machine gun—can only increase the chance of public support for restrictions on these weapons."

• • •

Sugarmann was preaching to the choir in the California legislature. Prior to the Stockton murders, California state senator David A. Roberti (D-Van Nuys) and assemblyman Mike Roos (D-Los Angeles) were working to enact greater restrictions than required by then-existing law on the sale and ownership of semiautomatic long guns of the type Sugarmann had labeled "assault weapons."

The National Rifle Association was confident that this pending "Roberti-Roos" legislation could be watered down. Dave Marshall, the NRA state liaison (who I had replaced in the northeast in 1984) was leading a convoluted closed-door lobbying effort to ensure that no outright ban, or inflexible registration law would pass that might impact the sale and ownership of a host of semiautomatic long guns— many of which looked like assault weapons but were basically target-shooting or hunting ("sporting") models.

But after Stockton, there was a groundswell of outrage that military-style weapons with high-capacity magazines were as easy to buy, sell, and swap as the .22 caliber target rifles I'd shot as a kid. The Roberti-Roos bill swept aside the NRA's efforts to limit its scope. The original bill was expanded and revitalized in the Sacramento committees and passed with a wide margin of votes on May 24, 1989. Governor George Deukmejian signed the Roberti-Roos Assault Weapons Control Act of 1989 into law the same day.

Although both pro- and antigun control organizations described the new law as a "ban," it allowed thousands of assault weapons legally held before June 1, 1989, to remain with their owners, provided the weapons were registered with the California Department of Justice by March 31, 1992. The law also prohibited the manufacture, sale, transfer, or importation into the state of fifty-six specific firearms designated as assault weapons. This list covered the most readily available military-style semiautomatic rifles and carbines: the AK "series" (including the Norinco 56S that Patrick Purdy used); all other AK-type domestic and import models; the Israeli-made UZI and Galil; the foreign and domestic derivatives of the Colt

AR-15; and a variety of other less-common semiautomatic inter-
mediate rifle-caliber guns. "Assault pistols" were also found on the
Roberti-Roos list, including the Intratec TEC-9 and similar external
magazine-fed 9 mm guns made famous (or notorious) on television
shows like *Miami Vice*.

As I read the mainstream news media commentary on the impact
of the Roberti-Roos law, I saw a pattern familiar from my tenure as an
NRA lobbyist in the northeast. Senior California law-enforcement
officials—like their counterparts in Massachusetts, New York, and
New Jersey—followed the policy line of their political leaders.
Because influential California politicians saw the law as a significant
gun control victory, these police officials touted its merits. These
senior officers implied that their officers were confiscating many
fewer assault weapons from criminals as the implementation date
approached. But hard before-and-after numbers were difficult to
obtain. This did not stop the *Washington Post* from proclaiming "a
dramatic decline in the illegal use of AK-47s, Uzis and other
semiautomatic firearms that had been favored by drug dealers and
gang members throughout the country."

When I read that quote and scanned the list of fifty-six weapons
on the Roberti-Roos list, it was obvious (to me, at least) that Josh
Sugarmann had scored important points. People would take comfort
believing that a significant public safety trend had begun in California
and would probably sweep the country, ridding our crime-plagued
streets of all menacing military firearms. But I quickly realized that
this was not the case. The word in gun circles was that certain
manufacturers were already renaming or slightly altering their
affected models to eliminate prohibited nomenclature.

This reminded me of the "red car" fallacy in logic. Red cars are
involved in a disproportionate number of accidents; therefore, red
cars must be *inherently* dangerous. So it follows that road safety can
be improved by banning red cars. This progression of logic, of course,
ignores the fact that young people prefer flashy red cars and that they
are the least experienced, riskiest drivers.

Similarly, banning a list of specific firearms by *name* would
supposedly decrease gun deaths. But what if the manufacturer simply
changed the name? And as Roberti-Roos took effect, this was exactly
what was happening. If a criminal switched from a flashy TEC-9 to a

traditional looking Smith & Wesson 9 mm, he remained just as dangerous.

This trend to ban semiautomatic firearms alarmed my friends in rifle and pistol clubs—Jerry Preiser, Rodger Iverson, and others— who were technically well versed in weapons.

"If Purdy had been shooting a hundred-year-old pump shotgun with double-aught buckshot," Rodger said, "he could have fired more 'bullets' in less time than an AK or MAC-9."

He had a point. A perfectly legal pump shotgun could fire 00 (double-O) buckshot shells, each containing twelve .33 caliber bullets. By working the slide as quickly as possible, the venerable pump would blast out six shells in less than ten seconds, producing a volume of fire greater than a modern "assault weapon." But no one was talking about banning Grandpa's duck gun. At least not yet.

The NRA response to the Roberti-Roos law was predictable. The association launched an immediate legal challenge, *Fresno Rifle and Pistol Club v. Van de Kamp,* on the grounds that the law violated the Second Amendment guarantee of the right to keep and bear arms. The Fresno Club was an NRA affiliate and Van de Kamp was the California attorney general. This lawsuit ran into serious resistance almost immediately, but the National Rifle Association continued to litigate—which, of course, presented the opportunity to use the legal confrontation as the core of a well-orchestrated fund-raising campaign.

(Lawsuits—and their protracted appeals—gave the NRA the chance to shake the membership's money tree. In the case of the Roberti-Roos litigation, the suits and appeals would drag on for twelve years before the U.S. Supreme Court finally sided with California courts and the association's legal challenge to the assault weapons ban was rejected. But twelve years was a long time when it came to mailing out fund-raisers.)

• • •

In the U.S. Senate, senators Howard Metzenbaum (D-Ohio) and Dennis DeConcini (D-Arizona), formerly an NRA "A"-rated senator and past friend of Harlon Carter, were sponsoring bills to ban the sale and possession of semiautomatic firearms virtually identical to those on the Roberti-Roos list. A fund-raiser mailed under the signature of Wayne LaPierre, executive director of the NRA's Institute of Legislative Action, asked members to contribute and also to "tell your senators that the right to own a firearm is guaranteed by our Constitution and *nothing* should be done to abridge your Second Amendment rights." To further assure that the pending legislation would be stopped, ILA's letter offered a laundry list of contribution options, ranging from $5.95 for a 900 telephone number registration on the NRA Minuteman Alert Team (an automated call system advising on the status of these pending bills) to much larger contributions to the NRA Institute's political action committee, starting at $150. The ILA provided a prepaid business reply envelope for the contributions, which bore a computer-written cursive text in red ink, "Your 25¢ stamp will save us money!" This hokey fund-raiser's gimmick had two advantages: If people did use their own stamps, the NRA could save a lot of money. And the minor contribution would enhance members' sense of personal involvement in a larger crusade. The association would win on both counts, especially because the drive to ban semiautomatic assault weapons then spreading across the country and in Congress gave the NRA a Second Amendment rights issue much more compelling than the KTW "cop-killer" bullet or Glock "plastic gun" controversies.

•　　•　　•

So one would have expected that the National Rifle Association could have used the assault weapons controversy as an especially effective fund-raising and membership-recruiting tool. But that was not the case. The board of directors was displeased that, under Warren Cassidy's leadership, membership had dropped from almost 3 million at the time of the Volkmer-McClure victory to 2.7 million. It took annual expenditures of $13 to $15 million to add another hundred thousand members in 1988; most had joined in response to the perceived threat of state gun bans, not expensive solicitations.

There was no doubt that the anti–assault weapons forces were a growing threat. Gun control groups and individuals—including senior law-enforcement officers beholden to urban politicians— quickly developed a common mantra: high-power military-style assault rifles were the criminals' "weapons of choice." As I read their statements, I found this reasoning both illogical and disingenuous. Until very recently, organizations like Handgun Control, Inc., had campaigned to ban the sale of cheap small-caliber Saturday night special pistols because *these* guns were supposedly the criminals' preferred weapons. Now they were saying that criminals preferred expensive, high-powered, hard-to-conceal assault weapons.

The NRA valued this dichotomy. It revealed that antigun forces were either technically ignorant or deceitful—or both (as with the anti-KTW and Glock pistol campaigns). And the association's leadership hoped this revelation would stimulate badly needed contributions and spur membership growth.

As Warren Cassidy editorialized in the NRA's publications, those calling for the ban on assault weapons really *did* seek to confiscate all privately owned firearms in the United States. So the gun grabbers had cleverly manipulated the relationship between guns like the AK-47, AR-15, and the UZI and crime to accomplish their goal.

But there were even more impressive statistics that proved the opposite relationship. After the Stockton shootings, Eric C. Morgan, a North Carolina attorney and a recognized firearms legal scholar, wrote a well-researched and influential paper in the *American Journal of Criminal Law* on the pros and cons of banning assault weapons. Besides the questionable constitutionality of the Roberti-Roos act, Morgan demonstrated that "empirical evidence fails to support the legislative response" of such gun bans. In other words, there was no sense trying to fix a nonexistent problem.

"Semiautomatic military-style rifles, though sinister in appearance, are simply not the 'weapons of choice' of criminals and drug dealers." In 1988, for example, Morgan noted that only 3 percent of the guns that Los Angeles police seized from criminals fell under even the most expansive definition of assault weapon. Only 2.2 percent of the firearms San Francisco police confiscated that year were military-style semiautomatics, while such weapons made up only 1 percent of the almost five thousand guns that the San Diego police had seized in 1988, and were not a significant factor in the city's 144 homicides. On average, police in Akron, Ohio, took about four hundred weapons off the street from criminals each year: only

2 percent met any legal definition of the assault weapon (high-capacity magazine, pistol grip, military appearance, etc.).

But what about cities with rampant street crime and violent drug problems? New York City police confiscated 16,370 guns in 1988; only 1,028 of them were rifles, Morgan noted in his article, and far fewer could be defined as assault weapons. Even more dramatically, Washington, D.C., police seized more than three thousand weapons in 1988 but not one was an assault rifle. Yet homicide raged on the capital's streets. Further, Morgan argued, based on nationwide crime statistics, only "4 percent of all homicides in the United States involve rifles of any type, and less than half of 1 percent of those rifles could be considered military look-alike semiautomatic rifles." To emphasize his point, Morgan cited the 1987 *FBI Uniform Crime Reports* that revealed Americans were much more likely to be killed by a knife or a blunt object than any type of rifle.

"While they may appear menacing," Morgan concluded, "both local and national crime statistics do not indicate that the so-called assault rifles are a serious crime or drug problem."

Stated more colorfully, Joseph Constance, a deputy police chief in Trenton, New Jersey, testified to the U.S. Senate Judiciary Committee debating this issue, "My officers are more likely to confront an escaped tiger from the local zoo than to confront an assault rifle in the hands of a drug-crazed killer on the streets."

Joe Constance, whom I came to know and respect, was *not* an NRA shill. In fact, as a gun-owning cop, he avoided membership in the association so that the connection would not tarnish his position of political neutrality. And Eric Morgan was not a polemicist: his paper was rigorously sourced with scores of footnotes. It could have served as the basis of a rational debate on the issue. But it was in the interest of neither the NRA nor the antigun groups to conduct such an unemotional national debate.

•   •   •

On March 13, 1989, my old friend William Bennett was sworn in as the country's first director of the Office of National Drug Control Policy, a position that the media immediately dubbed the Drug Czar. That night as I watched the television news coverage of Bill's swearing-in ceremony at the White House, I thought about our last meeting. His aide in that Nashville hotel room had taken careful notes when I'd recommended that Bennett's political future depended on getting "a solid grounding" in law enforcement and foreign policy. Becoming drug czar involved both.

Bill's up and running, I thought.

But the next day I was stunned to read in the *Washington Post* that Bennett had prevailed on Treasury Secretary Nick Brady, who oversaw the Bureau of Alcohol, Tobacco, and Firearms, to ban the import of foreign-made semiautomatic weapons on a list that was virtually identical to that in the Roberti-Roos Act.

Bennett's stated reason for this action was dramatic and attracted widespread positive media coverage. Assault weapons, he stated, "were the 'weapons of choice' of drug dealers and other criminals." To emphasize his point, Bennett added, "There are a lot of policemen and chiefs out there who are saying . . . the main purpose of these weapons is carnage and mayhem."

This ban, although officially "temporary," was seen as a sudden departure from Bush administration policy. Only a month before, President George H. W. Bush had announced that he would favor "no new restrictions on guns" despite the growing public outrage following the Stockton shootings. Press accounts noted that Bush was a life member of the National Rifle Association who had sided with the group in opposing legislation restricting such firearms. But few reporters got inside politics deeply enough to reveal that Bush had played catch-up in early 1988 (before the nominating season began) by becoming an NRA life member in a White House ceremony prominently featured in the *American Rifleman*. His campaign office answered the NRA's political preference questionnaire perfectly. He promised to oppose gun bans and registration, waiting periods for firearms purchase, and all other types of gun control.

This affirmation of the NRA had sparked the association to drum up grassroots support for Bush during the fall campaign. In fact, the association spent more than $6 million—more than in any past presidential election—backing Bush and bashing Dukakis's antigun position. A lot of this money went to rural radio ads and on millions of DEFEND FIREARMS—DEFEAT DUKAKIS bumper stickers (which often outnumbered bumper stickers from either of the Bush and Dukakis campaigns). These messages stressed that Bush was the candidate who would "protect" citizens' Second Amendment rights, while Dukakis represented the liberal northeast gun-grabber element in U.S. politics.

In the end, Bush won an electoral vote landslide (426 to 111) but a much slimmer popular vote margin (48,882,828 to 41,807,430). The NRA could justifiably claim that it had swung millions of rural and blue-collar pro-gun Democrats in states such as Michigan, Pennsylvania, Illinois, and Maryland into the Bush camp.

Bush was elected in November 1988, but only four months later, his administration had apparently turned its back on the association by calling for the import ban. Clearly, this was embarrassing to the White House. From friends in Washington, however, I learned that Bill Bennett's action had in fact caught the White House flat-footed. On Tuesday, March 14, 1989, just one day after his swearing in, Bennett telephoned Treasury Secretary Nicholas Brady and reportedly told him, "Why don't we suspend the imports for now?" Bennett added, "Let's have a little cooling-off period." Only later, Bennett told the *Washington Post*, did he call Brady and White House deputy chief of staff Andy Card to announce his decision.

But the *Post* received a different account from Card, who said Bennett raised the issue to Bush in general terms at the swearing-in, and then called on Tuesday "with the details," which Card presented to his boss, John Sununu, and to the president, both of whom "thought it was appropriate." Hardly a solid endorsement: obviously, there was some serious back-pedaling going on.

And Bill Bennett did not make things easier by adding that he had made the decision on the import ban independently and that Sununu had given him such freedom of action: "When there's something that's very important for us to know about, let us know," Bennett told *Post* reporter Michael Isikoff. "The locution is, 'let us know,' not 'don't act until we say act.'"

To a lot of people on Pennsylvania Avenue and Capitol Hill, Bennett's version sounded like he had permission to fire (loose cannons) when ready. Over the coming weeks, Bennett tried to work damage control, reminding everyone who'd listen that his action was only "temporary," but in so doing, he lost support on both sides of the debate.

In March, I went to Washington on my regular monthly trip for the Sporting Goods Manufacturers Association. I checked in as usual at the NRA to catch up on the latest gossip and politics (the endlessly churning internal power struggles), but also to learn about the association's reaction to Bennett's import ban. As always, I booked into the Park Terrace Hotel at 1515 Rhode Island Avenue NW because it was across the street from the NRA's headquarters at 1600 Rhode Island Avenue. As I was official family, there was no need to stop for a headquarters escort, and I greeted just about everyone I met. On the seventh floor, ILA—my old stomping grounds—I usually spent some time with Rick Manning (now covering New Jersey), Chuck Cunningham—"Hi, Richie, how *aawrr* ya?" a good-natured send up of my Long Island accent—and with Rich Gardiner in the general counsel's office.

But today, I went straight to Wayne LaPierre's office. Laurie, his receptionist, looked a bit more stressed than usual.

"How's his schedule?" I asked.

"Back to back," she said. "But when Mary Corrigan gets out, why don't you poke your head in?"

I waited a couple of minutes in the hall chatting with Mary Rose Jennison, ILA's fiscal officer and just an all-around sweetheart. Mary Corrigan emerged with a gaggle of fund-raising consultants. "Oh-oh, trouble from Florida has arrived," she exclaimed, grinning.

I guessed where this was headed.

"Weren't you the big Bennett promoter?" she pointedly remarked.

"Yeah, I know, with friends like those, who needs enemies?" I limply threw back. "Anyway, I have a couple of ideas I want to run by Wayne, do you have a minute to come back in?"

Wayne was fidgeting between his desk and his workbench, "Hi, Richie. How's the fight going?"

"Well, not so good nationally at the moment," I said. "That's what I want to talk to you about."

I sat down and reviewed the Bennett situation, as I knew it. "Bill may be a movement conservative, but he's still from Brooklyn and knows nothing about guns and even less about the policy of guns."

Mary and Wayne were listening intently.

"Look, no way he did this on his own," I continued. "Someone put him up to it, and I think I know who . . . Chuck Wexler is on Bennett's staff. He's a really old friend from B.U. days. I was on student government with Chuck, and he eventually became an aide to DiGrazia, the old Boston police commissioner whom we had a few run-ins with, but get this—for the past couple of years, Wexler was aide de camp to the president of the IACP, Jerald Vaughn." That was the International Association of Chiefs of Police, a solidly antigun body of political appointees with whom the NRA had been feuding for years.

Mary and Wayne were getting very interested now.

"Yeah," I added, "Nobody over there has forgotten the pissing contest that Wexler's boss and Cassidy got into over Volkmer-McClure and Glocks, and all this may well be payback back time from Wexler now."

"Makes sense to me," Mary said.

Wayne, as was his habit, did not initially comment.

"Wexler's not just anti-gun," I continued. "He's probably got a hard-on the length of Pennsylvania Avenue for us. When I told him I was working as an NRA lobbyist, he laughed and said, 'C'mon, Richie, what are you really doing?' When I made clear that I was serious, he said, 'I really shouldn't be talking to you.' That's the level of his discomfort!"

"How can we use this to get Bennett off his import ban kick?" Mary asked.

Wayne jumped in, "You don't ditch the girl who 'brung' you to the party as soon as you arrive. We worked our butts off for Bush last fall. Hell, we'd be better off with Dukakis. At least this would have been expected and now we're goin' to have a devil of a time keeping the Republicans in line on the Hill."

"The squishy ones anyway," Mary added.

"Look," I said, "here's what I'm planning to do. In two weeks, Roy Innis will be in town and I'm coming back. He's scheduling a meeting with Bennett and I'm going with him. I'm working on the talking points for Roy and in my quasi-official public affairs NRA role. I can suggest some face-saving strategies to help Bennett and prevent this from escalating into a nuclear disaster."

"What do you need from us?" Wayne asked.

"Prayers that he's not cornered himself so far he can't wiggle out," I said, only half joking.

At moments like these, I always remembered Speaker of the House Tip O'Neil's comment on lobbying: "If you can't accept the fact that politicians will drink your booze, eat your food, screw your women, and then vote against you, you're in the wrong business!"

On my way out, I turned back to Wayne. "We've already gotten fucked on this. If we can't turn it around with a Republican president that we helped elect—an NRA Life Member to boot—what the hell are we going to do with Democrats? We've got even less leverage with them."

Wayne shrugged. "Good luck. Stay in touch." (And then his signature message):

"I'm with ya' on this one."

Coming from Wayne, I knew perfectly well that meant: "Feldman, you are *on your own!*"

Although the National Rifle Association remained outraged that Bennett had betrayed them, they would not open a public breach with the White House. Wayne took the lead, telling the press that at least Bennett's action "should put a stop to the media hysteria surrounding the semiautomatic version of the AK-47 rifle, and should provide an atmosphere for a reasoned and sensible debate on this issue."

When I heard an NRA spokesperson talking about "a reasoned and sensible debate," it was clear that they'd absorbed a body blow and were seething.

Bill Bennett was basically a really good guy and an old friend. If I could just speak with him with his hackles down, I was sure I could work out a peaceful compromise. Feldman's Rule # 7 for lobbyists: "Always believe you can succeed, even if logic and wisdom counsel otherwise." Oh well, my paycheck wasn't dependent upon the gun lobby, but Wayne's was.

About two weeks later, I hooked up with Roy Innis and his aide, Cyril Boynes, with whom I had worked so closely during the Bernie Goetz and Volkmer-McClure campaigns. We met at the NRA's headquarters in the morning and took a taxi over to the office of the director of National Drug Policy. The office wasn't even near the White House but up on Connecticut Avenue in a fairly small, nondescript, but recently renovated building. We were quickly ushered into a conference room where a secretary asked if we'd like any refreshments. I wanted coffee, but wondered if my sudden overwhelming desire for caffeine would tip them off regarding my past predilections for mind-enhancing drugs—after all, I found myself in what a charter member of the sixties generation would consider the Belly of the Beast—so I requested water.

Bennett charged into the room, greeting Roy and two staffers, and then stopped, looking a little startled to see me.

So I took the lead. "Bill, I'm here to try to bring peace between a couple of my friends who ought not be at war."

Bennett seemed unimpressed.

Roy started off talking about the crisis with gangs and drugs. He explained that "guns are a huge problem in New York City with criminals, but not with decent citizens, particularly poor ghetto citizens who *need* guns for protection more than wealthy suburbanites. Banning guns to control criminals has never worked, will never work and only alienates the good, decent folks who want them for protection and are already on your side in the fight against drugs."

Clear and to the point, I thought. Bennett went into his canned offensive. "All right, but who needs military-style assault weapons for self-defense?"

Yeah, I thought, and who needs the latest editions of the Bible to feel close to God? And who needs a house in the country when you live in D.C.? And who needs two cars when you can only drive one at a time? When the hell did *need* become the critical criteria for private property ownership in the United States?

As the conversation progressed, I became upset. Bennett was digging in his heals and didn't seem interested in making peace with the big bad "gun lobby." He actually appeared to be enjoying the controversy and resultant media attention. Try as we might, our perspective on this issue was not falling on fertile ears. "You know," I said, upping the ante, "we wouldn't be here today if this policy had been vetted by the administration before it was announced." (Of course, I knew it hadn't because I'd been told as much by the deputy chief of staff, Andy Card.)

Bennett interrupted, "Everyone was on board about this decision and it's the *right* one!" His tone was both defensive and harsh. "It was also my considered judgment that at least some of these assault weapons would end up in the wrong hands. There's no question that criminals traffic in these guns. Can't you see that?"

Well, I hadn't meant to get personal, but he seemed awfully touchy on that subject.

We spent another forty-five minutes going nowhere, certainly not reaching an agreement on how to proceed other than agreeing that it wasn't in the Bush administration's best interest to continue this public feud. It was not the most productive meeting I had ever attended.

But Roy felt that the message he'd wanted to transmit had come across. "Richie, why the long face?" he asked in the cab back to NRA.

"We failed," I said. "Bennett really didn't hear a damn word of what we were saying. This sucks and it portends very poorly for Bush's administration and our pro-gun agenda for the future. Why worry about Democrats if we have Republicans out to fuck us like this? Hell, if Bush doesn't have a dork like Dukakis running against him in '92, he'll be lucky to get *any* of the gun vote, and if the Democrats have half a brain, they'll run a pro-gun Southerner, who'll kick his butt." I raised my fists in frustration. "This is so stupid. I just can't believe that one of the smartest guys I know fell into this trap, hook . . . line . . . and sinker . . . eeehhhhhhh!" I smashed my right fist into my left palm. "We're all fucked."

"Richie," Roy said, "don't let it get to you. We'll live through this one."

Maybe, I thought. But I couldn't help thinking that the next presidential election was less than four years away.

Almost as if to tell the NRA what the other side was thinking, the Violence Policy Center and Handgun Control, Inc., took maximum advantage of this opportunity to remind potential supporters that even the gun-friendly Bush administration had reversed itself on assault weapons. And because the DeConcini and Metzenbaum federal assault weapons bans were pending in the Senate, the antigun lobbies stressed that this was not the time to slack off on contributions.

In the initial months of the Bennett import ban, the BATF reviewed the weapons on the list to determine if they met the provisions of the 1968 Gun Control Act, which required that imported firearms were "generally recognized as particularly suitable for, or readily adaptable to, sporting purposes." Having worked as a government attorney, I saw that only a committee of bureaucrats with law diplomas on their office-cubicle walls could have crafted such language.

•　•　•

The mood at the NRA during this period was complex. For the association's leadership, the assault weapons debate was reminiscent of the "cop-killer" bullet and "plastic gun" controversies, in which the NRA had reaped the reward in increased membership and contributions. As long as the association could convince members, potential members, and contributors that the gun control groups trying to ban private ownership of assault weapons *actually* sought to abolish all privately owned firearms, the issue would play an important role in the NRA's financial and political success.

But there were also hidden dangers in this position. If the antigun forces did succeed in forging a political alliance that pushed a sweeping federal assault weapons ban through Congress—defeating concerted NRA opposition in the process—the association would have suffered a major blow to its prestige, and by extension to its political power.

During this period, I wasn't blindly naive in my support for the NRA. (Although I would come to distrust its entrenched—and exceedingly well compensated—leaders in coming years.) And I never doubted that the association would try to milk the assault weapons issue for all it was worth in terms of donations and new membership—after all, they really did need both—as did their opponents. But I also recognized that there were Second Amendment fundamentalists a lot more zealous than the NRA, in particular, Neal Knox and Tanya Metaksa. Both seemed like hyenas out there on the edge of the public debate waiting for the association's leadership to weaken so they could rush in and strike. Executive Vice President Warren Cassidy was already in a shaky position, and the prospect of Knox and Metaksa filling a leadership vacuum at 1600 Rhode Island Avenue was appalling. So, despite emerging misgivings, I kept soldiering on, hoping that the NRA leadership issues would be resolved before the organization was crippled.

Cassidy's basic problem lay in his leadership style and track record. Some saw him as coldly aloof, a New England elitist who made arbitrary decisions; to others Cassidy was more interested in hobnobbing with Capitol Hill celebrities—on the golf course of the Congressional Country Club than in shooting sporting clays at NRA-sponsored gun clubs. Whatever Cassidy's perceived faults, they could have been excused if he'd managed to increase the revenue flow and swell the membership. But by late 1989, the NRA was doing neither.

As the association's former public affairs director Johnny Aquilino put it in his new NRA-watchdog publication, *Insider Gun News*:

Knowledgeable life and benefactor members argue that a conservative estimate of NRA membership should be at least five million. The traditional equation is that NRA membership rises in direct proportion to anti-gun threats. That rise, of course, presupposes that the NRA leadership can astutely tie a sense of urgency due to the anti-gun threats to its membership pleas. Never in history have the anti-gun groups enjoyed such success or publicity . . . and never has NRA failed so completely to convert those opportunities into memberships. Nor has it spent so much with so little to show.

A stagnant NRA membership equals diminished political and legislative clout when anti-gun initiatives are on the rise. A case can be made that by encouraging, approving, or tolerating the failing membership recruitment effort under Cassidy, NRA's Directors open themselves to charges that they not only failed in their fiduciary responsibility, but also shirked their duty to fully protect the political and legislative rights of their constituents.

Since I considered both Warren Cassidy and Johnny Aquilino friends, I took no pleasure in reading these words. But I had to recognize that they were powerful talking points for those seeking to oust Cassidy.

• • •

I finished working for the Sporting Goods Council in December 1989 and got a call from Rick Manning a few weeks later. In January 1990, Rick was still the NRA's state liaison to New Jersey, my old turf.

"Richie," he said, "the shit's about to hit the fan up here. Have you been following Jim Florio's media crusade against semiautos?" Like most members of the NRA, Rick hated using the contrived—and inaccurate—term "assault weapons."

"I had been, Rick, but I've kind of lost track recently," I admitted. "What's happening?"

Newly elected Democratic governor James Florio was a former prosecutor who had tried to reform his party's corrupt machine politics and then gone on to serve as a congressman in Washington. Back in 1981 in his failed run for governor, the NRA endorsed him over Tom Kean, the Republican. Florio didn't have much charisma, but he'd been able to assemble enough support to win the 1989 off-year statehouse gubernatorial race.

"We're about to get another Roberti-Roos rammed down our throats," Rick explained, "*that's* what's happening."

Florio's election victory brought in a large number of Democratic politicians on his coattails, so he was confident he had enough support in the Trenton legislature for a sweeping ban on semiautomatic weapons. And Florio's confidence also rested on the fact that the New Jersey state senate had passed its own version of a semiauto ban in 1989, only to have it blocked in the Republican-controlled State Assembly, which was now back in Democratic hands.

Like the California Roberti-Roos Act, Florio's draft New Jersey law would outlaw the manufacture, sale, and possession of a long list of specific "assault weapons"—and also firearms that fell into less specific categories. But Florio's proposed new gun ban was much harsher in other ways, and contained inflexible confiscation provisions—without compensation—for guns that were currently legal, and which were used for both hunting and competitive shooting. Further, a number of gun collectors prized their European- or Israeli-made semiautomatic rifles both for their intrinsic and historic value. But the pending law proposed that owners of the weapons either render them "permanently inoperable," sell them to out-of-state buyers, or surrender them to law enforcement within three months of the bill's passage or face prosecution on felony charges.

And then there was the fear of a widening ring of confiscation, not just of military "style" weapons but also all semiautomatic long guns, including models of shotguns and rifles very popular with waterfowl and deer hunters.

"Richie," Rick Manning told me at a strategy session early in our campaign, "Florio wants to turn a bunch of honest citizens into crooks."

Rodger Iverson leaned back in his chair and stroked his chin. "Jim Florio might have heard the expression 'shit storm' before," he said. "But he hasn't seen one yet. That's about to change."

However, Governor Florio and the bill's sponsor, Democratic state senator John Russo, remained inflexible about the need to cleanse New Jersey of assault weapons.

"They are the weapons of choice of the drug dealers," Florio told the *New York Times*. "As far as I'm concerned, if we care about the streets and safe communities, we have to get these weapons of war out of the hands of criminals."

Boy, I thought, *he pushed all the buttons on that one: safe streets . . . "weapons of war" . . . heavily armed criminals.*

Florio's crusade would be his administration's first crucial test. If he lost, he would begin his four-year term badly weakened.

Equally, the struggle over Florio's assault weapons bill in the state legislature would be a major test for the National Rifle Association following the Roberti-Roos debacle in California. We had enjoyed considerable success in New Jersey during the long Volkmer-McClure struggle—right in the backyards of Congressmen Peter Rodino and William Hughes. Now, with the energetic help of the NRA's activists like Rodger Iverson, John Anderson, and Bob Mac-Kinnon, I knew we could wage political guerrilla warfare on an unprecedented scale.

The NRA thought so, too. Manning persuaded LaPierre to hire me as a consultant for the New Jersey battle. I would organize the grassroots activists while Rick worked directly with the legislature inside the statehouse. "Mr. Inside and Mr. Outside," we joked. But there was a solid foundation to these nicknames. Rick was most effective sitting face-to-face with individual legislators, patiently explaining why it was in their best interests to help defeat the new governor's sweeping—and probably unconstitutional—assault on Second Amendment rights. I earned my pay keeping the activists pumped up, organizing street demonstrations, and orchestrating letters to the editor in local papers and call-ins to radio talk shows.

All this effort had to be coordinated, calibrated, and adjusted depending on our latest political intelligence and projected outcomes as Florio's draft bills worked their way through the state senate and assembly committees. In general, New Jersey Republicans leaned toward the NRA's position while Democrats were predisposed to follow Florio's lead—as long as he showed leadership. Our job was to weaken him by proving that large blocks of voters opposed his radical position on semiautomatic firearms. And we hoped that we could muster enough resistance to the gun bill that his own administration would dilute it to a mere token measure even if it became law.

To make our work even more interesting, Florio had made passage of his assault weapons ban his number-one legislative priority. This was politically astute: for the first time in several years, the Democrats controlled both the New Jersey senate and assembly, and Florio intended to force his party colleagues to stand up and be counted early in his administration.

"Whatever happens in Trenton this spring," Manning announced, "I hope we can cut down some of the bozos who oppose us."

(In those days, we still belonged to the Take No Prisoners School of Politics.)

●   ●   ●

As Florio's semiauto ban was being minced and kneaded in the sausage machines of the legislature, we lined up our opposing forces. Our efforts became urgent when a senate committee passed a version of a bill almost identical to Florio's original draconian proposal. Although votes on the senate and assembly floors had not been scheduled, we could see them coming. So we had to demonstrate that we, too, had clout.

Our first big demonstration of power was the mass rally that I helped organize on Monday, March 19, 1990, in Trenton.

Drawing on the membership of the Coalition of New Jersey Sportsmen, we filled the courtyard of the statehouse annex with a zealous, boisterous but well-mannered crowd. They arrived in hundreds of chartered vans and buses from across the state. Pro-Florio senior police officials estimated the turnout at "more than two thousand," but I'd seen enough rallies to recognize the flag-waving pro-gun activists undoubtedly numbered many more (six to eight thousand). The crowd overflowed the courtyard, spilling onto State Street, which was completely blocked to traffic for over three hours. When the chants of "*Free*-dom" and "N-R-A! N-R-A! N-R-A!" echoed off the stone pillars of the surrounding office complex, legislators debating the bill inside had difficulty hearing, despite their public address systems. As soon as the streets filled, the buzz spread that this was the biggest rally in New Jersey history.

There were a lot of NRA caps in the crowd, but Coalition of New Jersey Sportsmen caps and jackets were equally prominent. And the signs the demonstrators carried were meant to send a message to any pro-gun ban politician in the statehouse: GO AHEAD, MAKE MY DAY. JUST TRY TO TAKE MY GUNS AWAY.

Another hand-printed sign held aloft by two men in blaze orange hunters' caps and plaid lumberjack shirts was equally dramatic: FEAR A GOVERNMENT THAT FEARS YOUR GUNS.

The TV crews loved it. They zeroed in on one burly guy in a Teamsters vest waving the sign: TAKE MY WIFE, NOT MY SHOTGUN.

We'd set up a raised podium at the top of the steps to the annex with a powerful PA system and decorated it with red-white-and-blue bunting. Roy Innis was one of our first speakers. As always, Roy drew energy from an enthusiastic crowd. Carefully building his argument, Roy noted that as the national chairman of the Congress of Racial Equality, he knew how minorities faced discrimination and how people tried to deny them their civil rights.

"And among the most fundamental of civil rights are gun rights," Roy thundered, hardly needing the microphone. The crowd thundered back, whooping, hollering, and clapping for minutes. "If you want to reduce crime," Roy continued, "stop making laws that allow guns in the hands of criminals and that say guns in the hands of decent people are illegal."

Once more the crowd erupted. But people fell silent when Roy explained that many more blacks than whites were victims of violent crime. And that silence became absolute when he revealed that criminals had shot two of his sons, Alexander and Roy Jr., one in the Bronx, and the other in Harlem. But the witnesses to the shootings had been afraid to testify because they'd had no weapons for self-defense. "Blacks have a common bond with the people that are here today," he concluded. "It's important to show blacks that all of us have to uphold the Second Amendment."

When he finished speaking, a fife-and-drum corps in Revolutionary War tri-corner hats played "Yankee Doodle" and "The Battle Hymn of the Republic."

The most enthusiastic response from the crowd was for Washington Township police officer Jon Schramm, who took the podium wearing his uniform, his badge, and his gun belt. Schramm hefted a thick petition with the names of two thousand other officers who opposed the Florio gun ban. "We're not outgunned by you people," he told the crowd. Schramm emphasized that the state's resources would be better directed against criminals, not the law-abiding citizens filling the courtyard. The photograph of Innis, Schramm, and Warren Cassidy's arms raised was the one all the papers featured the following day.

I had worked with Trenton's deputy chief of police Joe Constance to obtain all the required permits for the rally. His cooperation had been outstanding, another indication that New Jersey's uniformed cops were firmly against the ban. Many of them were hunters or gun collectors, Joe had explained, and they feared that the Florio administration really did intend to confiscate their guns.

"This bill is a piece of crap, Richie," Chief Constance told me. Referring to Florio and his cronies, he added, "I can't *stand* those people. They're gonna be taking away our guns. But we won't forget at the next election."

In fact, the main rank-and-file police officer organizations had either voiced specific opposition to the bill or refused to join the Florio camp. Vincent Frammigen, president of the New Jersey Lodge of the Fraternal Order of Police, which had ten thousand members, told the *New York Times*, "We already have one of the strictest gun control laws in the country. Why are we trying to make it stronger if we can't enforce the one we have?"

Good question. We could only hope the politicians in Trenton were listening.

Even if they weren't listening, those senators and assembly members were certainly getting a lot of calls. One of our tactics was to tie up the statehouse office phone lines from early in the morning until night, using volunteers to stress their opposition to the pending law.

• • •

But Governor Florio had enough political capital to move a slightly amended version of his bill through legislative committees toward a final vote in May. We had to find a way to keep the momentum of the March rally rolling.

The annual dinner of the Coalition of New Jersey Sportsmen on May 12 seemed like a good opportunity to set up another rally to stop the bill.

"Who can we get as speaker that will draw the media and get the politicians' attention?" I asked.

"I know just the guy," Rick Manning said. "Charlton Heston."

Heston had given a great speech at the 1989 NRA members meeting in St. Louis, after which he'd been presented a beautiful handcrafted musket. Lifting the gleaming muzzle-loader high over his head, Heston had intoned in his best Moses-with-the-Tablets voice: "From my cold, dead hands!" In other words, the gun grabbers would have to kill him to trample his Second Amendment rights. The crowd in St. Louis—myself included—had gone nuts.

We hoped Heston could ignite the same spark in New Jersey.

• • •

Up close, Charlton Heston did not look ten feet tall, as he had to me watching *The Ten Commandments* years earlier. But Heston definitely seemed larger than life as I joined the Sportsmen Coalition's and the NRA's officials who escorted him from the press conference at the Pines Manor in Edison and into the banquet hall on May 12. The hall erupted in cheers as they made their way to the head table. Heston might as well have been Moses parting the Red Sea.

There were so many standing ovations during his keynote speech that Heston remained at the podium twice as long as scheduled.

Unlike his Hollywood contemporary, Ronald Reagan, Heston spoke with a teleprompter. He described how he had hunted "only to put food on the table" as a kid in Michigan during the Depression. And he spoke of the Army Colt .45 pistol he'd brought back from duty as a bomber gunner during World War II.

"To this day," he told the crowd, "I sleep with that .45 beside my bed. I figure I earned the right to do so."

This unleashed applause that rattled the chandeliers.

Then Heston launched into the heart of his remarks.

He ridiculed the claim that semiautomatic rifles had ever been the "weapon of choice" of drug dealers and other violent criminals. "Law-abiding citizens are not your problem, Governor. We do not commit crimes, and resent being treated like criminals." Heston shifted his focus to stare directly at the minicams from the three local-network stations. "Governor, leave the honest people of New Jersey alone and start worrying about keeping violent criminals where they belong—behind bars."

Again, the applause was almost painfully loud. "Seventy million gun owners in America have a personal stake in our Second Amendment rights," Heston proclaimed, and then paused for dramatic effect. "But *every* American has a stake in the future of Democracy."

We had timed the event for maximum media exposure. Heston's prebanquet press conference and keynote speech made the local TV news, and the Sunday morning papers. By Monday, the Assembly Judiciary Committee was scheduled to resume considering the most stringent assault weapons ban in the country. There were no grand-father clauses, as with the Roberti-Roos Act, which allowed people to retain possession of the firearms they owned before the law's passage. Confiscation in one form or another remained a hallmark of Florio's bill.

Thursday, May 17, was the big test. Florio and his legislative allies were working their best legerdemain, shuffling the language of amendments like card sharks. We had tried to marshal a mass rally outside the statehouse annex as big as the March demonstration. But it was clear that this crowd was less than half as large. They were enthusiastic, however. While the politicians heard testimony for and against the bill, our troops packed the committee room visitors' galleries and corridors outside. Once more, witnesses for the

Coalition of New Jersey Sportsmen spoke against the bill. And the New Jersey Fraternal Order of Police (FOP) came down in firm opposition.

"This bill is not going to stop a single crime, or keep a single drug dealer from getting one of these guns," the FOP's legislative chairman Danny Schick told the assembly committee. "You're going to turn government against law-abiding citizens."

Although we had fewer demonstrators than in March, we were probably better organized. Our sound guy had hooked up the public address system on a pickup truck in the courtyard to intercept the FM feed of the deliberations normally broadcast to staffers throughout the statehouse complex. As legislators debated crucial points, chants of "Vote no" and "No way" echoed from the courtyard outside.

But at the end of the day, we lost by the narrowest possible margin in the senate, 21–17 of the forty-member body. Seeing which way the wind had blown, the Democrats carried the day more decisively that afternoon in the assembly, passing the measure 43–33 with 7 abstentions. Obviously Florio had won a crucial victory.

A local television reporter thrust a microphone at Rodger Iverson as he came out of the statehouse.

"How do you feel about your defeat?" she asked.

"How do I *feel*?" He glared at the young woman. "Like a two-dollar whore at sunrise."

• • •

The reaction at 1600 Rhode Island Avenue was just as grim. It could be argued that the NRA had been blindsided by the Roberti-Roos Act after the Stockton murders and had not prepared a vigorous legislative defense and counterattack.

But this hadn't been the case in New Jersey. We had worked the statehouse, office by office; we'd filled the streets with demonstrators; we'd flooded legislators' mailboxes with postcards and jammed their phone lines, urging them to vote against the Florio gun ban. We had brought in Roy Innis, an icon of the civil rights struggle. And we'd called on Charlton Heston—Moses himself.

In addition, we had made it clear that the politicians voting against us would face stiff reelection battles when their terms expired in 1991. Immediately after Florio's gun-bill victory, it was doubtful that many New Jersey legislators took this threat seriously.

But before the next election they would.

•   •   •

Within a month of Governor Florio's victory in the assault weapons fight, he found himself caught in a struggle much more threatening to his political future—and there was a definite link between the two battles. I know this for a fact because I helped forge the links of that connection.

When Florio ran for election in 1989, he promised the voters of New Jersey that he would not raise taxes. But by June 1990, less than six months after taking office, he found it necessary to push a $2.8 billion tax package through the Trenton legislature. This was needed to close a huge budget gap and to provide $1.1 billion in court-mandated aid to underfunded public schools.

The public uproar was spontaneous, loud, and vigorous. Out of the clamor a vigorous antitax grassroots group, calling itself Hands Across New Jersey, coalesced to protest the tax hike all across the state, beginning with a massive rally in Trenton on Sunday, July 2, 1990.

Just before the big Trenton rally, I joined Rick Manning, Rodger Iverson, Rich Miller from the Sportsmen's Coalition, and state Republican party chairman assemblyman Bob Franks in his Trenton office. The Hands Across New Jersey rally had nothing to do with guns, of course, but we were there at Assemblyman Franks's behest to attack Jim Florio, not defend the Second Amendment.

Manning assured us that there would be NRA money available to support the effort. And Iverson and Miller promised to supply bodies whenever and wherever they were needed to bolster the ranks of the "Hands" demonstrations.

"Richie," Manning said, "you're going to have to help these people. They really are grassroots and not ready for prime time."

"Not yet," I said. "But they will be."

Bob Franks was a moderate Republican and had friends on both sides of the aisle. He promised to keep me supplied with intelligence from inside the Florio administration and also to raise money to support my effort.

Hands Across New Jersey had two chairs, a postal worker named John Budzash, and a woman named Pat Ralston. They had "met" on a radio call-in show, full of indignation at Florio and confidently determined that they could reverse his tax policy. But, listening to them speak, it was clear, as Rich Manning had noted, that they really were amateurs.

This bunch will implode before it succeeds.

When the big Trenton rally did come, it produced more heat than light, a lot of disjointed promises, but no cohesive plan. Addressing the crowd, however, John Budzash called for a complete audit of the state government, "to see where our money goes." And he threatened Florio that the group would present a petition against taxes signed by 1 million voters.

Jon Shure, Florio's communications director, told the media that the Hands rally had been organized by the Republicans, but he didn't spot anybody from the Sportsmen's Coalition or the NRA in the huge crowd. Coloring the movement with the taint of the NRA would damage its grassroots image. And we didn't want that because Rodger Iverson and I planned to lend Hands Across New Jersey all the help we could. One of our first contributions was a jumbo red-white-and-blue bumper sticker reminiscent of NRA-ILA products:

TAX REVOLT NOW!
HANDS ACROSS NEW JERSEY

Over the coming weeks and months, I worked out of a cubicle next to Bobby Franks's district office organizing Hands rallies around New Jersey. Going back to my law school days and drawing on my experience as an NRA lobbyist, I made sure the group followed up on all the niggling details—sending press releases before deadlines, obtaining rally permits, etc. But I had to be careful not to appear *too* well organized or professional. After all, this was a grassroots outfit.

"Act like you don't know me," I told members. And I warned Rodger Iverson and his crew, "Don't come over and talk to me at a rally."

Writing press releases and flyers was one of my main jobs. But unlike what I'd helped produce for the NRA, we had to give the

Hands documents a rough edge. I always made sure to misspell at least one word, "frivilous" or "wastefull." And we turned out several mailers with blurry, obsolete dot-matrix printers on rough paper stock.

One of our funniest innovations was the "Flush Florio" toilet paper rolls we distributed before rallies. After all, Florio's tax bill had put a sales tax on toilet paper, so he got more than taxes back when demonstrators decorated his office complex with the rolls.

By the time I left New Jersey after that fall's special elections, Hands Across New Jersey was still running and the internal warfare had remained "internal." In one of the special elections, a state senate candidate, Democratic assemblyman Ed Salmon, who had voted for the gun ban in May, was running against former state senator Jim Cafiero, who'd been an opponent of the gun ban. We plastered the South Jersey district with "Can Salmon" and "Smoke Salmon" bumper stickers and posters. In another special election, Hands Across New Jersey asked the state attorney general for a special watch of Democratic assemblyman Cyril Yannarelli and his staff. We wanted the extra scrutiny because Yannarelli had been recently indicted on voter registration fraud.

I knew we'd been making progress, but I was surprised just how effective Hands proved in both the New Jersey special elections and the federal election that November. Both Salmon and Yannarelli lost. And, fueled by antitax zeal, voters almost defeated popular Democratic senator Bill Bradley. He won by a slim margin over Republican newcomer Christine Todd Whitman, the candidate Hands Across New Jersey had endorsed. Several Democratic congressmen also scraped through.

But I did not escape completely under the radar. Rick Linsk, the Trenton reporter for the *Asbury Park Press*, exposed the fact that I— an ex-NRA lobbyist—had been "advising the anti-tax group Hands Across New Jersey."

Although he was on to something, Linsk could not find a smoking gun—pun intended. There was no money or paper trail linking Hands to the NRA, and I told Rick Linsk that I was involved with Hands "as a citizen," adding that, "I encourage lots of people to be involved as citizens."

John Budzash told the paper that I had not given Hands Across New Jersey any money or legal advice, but that I had been a "calming influence."

Feeling anything but calm, I got the hell out of New Jersey.

In 1992, New Jersey Republican state chairman Bobby Franks—who had helped arrange my involvement with Hands—was running for Congress. He attacked his pro-gun opponent for taking support from the NRA. Franks claimed he had never received such support because he had "refused to abide by their dangerous position on gun control." But apparently that hadn't stopped Franks from using two of the NRA's lobbyists and the Coalition of New Jersey Sportsmen to work undercover for him in the Hands Across New Jersey's campaign against Jim Florio.

I went through the roof when I heard Franks's hypocrisy. So I called several New Jersey reporters and informed them that Franks was not only a liar but a "damned liar."

I then proceeded to answer honestly the reporters' questions about my involvement with Hands Across New Jersey. But I didn't volunteer anything. There's a maxim in both the law and politics: "Don't answer questions that nobody asks."

• • •

The final outcome of Governor Florio's ill-advised assault weapons ban and the Hands Across New Jersey tax revolt came in the 1993 election. Two days before the November gubernatorial vote, the NRA used an obscure facet of New Jersey election law to finance a $100,000 anti-Florio phone bank—manned in part by Sportsmen Coalition volunteers. Florio was defeated in his bid for a second term, losing badly to Christine Todd Whitman.

But politicians in the state had learned a lesson: cross the National Rifle Association at your own peril.

The adage that the acronym NRA represented "**Never Re**-elected **A**gain" for politicians who dared cross the organization had never seemed more valid.

(During the election campaign, the National Rifle Association lambasted Florio in ads that claimed Florio had scapegoated the association: "Jim Florio, you can't run away from your records by running against the NRA." The ad listed a series of the governor's policy blunders, each followed by a tagline that read, "Blame the NRA." This was persuasive political propaganda. The only problem was that the NRA—in the person of Richard J. Feldman, Esquire—*had* in fact been working beneath the surface to undercut Jim Florio.)

8

THE NEW NRA

RA Headquarters: In January 1991, I was back in Washington, working as a consultant for the National Rifle Association to help defeat a proposed gun control bill in Virginia. The bill was an effort of the "Brady Bunch," the NRA's derisive epithet for Handgun Control, Inc. (HCI), and it mirrored national legislation pending in congressional committees establishing mandatory background checks and waiting periods for the purchase of all revolvers and semiautomatic pistols.

Sarah Brady, whose husband, Jim, had been brain damaged and disabled in the 1981 assassination attempt on President Ronald Reagan, had become the force behind the campaign when she became HCI's chairperson in 1990. The Brady campaign sought simplistic, even counterproductive answers to complex criminal justice and civil liberty problems. The federal legislation, known as the Brady Bill, had been pending in Congress since the mid-1980s, and the NRA hoped to continue stalling it.

But in Virginia, a coalition of politicians decided to push a similar state law through the House of Delegates and the General Assembly now that newly elected Democratic governor Douglas Wilder had taken office. But the NRA had other plans.

I was put in charge of "special operations," while state liaison Chuck Cunningham ran the lobbying in Richmond—just as Rick Manning had in the Trenton fight. My focus was on the grassroots: gun shops, gun clubs, and gun shows. And once you got away from the suburban yuppie crust of northern Virginia, these grassroots ran wide and deep, especially in the Shenandoah Valley and in the southwest.

Given the composition of the two legislative houses in Richmond, I realized that we could align the pro-gun "shit-kicker" rural and small-town politicians against their urban-suburban counterparts to prevent the bill's passage. But to get out to those far-flung counties and virtually beat the bushes for support, I was going to need more NRA staff who knew guns and who could get the message across that the proposed waiting period and background check represented a dangerous erosion of Second Amendment rights.

I needed people who could cover the territory, spread the word, speak at the gun clubs, and pump up the troops. I got four additional field reps assigned to the project—no nickel and diming here! We had to make it clear to the elected representatives in Richmond that a sizable and politically energized body of their constituents' priorities changed and were against the mini–Brady Bill. But as the political sands shifted in Richmond, I had to find a way to remain in contact with all the extra field representatives I brought on board. Snow-covered Appalachia was a formidable barrier, and in those days the field reps would stop at a roadside phone once or twice a day and call in. So I got them all beepers in order to communicate with me.

"You're a hero, Richie," Chuck Cunningham told me.

Heroic or not, our campaign was working. Rural state delegates and members of the senate who'd always felt (correctly) like country cousins to their city lawyer and businessman colleagues, now experienced the power of having grassroots opposition one morning and warm gratitude for switching their public position by early afternoon. When the mini–Brady Bill came up for a vote in Richmond, it was defeated by a 58–42 vote. This proved again the old adage (to paraphrase), that when you "grab 'em by the groceries, their hearts and minds will follow"—or put another way, "they don't need to see the light, just feel the heat!!"

●   ●   ●

After the Virginia victory, the NRA appointed me to coordinate the association's efforts in Washington to defeat the Brady Bill on Capitol Hill.

But this wouldn't be a cakewalk. The bill was gathering a head of steam in Congress, and we desperately needed to derail it. President George H. W. Bush wasn't feeling too kindly toward the NRA after the vituperation over Bill Bennett's semiautomatic import ban. The Democratic leadership on Capitol Hill was out to screw us because of our obvious support for Republicans in the 1988 and 1990 elections. Furthermore, national polls (Gallup, media-sponsored surveys, etc.) showed great public support for background checks. What the pollsters did not know, and we kept closely guarded, was the fact that our own polling showed that gun owners and even a majority of NRA members supported background checks.

I would run the anti–Brady Bill campaign as I had run other operations but on the federal level. This meant that I would be the locus of information between the NRA's lobbyists and multiple pro-gun groups, as well as activists in the states. I would ensure that, as the situation changed (which it inevitably would), information would be effectively and rapidly transmitted in both directions.

This was probably the most challenging assignment of my life. I would have to coordinate what I now saw as the multifaced monster that the NRA was becoming. The Institute for Legislative Action had expanded, literally outgrowing its seventh-floor quarters. Field operations were not as big but still had many more people than when I was a full-time staff member.

•   •   •

In one version or another, the Brady Bill (HR-7) had retained the same basic provisions for years: a five-business-day waiting period. This meant that people trying to purchase a handgun from a federal firearms licensee would undergo a background check to verify that the information the buyer put on the Form 4473 was correct and that he or she was not a convicted felon, had never been committed to a mental institution, and so on. The Brady Bill required the dealer to obtain either local police approval or a green light from state records.

Studying HCI's fund-raising mailers on the bill, it was clear that Sarah Brady and her colleagues believed its passage would prevent the steady expansion of both legal and illegal handgun sales in the country. Indeed, the reduction of all gun sales was obviously their unstated objective. But, if they could curtail the illegal sale of handguns to criminals and others who weren't supposed to have them, then what HCI called America's appalling legacy of gun violence, could be reversed.

This was a noble goal.

But one of the main problems, as I (and the NRA) saw it, was that the Brady Bill would actually do little to prevent handgun violence. First, the legislation would not apply to gun sales between private persons, but only to transactions involving a federal firearms licensee. So there was absolutely nothing in the Act to prevent someone legally allowed to buy a gun from undergoing the waiting period and background check, taking possession of the weapon, and later selling it to an individual who would have never passed legal muster. We called this process "Buy and Lie."

Another major flaw in the Brady Bill was that it would *not* apply to eighteen states and the District of Columbia, which were "Brady exempt" because they either already had waiting periods, strict licensing regulations, or outright prohibitions on private handgun purchases and possession. But, despite these stringent gun control laws, these jurisdictions accounted for almost two thirds of violent crime and more than half the murders in the United States.

California was a good case in point. The waiting period had risen over the decades to a full fifteen days, yet the state had one of the highest rates of gun violence (including murder) in the country. And *all* handgun sales—retail and private—were officially covered by the waiting period.

New York State had the second-highest rate of murders and other violence in the country. And New York City, which had its own much stricter licensing system and background checks (to the point of being abusive), had the highest per-capita percentage of murders and violent crimes in the state.

As for background checks, in 1991, computerized databases of criminal records were sketchy, and records of mental commitment even thinner. So, an overworked clerk in Milwaukee or St. Louis scouring the state's paper files of criminal records might find nothing and inadvertently approve the sale of a handgun to a felon or a mentally deranged individual.

Still, the Brady Bill had strong symbolic "feel good" appeal.

At the time, there was promising information technology being developed that would eliminate the need for waiting periods. Described as "point of purchase" or "instant" background checks, this system would connect the federal firearms licensee selling the gun with the FBI's computerized National Crime Information Center (NCIC) in Clarksburg, West Virginia, which just happened to be the home state of Congressman Harley O. Staggers Jr. Staggers had sponsored an "instant check" bill in opposition to the Brady legislation. Even though the NRA publicly opposed both background checks *and* waiting periods, inside the NRA's headquarters and behind the closed doors of congressional offices we supported—and lobbied for—the Staggers legislation in lieu of the Brady Bill's waiting periods—the lesser evil.

Jim Baker was the NRA's main proponent of the Staggers Bill, but he kept a low public profile on this.

●   ●   ●

As we worked with members of Congress who were considering that session's version of the Brady Bill, we had plenty of persuasive material to back our arguments. But, as with other campaigns—"cop-killer" bullets and "plastic guns"—the NRA had to be careful not to present *too* logical a case because we needed the Brady Bill as a fund-raising tool. Although the ILA held its contribution figures close to the vest, everyone on the seventh floor knew that the effort against the Brady Bill had raised millions since the mid-1980s. Federal lobbying regulations required us to report the amount spent on directly "influencing" legislation before Congress, and we were already over the multimillion-dollar level.

Handgun Control, Inc., was raising funds and spending less, but it was taking in enough to expand its Washington lobbying operation, increase its membership (through groups, rather than individuals), and generally become the big kid on the block among antigun organizations. With their increasingly well-funded staff growing, they had no reason to gnash their teeth and moan too much when the Brady Bill sputtered and stalled yet again on Capitol Hill—their time would come.

But they did get some good news when former president Ronald Reagan came to town to receive an honorary degree from George Washington University. Asked about the Brady Bill, Reagan told *USA Today*, "It's just plain common sense that there be a waiting period to allow local law enforcement officials to conduct background checks on those who wish to buy a handgun." Reagan added, "You know I am a member of the NRA and my position on the right to bear arms is well-known. But I want you to know something else. I support the Brady Bill and I urge the Congress to enact it without delay."

"Jeeze," I told Jim Baker, handing him the newspaper, "HCI's probably going to make billboards out of this."

"I'm more concerned with voting members of Congress than with former presidents," Jim said.

"Well," I said, "have you been reading the crap coming out of the Brady Campaign lately? Now they're calling guns 'the only commercially marketed product designed solely to kill.' What the hell's wrong with killing a rapist breaking into your home? Or some pervert trying to abduct your kid? I suppose they think reasoning with armed felons while you're waiting for the cops to come after calling 911 is a better solution."

We often mocked the opposition's spongy logic, but deep down, we were glad they were such squishy-minded liberals who simply hadn't mastered the technical language within the firearm community. Over the years, HCI had gone from Saturday night specials to assault weapons as being the criminals' "weapons of choice." Now the issue de jour was handguns purchased from federal firearms licensees.

That set up a profitable them-and-us division. Let them collect their funds and sign up members; we'd do the same—in spades.

I recognized and appreciated this aspect of the relationship between the NRA and HCI that winter. At one of our Brady Bill coordination meetings with Wayne LaPierre, Jim Baker, Tony Madda, the deputy director of field operations, and Mary Corrigan of member services I tossed an envelope and its contents on the conference room table. It was an HCI fund-raising mailer. There was a dramatic statement in lurid purple ink on the face of the envelope: ENCLOSED: YOUR FIRST REAL CHANCE TO TELL THE NATIONAL RIFLE ASSOCIA-TION TO GO TO HELL! The multipage fund-raising letter highlighted the merits of the Brady Bill and castigated the National Rifle Association with its "$80 million budget," of which "$12 million is spent on lobbying alone." The solicitation insert had check-off boxes running from "$35 (the price of a Saturday night special)" through $100 to "other $."

The ILA had also collected a selection of viciously satirical newspaper and magazine cartoons that attacked the NRA. In one, a thuggish bruiser clutching a short-barreled Saturday night special mocked the "I'm the NRA" ad campaign.

"Dead-Eye Jones: Husband, Father, Convicted Felon, Owner of the Hard-Nosed Ammo and Liquor Shop (Home of the Pistol and Six-Pack Special—$9.95) A Life Member of the NRA."

The other cartoons were just as nasty. One showed three drooling psychopaths brandishing guns and proclaiming, "I threaten to kill the President!" Beside them a pipe-smoking gentleman in a three-piece suit (evocative of the NRA's executive vice president Warren Cassidy) announced, "I voted against banning handguns!" The punch line at the bottom read, "Will the REAL psycho please stand up."

And on and on, the NRA members were mocking assassinated political leaders, the NRA members were in prison cells with guns on their cell walls, and other scurrilous attacks.

"It's hard to believe that some of this crap was actually published as editorial cartoons," I said.

Tony nodded. But Mary Corrigan and Wayne were studying the cartoons, reading the captions carefully.

"You know," Mary reflected, "these could be very useful in fund-raising."

I was overworked and tired, so I didn't immediately get her point. But Wayne certainly did. He spread the cartoons out on the table again. "These could really rile up the membership. Each one *personally* attacks an NRA member. And members who are angry send money, money that we need to fight that bill."

Now I saw the logic of the argument. The membership was divided on the Brady Bill. But the activists were clearly opposed to it. And they were our most reliable contributors—who were most generous when either frightened or angry. We hoped to use the cartoons to transform some of that anger into generous contributions.

That month, a fund-raising letter based on the "vicious cartoons . . . trying to sway public opinion by portraying NRA as a bunch of crazy, shoot-'em-up old west cowboys" went out to the full membership. The requested contributions ranged from $100 down to $15. The returns came in fast and heavy. "A very good mailing" indeed.

• • •

Meanwhile, everything wasn't running so smoothly at the NRA's headquarters. For much of the previous year, rumors had been swirling hot and fast that Executive Vice President J. Warren Cassidy was under an increasingly fierce attack. It was no secret that Cassidy was barely on speaking terms with the NRA's chief lobbyists, Wayne LaPierre and Jim Baker. The tensions building up over member-ship—and dues—losses, as well as computer-system snafus and political defeats had everyone feeling the pressure. And, although Cassidy was trying to isolate and neutralize factions on the board that blamed him for these problems—"divide and conquer, and then divide and stomp," we joked—he had become the one who was increasingly isolated.

There were multiple sources to his troubles, but one factor stood out over all the others. Cassidy could come across as arrogant. In the past, he could dominate the board and cow the staff, but now board members and staff alike were becoming increasingly angry and resentful. Making matters worse, in addition to the membership losses, reports were circulating that Warren and his allies in the treasurer's and data processing offices were carefully crafting docu-ments to mislead the board on the NRA's financial health. This last-ditch effort—if the rumors were true—was bound to fail.

When the NRA's president Joe Foss—a World War II Medal of Honor winner and Cassidy ally—left office at the end of his term, the new president, Dick Riley, was much less sympathetic to Cassidy. Riley demanded and received a new and more accurate membership count since Cassidy had taken office. The directors were stunned that membership had officially dropped below 2.4 million. Grumbling on the board became loud, especially because of the expensive promotional campaigns that had bled the treasury just to maintain that shrinking membership list. But the hard dollar outlays were less important than the public perception that the National Rifle Association—Washington's reputed lobbying juggernaut—was losing its grassroots support. Cassidy targeted Laurel Smith, director of membership, to take the blame for the debacle. In reality, a lot of the cash hemorrhage was due to a badly flawed data processing operation, which Cassidy, as CEO had approved. Eventually, Smith was fired.

Meanwhile, Neal Knox was lurking out in the boondocks like a hungry coyote, writing vituperative articles and columns about Cassidy's mismanagement and skullduggery. These were early Internet days, and both Knox and Tanya Metaksa had online "bulletin board" sites from which they could snipe at the NRA leadership. In one article published in *Guns & Ammo*, Knox detailed the split between Cassidy and his factions and their opposing groups at 1600 Rhode Island Avenue. Cassidy tried to rally *his* troops by having Riley, Second Vice President Bob Corbin, and Wayne LaPierre sign off on a letter that disputed the Knox column. They refused, and the breach grew deeper and wider.

But Warren Cassidy might well have survived these troubles if not for private peccadilloes that developed into an embarrassing and well-publicized lawsuit. The matter began when Marsha Beasley, head of the NRA's Education and Training Division, ran afoul of Cassidy who reportedly told her that he was worried that such a "young girl" (Beasley was thirty-one) had taken this important position. Eventually, Cassidy fired her—without credible grounds, Beasley alleged. She initiated a wrongful dismissal suit, which cited Cassidy's unethical conduct involving female staff. In essence, Beasley and her attorney claimed that Cassidy rewarded those women with whom he had affairs and punished those who rebuffed him.

Beasley's lawyer deposed Cassidy. Once that deposition had been taken, Cassidy was in an extremely vulnerable position—similar to that of his predecessor, Ray Arnett, who had also had alleged amorous problems while executive vice president. Cassidy's attorneys advised him to settle in order to seal the deposition. He did so. Although we didn't get all the details on the seventh floor, the relevant issue of Johnny Aquilino's *Insider Gun News* quickly provided them. Beasley would receive $100,000 plus three years' salary at $45,000 per year, as well as legal fees to both her attorney and the NRA's outside counsel—a sum of more than $500,000, all of which eventually came from the NRA's members' dues.

The previously divided board could not tolerate this. At the end of January 1991, a chagrined J. Warren Cassidy—obviously shorn of hubris—made a brief statement to the NRA's staff. He was resigning effective February 22 for "personal" reasons. Gary Anderson, a former Olympic Gold Medalist shooter and now a quiet manager who ran general operations, would replace Cassidy until a new executive vice president would be elected in April.

●   ●   ●

The question now was whom would the board elect? Anderson's name was floated around, but he wasn't well known among the membership, other than the negative connotation that Harlon Carter had considered him ineffective.

As I came and went on the seventh floor, working on my Brady campaign lobbying, I heard whispers that both Wayne LaPierre and Jim Baker were being considered for the job. This possibility seemed simultaneously logical and improbable. The position of the NRA's executive vice president required a person (almost certainly a man) with considerable charisma and managerial skill. The job was much more akin to that of an effective corporate CEO than to a political ideologue. In other words, the new executive vice president had to deal well with people in public, manage a large staff and budget, and inspire a growing membership both to man the grassroots ramparts when required, and, of course, keep those checks and money orders coming.

I had known Wayne LaPierre since 1984, and in those years, he had barely progressed past the "policy wonk" stage. Wayne reminded me of an introverted chess champion who was so absorbed in the game that he'd forgotten to eat—or to vary his wardrobe beyond the same old, rumpled blue suit. Inspiring, Wayne was not. At this stage in his career, he was a mediocre public speaker at best. And, his experience in the NRA had been limited to the Institute for

Legislative Action. He had rarely dealt with the other divisions on substantive issues, including budget allocations. Johnny Aquilino nailed this in the *Insider Gun News* when he said, "LaPierre is too one-dimensional to be an effective EVP, too political/ILA oriented."

As for Jim Baker, he did have charisma and what we now call "people skills." He looked good and spoke well. But there was a problem, which Aquilino also pointed out, "Federal Lobbyist Jim Baker has sufficient vision to balance the many aspects of NRA. But, he's the gem in the NRA's lobby crown. His best use would be as head of ILA."

What people outside headquarters—including Johnny—didn't recognize was that the board sought peace and harmony above all else.

One more scandal and the whole battered organization might collapse. Considered in this light, Wayne LaPierre looked like a safe bet. But Wayne's candidacy was not unblemished. In 1988, the *Washington Post* published a front page story revealing that a federal grand jury was investigating a questionable 1986 arms deal in which—according to the *Post*—he had almost certainly been involved.

The transaction was murky to say the least. In 1985, Wayne LaPierre and Rene Carlos Vos, a former Alabama gun dealer incorporated Blue Sky Productions ostensibly to promote rock concerts. However, the "production" company also had close but indirect ties to an Alexandria, Virginia, gun shop, Old Town Armory, which was licensed to sell fully automatic weapons to qualified buyers and conventional firearms to foreign diplomats. One of the investors in the gun shop was Representative William Dickinson (R-Alabama), a friend of Vos. Another investor in the business was Anthony Speros Makris, a former deputy assistant secretary of defense for House affairs (and a growing confidant of Charlton Heston).

Wearing his Blue Sky Productions hat, Vos helped negotiate a deal to buy two hundred thousand surplus M1 Garand semiautomatic rifles from a South Korean arms exporter. This was a fantastic investment opportunity: Blue Sky would pay between $51 and $76 for each M1, depending on its condition; an M1 in good condition sold for at least $300. The math wasn't hard. Blue Sky Productions stood to make more than $60 million. Wayne LaPierre kept a low profile in this deal, of course, but he recognized the immense profits to be made, as the Volkmer-McClure legislation became law. The law authorized importation of these military weapons as "curios or relics."

At the time, however, I hadn't thought of Wayne as notably avaricious. He didn't live ostentatiously; he didn't gamble. I always assumed he wasn't overly interested in money. A decade later, I learned just how wrong I'd been on *that* score.

When the first shipment of 40,000 imported M1 rifles from Korea was blocked in customs in 1986, Blue Sky's allies in the State Department and the Pentagon helped free them. But the Customs Service and the Bureau of Alcohol, Tobacco, and Firearms embargoed the second shipment of 160,000 rifles on the Seattle docks, even though a number of influential congressmen signed a letter to Treasury Secretary James A. Baker III requesting that he intervene. The deal seemed to be crumbling; at least one lawsuit was a distinct possibility. And the whiff of corruption involving the NRA's "Goody Two-shoes," Wayne LaPierre, was rising in northwest Washington, D.C.

Rene Vos was subpoenaed to testify (under an immunity grant) before a federal grand jury investigating the Blue Sky arms deal. Then, in November 1987, Vos was killed in what the *Post* called a "puzzling" light plane crash in which his flight instructor also died. The FBI quickly began to investigate whether Vos had committed suicide, taking the hapless instructor with him, or if a "third party" had sabotaged the plane. Their results were labeled "inconclusive."

When the *Washington Post* interviewed an understandably nervous LaPierre, he claimed to have "severed ties" with Blue Sky in the spring of 1986 before the Korean arms deal was completed. That was possible because Warren Cassidy almost fired Wayne when rumors of his involvement with Blue Sky and Vos surfaced during the last stages of the Volkmer-McClure fight.

The grand jury did not indict Wayne LaPierre. He slid back from under the microscope slide and retreated to his office at the NRA's headquarters.

Aside from his abortive foray in the high-stakes international arms business, Wayne did well in his NRA assignment. Under his leadership, ILA had collected substantial contributions. But most important, Wayne was bland. He was single, and even those who had worked with him for years never knew if he dated or not.

"He's definitely not a womanizer," the private joke around the ILA had it. "He doesn't look or act gay. There's a good chance he's just asexual—you know, like an amoeba."

That, I thought, *would probably fit the board's ticket just right.* There was substance beneath this rough humor. Like an amoeba, Wayne LaPierre seemed to lack a spine, a solid core. Wayne really did prefer to go with the flow, as the saying went. He hated personal confrontations and was said to have relied on the personnel department to fire an ineffective secretary rather than facing the unfortunate woman himself. Wayne was also very partial to consultants. With the Ackerman-McQueen advertising agency now firmly implanted in the NRA, word on the street was that the agency was quietly managing Wayne's campaign for executive vice president. Brad O'Leary, who had done fund-raising at the Republican National Committee, had tutored him on raising money for the ILA (read Wayne) and O'Leary was also in on the push to make Wayne "king."

It was interesting to note that Tony Makris would shortly become Ack-Mac's vice president. For Wayne LaPierre, having Makris as an energetic and politically astute ally was invaluable—and Makris unlocked the Heston tree, whenever needed, whatever the financial cost—to be born by the association at a later date.

In the coming months and years, just how valuable this relationship was to Ackerman-McQueen would become apparent to everyone watching the NRA.

● ● ●

It wasn't long before Bill Bridgewater, who headed the National Alliance of Stocking Gun Dealers, called me in Washington. In theory, he was just another activist gun dealer, owner of the Croatan Rod & Gun Shop in North Carolina. But because National Alliance represented twelve thousand retailers who "stocked" guns in their stores, he was becoming an industry heavyweight—and one of the driving forces behind the American Shooting Sports Coalition. I had originally been offered the job as the new ASSC's executive director but hadn't been finished with my tort reform work at the Coalition of

Americans to Protect Sports (CAPS), so I had recommended Manny Kapelsohn.

Manny was probably a certified genius and one of America's premier forensic lawyers in cases involving firearms. And he had more hands-on experience with guns, principally in police training, than most other law-enforcement instructors.

But Manny had not functioned well in a disparate organization like the ASSC.

"He just didn't work out," Bill said. "Manny actually resigned after the summer of '90 but stayed on for the SHOT Show in January of '91."

The huge SHOT (Shooting, Hunting and Outdoor Trade) Show was held each year in Las Vegas, Dallas, Houston, Atlanta, or Orlando—most often in Vegas. It brought together the entire U.S. firearms industry from replica musket makers to manufacturers of top-end, custom-made hunting rifles—and everything in between. When I'd heard of Manny's resignation earlier, I was saddened but not terribly surprised.

The ASSC combined unlikely—often competitive—firearms and ammunition manufacturers (both foreign and domestic), importers, distributors, and retailers. Naturally, the interests of the domestic manufacturers, the foreign companies, the importers, the whole-salers, and the retailers often diverged. This was a little like harnessing Hamas and B'nai Brith to pull the same sled. The ASSC's stated goal (as established at the Atlanta conference I'd attended), was to unify the diverse elements of the shooting industry and to lobby for "reasonable" gun laws at the federal and state levels, while opposing legislation that would unreasonably curtail firearms ownership and use by law-abiding citizens. The ASSC also sought "reform of the nation's criminal justice system aimed at ultimately reducing drug and crime problems" while pledging to "cooperate with other groups [implicitly the NRA] sharing the same objectives."

In fact, I had originally envisioned the organization as the Institute for Legislative Action of the gun industry. I knew I had the experience to do the job, and I was confident I would do well in the job interviews.

I had my chance to meet the ASSC's selection committee as they interviewed the executive director candidates in yet another

anonymous rented conference room, this one at the Piedmont Airlines lounge in Charlotte, North Carolina. The board took a fax vote
on my appointment a couple of days after my interview. Everyone
was enthusiastic and figured that I knew the firearm policy issues as
well as how to run a trade association. I accepted the position with the
proviso that it not be announced until the NRA's show in San Antonio
about a month later. I wanted to provide a smooth exit from my NRA
consultancy into my new industry role.

• • •

When I accepted the job, I made a couple of requests. First, I wanted
to continue working out of West Palm Beach. Ostensibly, the reason
for remaining in the South was to be near several of the ASSC's key
board members, including Mike Saporito (RSR Wholesale in
Orlando) and Bill Bridgewater. But I also wanted to avoid being
swallowed by the NRA in Washington. The National Rifle Association
had entered what I saw as a "siege mentality" bunker with the loss
of the state assault weapons fights, declining membership, and
the internal imbroglios. I didn't want the ASSC publicly connected
to the NRA even though we would be lobbying the same issues.
And, although I considered Jim Baker and Wayne LaPierre friends,
the association's obsession with hegemony on all aspects of gun
politics might well lead us crossways sooner or later—probably
sooner.

But by keeping my operation small and away from D.C., I might
stay below the NRA's radar. Also, there were already enough
alphabet-soup gun groups in Washington, and I wanted the cachet
of being the "not inside the Beltway" organization.

The board of the ASSC readily agreed to my conditions, and I
went to work setting up my new Florida office. One of my first tasks
was to meet the principal members of the organization. Unfortu-
nately, the ASSC had already acquired the undeserved reputation of
representing the "black gun" side of the industry. This sprang, in
part, from the roster of the group's officers, board, and leading
members in its first full year of operation, when Tom Conrad of
Intratec (maker of the evil-looking black polymer TEC-9 of *Miami
Vice* notoriety), Ron Stillwell of Colt's Manufacturing (the AR-15

"assault rifle"), and Evan Whilden of Action Arms (importer of the UZI) had attracted media attention.

But we also had prominent members from some of the most well-established and respected American and foreign gun makers like Smith & Wesson, Mossberg & Sons, Springfield Armory, Glock, Heckler & Koch, and SigArms.

Johnny Aquilino gave me a nice "welcome onboard" spread in his April *Insider Gun News*. In naming me its executive director, he said, the ASSC had scored a "10X!" (shooter's jargon for a bull's-eye).

"Feldman has more credentials than half of Capitol Hill . . . an attorney with a career crusading against fee-sucking liability lawyers. A former NRA state lobbyist and grassroots organizer, he managed to pull off the nearly impossible: he won respect of state associations, police and local politicians, minority groups, and NRA staff."

I'll never say no to flattery, Johnny, I thought. But then I felt a twinge of unease. Everybody above janitor at 1600 Rhode Island Avenue (and probably most of the people pushing brooms as well) read the *Insider Gun News*. The seventh and eighth floors would be particularly interested in what Aquilino had to say about me. He had been pretty ruthless commenting on the intrigues leading up to Warren Cassidy's canning. Now he was pulling out the stops to praise me. How would the NRA react?

I'd just have to wait and see.

•   •   •

In April 1991 at the annual meeting in San Antonio, the NRA's board of directors announced its choice of executive vice president: Wayne LaPierre. Nobody that I knew was particularly surprised. Wayne's only serious opposition had been Tom Washington, an energetic Michigan conservationist, sportsman, and longtime board member on the finance committee. He was a very capable guy, but Washington didn't have LaPierre's D.C. political connections.

Harlon Carter was in Wayne's camp, but Carter always played this close to the vest (he was also quite ill and would be dead by the fall). Tony Makris, soon to become a vice president of Ackerman-McQueen, was working on Wayne's campaign behind the scenes. And Brad O'Leary, the top-drawer Republican fund-raiser who'd earned so much raking in contributions for the ILA, was eager to work all the NRA fund-raising angles, particularly membership.

But Jim Jay Baker was Wayne's trump card. Jim had let it be known that he would leave the NRA if Wayne weren't elected executive vice president. Nobody wanted that. Jim was too valuable on Capitol Hill, the "yin" of the "yin and yang" lobbying team. And Jim complemented Wayne in another, more subtle way. He was an avid hunter, a shooter, and a savvy gun collector while Wayne had never been a "gunny." Wayne probably didn't know a 20-gauge quail gun from a .375 big game rifle, which was good because he didn't hunt. But knowledge of firearms and hunting experience had traditionally been required traits of the NRA's leaders. So, in a sense Wayne LaPierre and Jim Jay Baker were a two-for-one package.

Wayne's acceptance speech was not a stellar performance. At this stage of his career, he wasn't the accomplished public speaker he would later become. In the big San Antonio convention hall, he seemed stiff and small, although he was actually a pretty tall guy. Blinking behind his wide glasses, he missed several words in his prepared text and had to repeat phrases, which only drew more attention to the mistakes.

A lot of this sounded like "same old same old," and the applause was polite but unenthusiastic.

As they say down South, I thought, *Wayne's got a long row to hoe.* I even wondered if he'd last out his five-year term. (Did I ever miss the mark on that one.)

•　　•　　•

The Brady Bill was one of the main topics of discussion among members at the convention. The House version had just been passed in the Judiciary Subcommittee and was scheduled for Senate committee debate that spring.

In what would be my last public statement as an NRA spokesman, I told the Associated Press that the Staggers bill "accomplishes what most of the handgun control people at least say in public they want to do, which is to prevent criminals—that small number of criminals— from being able to obtain guns from legal sources." In other words, I had put the association on record that it sought the same ends as HCI but wanted to achieve them by different means.

That year's keynote speaker was Beaumont, Texas, Democratic congressman Jack Brooks, a senior House member and longtime friend of the NRA. He drew a standing ovation by praising the association for supporting the Second Amendment and the Bill of Rights, which he called "a bold and masterful plan of individual rights."

As the convention hall rang with applause, it was easy to believe that the National Rifle Association was again a unified organization—if you didn't know better.

• • •

It didn't take long for me to grasp that the American Shooting Sports Coalition and the NRA not only differed in our approaches to the major firearms issues; we also had fundamentally different clienteles. In theory at least, the National Rifle Association represented the best interests of firearms consumers, the American gun owners who were its members (and principal contributors). But the ASSC represented the industry, companies that survived or failed based on their profit margins. So, while the National Rifle Association advocated the easiest availability of federal firearms licenses (FFLs), which could only increase gun ownership, the ASSC opposed this. For each amateur "kitchen table" or "basement bandit" private FFL dealer, one of Bill Bridgewater's retailers lost business. To demonstrate just how easy it was to obtain a license, Bridgewater applied for and received an FFL in the name of his dog, embarrassing BATF officials no end.

It also drove Bridgewater crazy when the NRA held membership promotions to give away guns or free trips to the industry's SHOT Show. "That's just raiding our cash registers," he'd shout at me by phone.

• • •

Another fundamental difference that developed between the two organizations was our attitude to the press. The NRA could not only afford to antagonize the "liberal media," their membership support and fund-raising consistently increased when the media counter-attacked. But the companies making up the ASSC only lost when they were lumped under the negative umbrella of the "gun lobby," which was just another variation of the old "Merchants of Death" smear. (I always laughed at that and said, "Merchants of Freedom.") So getting into spitting contests with the press was not a useful strategy for us. I knew that improving the industry's media image was going to be one of my important, immediate, and long-term goals.

• • •

Wayne LaPierre's cozy relationship with the Ackerman-McQueen advertising agency—that had become the NRA's in-house public affairs department—grew closer in 1991. So did Ack-Mac's lucrative deal with the association, which many of us considered a blatant conflict of interest. Activists, board members, and staff would pro-pose ads addressing political issues. Ackerman-McQueen would create the material, and the word was that it would bill the NRA for both the creative work and for placement. Furthermore they were the association's "in-house" ad agency, literally on the second floor where public affairs used to be. Jim Baker and his deputy, Pat O'Mally, distrusted them with a vengeance, and had their office swept for bugs on a routine basis and once traced some "unex-plained" hard wires back to a junction box near the Ack-Mac operation. The ad agency had a pretty smooth deal: help establish the need for the campaign, and later, bill the association for this service.

(An NRA insider later confirmed that Ack-Mac had a no-contract monthly retainer and also billed to create and place the material—triple-dipping at its most lucrative—if true.)

The huge new publicity campaign for the NRA began in Sep-tember 1991 and continued through October 1992 in sixty-nine publications. I had to assume Ack-Mac was making a tidy profit. Interestingly, six of the ads ran in *Soldier of Fortune*, whose pub-lisher, Lieutenant Colonel Robert K. Brown (U.S. Army, Ret.), was an opponent of Neal Knox and a supporter of Wayne LaPierre. Mutual back scratching? Hey, if it walks like a duck . . .

• • •

Soon after coming on board at the ASSC, I paid my respects to the organization's officers like President Ron Stillwell (Colt's Manufacturing), Dr. Florian Deltgen (Heckler & Koch), and key board members such as Mike Saporito. Then I began communicating indirectly with our membership through an "ASSC Report" column in the National Association of Stocking Gun Dealer monthly newsletter, the *Alliance Voice.* I wanted to let our members know there was a new kid on the block.

In my first column—"Players and Victims"—I resorted to the same attention-grabbing tactics I'd used as a CAPS lobbyist. The newsletter was read by thousands in the gun industry who were curious if the ASSC had acquired any spine. I thought we had and said so. Those of us who manufactured, distributed, and sold firearms and ammunition— "the quintessential American industry"—need no longer feel ashamed to be called the gun lobby by critics and opponents. "I am proud to represent you," I stressed. Although the industry had unusually diverse elements, unity, not division, had to be our goal.

My columns continued, each month addressing a new issue. And the reaction of the industry was universally positive. In one of the most well-received columns, I discussed the gun industry's relationship with the "liberal" news media. The belief that every newspaper reporter, television correspondent, and editor was solidly opposed to firearms was an article of faith in the gun industry. But I had discovered in New Jersey, I wrote, that this was far from true. Among the statehouse media corps during the assault weapons ban fight, I'd found considerable technical ignorance about firearms, but also a willingness to learn. The New Jersey Dealers' Association had stepped in demonstrating that semiautomatic sporting guns—"auto loaders"—were not at all the same as machine guns. And in organized "touch and feel" sessions, the dealers allowed the media to handle Glock semiautomatic pistols, which made it amply clear from the weight of the metal, that these were not the plastic terrorist guns that most reporters had come to believe they were.

In closing, I told our members, "The time to establish relationships with the press is now—not in the heat of a legislative contest.

Most reporters want to be fair, even when they disagree with us . . . if we could do it in New Jersey, it can be accomplished anywhere in America—it's up to you!"

In writing this column I established a position that would become fundamental to the ASSC: the news media were not our natural enemies; they could be educated about the legitimate purpose of firearms in the hands of law-abiding citizens. Unlike the NRA, we did not need to antagonize the press to keep our membership supportive. We wanted allies, not permanent enemies.

•   •   •

One of my first responsibilities as executive director of the ASSC was to heal the hostility Bill Bridgewater had developed toward the National Rifle Association. He always felt that the NRA was after the little family dealer, who made up his association's membership. I thought that this stemmed from the NRA's ignorance and arrogance about a number of narrow issues to which they lacked sensitivity. So I proposed to Bill that I negotiate an NRA/industry membership promotion campaign.

"This would be a win-win situation, Bill," I said. "We'll all make money and the NRA will grow their membership numbers."

The deal was straightforward. Every retail gun dealer who signed up for the program would be issued NRA membership forms, which listed annual dues of $20. For each new member, the gun dealer got $5, the ASSC got $1, and Bill's National Alliance got another $1. That left the NRA $13, which was more than they would have received from their other promotions.

Bill, Wayne, and I signed the deal in the summer of 1991. We immediately signed up almost a thousand gun shops and more were joining each week. It looked like there'd be a period of closer, more equal relations between the NRA and the industry. But almost before the ink was dry on our agreement, there were problems. The NRA began a stealth effort to bypass our dealer-participation program. In monitoring the campaign, we found retailers who we had signed up that were now dealing directly with the NRA, cutting out the ASSC and National Alliance. This was a blatant breach of our agreement.

Bill Bridgewater called me from Havelock, North Carolina, furious. "Those little pricks are cheating us again," he thundered so loudly I had to jerk the receiver away from my ear.

"It's just some kind of a screw-up, no big deal," I insisted. "I'll call Baker and we'll go to D.C. and fix it. No problem."

"Yeah," Bill said skeptically. "We'll see about *that*."

I put down the phone, genuinely perplexed. Solving the dispute with Bridgewater had been a priority issue to the NRA. How could they be fucking this up so badly, so early into the relationship?

Two weeks later, Bill and I went down the seventh-floor corridor at the NRA's headquarters to Jim Baker's ILA office. As we entered, we encountered a couple of gatekeepers, including Pat O'Mally who eyed Bridgewater like a zoo exhibit. Bill Bridgewater was a hefty guy. His face was red with outrage, his brow knotted. Among those greeting us was Brad O'Leary of P.M. Consulting, who had been doing membership promotion as well as fund-raising after Wayne took over from Cassidy. *Now* I began to see what was happening: Brad had been working the NRA's membership account and wasn't about to give up his lucrative fee-per-member to resolve an issue with the industry.

Again, it wasn't until years later that I learned intriguing details of these events—which the NRA's inner circle had not wanted to share with the public, or with the board of directors. For his work in improving the anemic membership numbers, O'Leary was reportedly paid an amazing consultancy fee of $200,000 per *month*, plus per-"mailing" and new-member sign-up fees. In retrospect, it was no wonder that O'Leary had not wanted to share this incredibly good deal with outsiders from the ASSC.

Over the next hour of the meeting, we muddled through various "clarifications" that would "delineate" responsibilities to our "mutual satisfaction." Bill Bridgewater remained largely silent, his face still angry and constricted. But it seemed to me that we had patched up the misunderstandings.

Down on 16th Street, I walked Bill to his car. "See, I told you Baker would fix it," I said. "He's my buddy. We go back a long time."

Bill turned and sneered. "Baker is *not* your friend. Why is it that all you NRA types think the sun rises and sets on 1600? It doesn't!"

I was about to reply, but he wasn't finished yet. "Try and get that through your skull, Mr. *Industry* executive director."

Bill was proved right. The NRA/dealer program hobbled along for a while, but it was so badly undercut that it wasn't worth the aggravation, the cost, or the benefits. The NRA took from our program and gave it to O'Leary to milk as he pleased.

While my ASSC board was always concerned that we not interfere with the NRA and "individual" gun owners, the National Rifle Association didn't give a damn if they skimmed cream from the industry. Or as one major firearm publisher said to me, "The NRA is an ineffective ally, but a fierce competitor." There had been several cooperative programs, including the "round-up" (on contributions) and the "NRA Business Alliance" that tilted heavily in their direction. But they were always warning us to never invade their turf. For a while I had hoped that the relationship would change under Wayne. It did, going from bad to worse. Now their *mistakes* in dealing with the industry weren't mere gaffes, but intentional, high-handed interference.

●　●　●

Nevertheless, I remained on good personal terms with Jim Baker, Wayne LaPierre, as well as with all the key Second Amendment groups. At least three times a year we held secret meetings in Washington at my suite in the Park Terrace Hotel across from the NRA's headquarters. These "quilting bees" were frank (no-notes-taken), free-ranging discussions of gun politics and industry trends. Alan Gottlieb of the Citizens Committee for the Right to Keep and Bear Arms, Larry Pratt of the Gunowners of America, Joe Tartaro of *Gun Week*, Mike Saporito, my chairman, and even Neal Knox joined the NRA guys. We wanted to know where each group stood on an issue—so all of us could keep moving in the same general direction and avoid being sideswiped in legislative conflicts.

The Brady Bill was still gathering momentum in Congress in 1991. And it seemed inevitable that a federal assault weapons ban was in the offing, with New York congressman Charles Schumer and California congresswoman Barbara Boxer probably taking over the leadership on the Hill from Metzenbaum and DeConcini. None of us wanted these laws. But, again, the NRA and the fundamentalist Second Amendment organizations had a different agenda than the industry. We were in the business of selling a legal product, so we wanted a predictable regulatory foundation on which to conduct that business. But some of the quilting bee members liked to tilt at windmills. And the NRA needed continuing crises to keep up the membership rolls and raise funds—"Send $20 immediately, must have by Friday or else," depending on the issue du jour.

●   ●   ●

In his first major personalized fund-raiser, Wayne LaPierre signed a multipage appeal for contributions to commemorate the two hundredth anniversary of the Bill of Rights. In this request, Wayne referred repeatedly to "the *new* NRA."

"I come from the grassroots of gun ownership and hunting," he (or Ack-Mac/O'Leary wrote), presumably with a straight face. "And I intend to bring this entire organization back to its roots." Wayne also promised to meet two other challenges: "to make the NRA stronger," and, "to make the NRA effective enough to beat all antigun laws."

The fund-raiser closed with a postscript:

"If I'm going to succeed in building a new NRA, it's important that I hear from you today."

"Remember, when the Sarah Bradys and Ted Kennedys say too many Americans own guns—they are talking about YOU and me. They are talking about our freedoms. Please help me today. Thank you."

I dropped the fund-raiser on my desk, and then circled the words "the *new* NRA" with a red felt pen.

"It doesn't look very new to *me*," I said.

●   ●   ●

At noon on Wednesday, October 16, 1991, the two days before the House vote on the assault weapons bill, I was in Florida, talking on the phone with Bill Bridgewater. His wife, Carole, came into his office and I heard her voice, tense and brittle.

"There's been a terrible shooting at a cafeteria in Killeen, Texas . . . a lot of people shot."

I flipped on CNN with one hand and hit the speed-dial button on my phone with the other. My law school friend Paul Jannuzzo was now Glock USA's general counsel. George Hennard, the killer at Luby's Cafeteria in Killeen, had driven his pickup truck through the restaurant window and opened fire on the crowded lunch hour tables with a Ruger P89 and a Glock 17. (Glock was an ASSC board member, Ruger hadn't yet joined.) Twenty-two people—including the gunman, who'd shot himself after the police had wounded him—were known dead at the cafeteria. It would be then the worst firearm massacre in American history.

Paul's secretary told me he was in a meeting. "I need to speak to him *now*," I told her. "This is an emergency."

I'd hardly had time to tell Paul about the shooting before he interrupted. "Richie, the phone lines are already lighting up . . . reporters, TV . . . how should we respond?"

"Be respectful. Make sure to say that this was a terrible tragedy. Whatever you do, Paul, do *not* say 'no comment.' "

"What else?"

"Set up a press conference. Be open, not defensive; empathize with the victims and the community of Killeen. Obviously the killer was another crazy. Be sure to stress it was the criminal, not the gun. Tell the press how many police and law-enforcement agencies are now armed with Glocks. Hell, the cops probably used Glocks to wound him."

Paul (and Karl Walter, the CEO) followed my advice to the letter. For the next several news cycles, the story focused on George Hennard, the violent misogynist who had told a friend that he sought "the satisfaction of one day laughing in the face of those mostly white treacherous female vipers" in Killeen. There was hardly a mention of the Glock 17 pistol in these reports. On the floor of the House there was more discussion of the Glock—but more balanced—and we won the vote. However, a federal assault weapons ban was getting closer with every Congress.

•   •   •

In the spring of 1992, I hired Robert Ricker, a Sacramento-based, former assistant general counsel of the NRA to be the ASSC's West Coast representative. Bob knew both gun politics and the California legislature well. I needed him because there were several handgun manufacturers near Los Angeles that were under attack from Josh Sugarmann and the Violence Policy Center, and increasingly from the mainstream media.

That June, I was headed out to California, hoping to run up the new ASSC flag and see if anyone saluted. I cast about for a way to improve the group's image in a state where the press did not favor gun ownership. Then it occurred to me that former president Ronald Reagan had a ranch in the hills behind Santa Barbara—*and* he was known to like quality firearms. I called my old buddy from my Commerce Department days, Dennis LeBlanc. He was a former California highway patrol officer and now a lobbyist for Pacific Telesis. He also managed part of the ranch operations for Reagan.

"We'd like to present some guns to the president," I told LeBlanc. "What would he like?"

The word came back: a Colt single-action revolver, the quintessential Western six-shooter. I called Ron Stilwell at Colt's and he said they'd be honored. "We've given guns to every president since we've been in business."

I didn't ask what they had given to Jimmy Carter.

And, Ron said, we'd also like to present him with an AR-15 Sporter.

The presentation was scheduled for Thursday, June 18, 1992.

Bob Ricker contacted George Waite who owned the Beverly Hills Gun Shop, to complete the Form 4473 paperwork and to obtain clearance to transport the guns from the two sheriffs whose counties we would cross en route to Rancho del Cielo in Santa Barbara. This was only two weeks after the Rodney King riots that almost burned down South Central L.A., so we were a little nervous driving up the Coastal Highway with guns in the cars.

We arrived at the ranch while President Reagan was still out riding, but he soon arrived at the shaded patio beneath a huge old oak tree, looking fit and genuinely glad to meet us.

Like all good politicians, Reagan had memorized our names and addressed us with an easy confidence that dampened any nervousness we were feeling.

The presentation of the guns was more of a photo-op than a formal occasion—we all wore jeans. George Waite huddled with Ronald Reagan to complete the details of the Form 4473 gun transfer. "I'm afraid I have to ask you a bunch of stupid questions, sir," George said.

Reagan brushed aside the apology. "I understand. Just do your job," Reagan said.

"Have you ever been convicted of a felony?" And so it went.

And then we all sat down with soft drinks and he regaled us with Hollywood stories about some of the cowboy roles he'd played. "I always had a little trouble with the quick draw," he said, stroking the new Colt and beautifully tooled holster belt. "I'm a lefty but the directors all made me shoot right-handed."

When Reagan put on the holster rig and slid in the revolver, he had great difficulty pulling it out, as the leather was stiff. He motioned for me to help him, and I found myself with my hand on the gun pointed down at his leg. Well, I knew the six-shooter was unloaded, but all I could think of at that moment was, *I'm the first person since John Hinckley to point a gun at Ronald Reagan.* The revolver came out with just a little more leverage, and the president said, "Thanks."

The president also reminisced on the difference between screen love scenes in 1940s movies and the present. "Back then," he chuckled, "you gave the gal a nice kiss. Today, it looks like they're going to eat right through each other."

Since we'd already outstayed our scheduled thirty minutes, I stood up, thanked our host, and suggested that we leave.

"Sit down, sonny," Reagan said with a wide grin. "I'll let you know when we're done with ya."

More stories and we were bent over laughing in our chairs. "Hey, fellas," Reagan said, "come on in and see the house."

This was a real honor as the ranch house was small and very personally furnished with scuffed leather chairs, hardly a show place. One of the president's prize possessions was an Indian tomahawk, which he could twist and flip quite nimbly.

Ronald Reagan cordially walked us to our cars and shook hands with a word of personal thanks for each man.

Had the Constitution permitted, I realized, here was a leader who could have continued to win elections. That sunny afternoon in the foothills of the Santa Inez Mountains, I saw no hint of the darkness of the Alzheimer's that would soon steal his mind.

●   ●   ●

The 1992 presidential elections were among the strangest in U.S. history. Third-party candidate Ross Perot badly disrupted the process by entering the race, pulling out, and then reentering. While the NRA held off endorsing any candidate during this uncertain period, people privy to the inner workings of 1600 Rhode Island Avenue—including members of the quilting bee—knew that the association remained so embittered toward George Bush over the 1989 assault weapons import ban that they were unlikely to support him. Hearing these political musings, I always recalled that night at the Opryland Hotel in Nashville when Bill Bennett sought my advice on future career moves. There was a direct line between that meeting and Bennett's assault weapons import ban—which the NRA's activists considered nothing less than treachery by the Bush administration. So by 1992, the watchword among the NRA's activists had become "Anyone but Bush."

This further split an already divided electorate and the conventions nominated George H. W. Bush and William Jefferson Clinton. Bush was anathema to the loyal NRA rank and file. Ross Perot's erratic campaign style and personal eccentricities did not appeal to gun activists, so Bill Clinton began looking better. People remembered that the NRA had given him an "A" rating on its political preference charts during his Arkansas gubernatorial campaigns. He was positioned as a moderate southerner from a pro-hunting state, as was his running mate, Senator Al Gore of Tennessee.

But the Bush campaign remained arrogantly confident that ILA's Political Victory Fund would endorse the president's reelection well before Election Day. The White House attitude was simple and cocky: "Who else will they turn to?"

By the end of October, the National Rifle Association had still not endorsed a presidential candidate. The association was demonstrating its independent strength in cynical retaliation for Bush's 1989 betrayal. This lack of the NRA's grassroots support was a crucial factor in the election. On Tuesday, November 3, 1992, Bill Clinton won 43 percent of the popular vote and 370 electoral votes to Bush's 37 percent popular and 168 electoral. Ross Perot carried 18 percent of the popular vote but no electoral votes. Had the NRA chosen to energize its grassroots base to support Bush, it is likely he could have cut into Clinton's landslide in key Midwestern swing states and squashed Perot's surprisingly strong popular vote across the country. Polls revealed that a high percentage of gun owners had voted for the Clinton-Gore ticket.

After the election, Bill Clinton awkwardly cobbled together his transition team and cabinet: even before his January 1993 inauguration, many of us in the gun community began to worry that the NRA had made a terrible decision.

As it turned out, most of our worries were justified.

9

CONFLICT AND COOPERATION

On the chilly Sunday morning of February 28, 1993, a convoy of pickup trucks towing cattle trailers rolled into the Mount Carmel compound of the Branch Davidian sect near Waco, Texas. Heavily armed, black-clad agents of the Bureau of Alcohol, Tobacco, and Firearms jumped down from the trailers and formed teams to assault the Davidian's central building, a massive barnlike structure. The BATF had warrants to arrest the group's leader, David Koresh, and his principal followers on charges they had assembled an arsenal of illegal weapons in anticipation of an apocalyptic battle initiating the biblical end of times.

Koresh—born Vernon Wayne Howell in 1959—had transformed the obscure Seventh Day Adventists splinter faction into an abusive cult. He alone had authority to marry female members and to father children with them. It was Koresh who claimed unique visionary insight into the book of Revelations. The Davidians were said to indulge in child abuse: Koresh was rumored to have taken prepubescent girls as brides.

But it was persistent reports that the Mt. Carmel sect had fortified their compound and stockpiled grenades, ammunition, and assault weapons, some illegally converted to full-automatic fire, that finally initiated the BATF raid. The BATF's director Steven Higgins gave authorization to proceed with the arrests, even though the element of surprise had evaporated when Davidian members outside the compound informed Koresh of the impending raid.

As the agents tried to batter their way into the Mt. Carmel headquarters through barred doors and second-floor windows, gunfire erupted. Later, survivors on each side blamed the other for firing first. Whatever caused the shootout, the BATF proved to be both badly outgunned and short on tactical skill. Their small-caliber submachine guns and pistols were no match for the 7.62 mm semiautomatic weapons blasting through the wooden walls to strike the exposed agents.

Before the federal officers retreated, their ammunition exhausted, four members of the assault teams and six Davidians were dead. Badly wounded agents lay in the cattle trailers or across the hoods of the pickups for the television crews lining the road to tape. The raid had literally ended as a bloody fiasco.

And then the FBI took over and a long siege began.

I had moved the ASSC's headquarters to Atlanta the year before, and I was in my office early on the morning after the failed raid, sipping coffee as I flipped through the TV channels. The BATF was already taking a beating from congressmen interviewed on their way to the Hill, and the Clinton White House had not come forward in the agency's defense.

In my first phone call that morning, I told Frank Dugan, the adept contract lobbyist I'd hired in 1991 to be our eyes and ears in Washington, "Everyone's talking about guns in this deal. The White House will be looking for scapegoats, and I have no damn doubt whatsoever they'll find illegally purchased guns and 'assault weapons' . . . whether they have them or not!"

"And you can bet that the NRA will be itching for a fight before the dust settles," Dugan added.

The Waco raid was reminiscent of the 1992 combined U.S. Marshal Service/FBI siege and assault on white separatist Randy Weaver's mountain cabin on Ruby Ridge, Idaho. A BATF informant had tricked Weaver, a religious zealot and former Vietnam War Green Beret, into selling two shotguns with illegal, sawed-off barrels.

When Weaver refused to spy on the nearby Aryan Nation's compound in exchange for having the weapons charges dropped, he holed up with his family at the cabin. On August 21, 1992, the marshals and the FBI's hostage rescue team moved in. Weaver's wife, Vicki, and their son, Sam, age fourteen, were shot and killed, as was Marshal William Degan.

To gun control organizations, illegal guns were the cause of the Ruby Ridge tragedy. Gun rights activists, especially the National Rifle Association and the pro-gun press—including Robert K. Brown of *Soldier of Fortune* magazine and columnist Neal Knox—saw the entire sad chain of events as emblematic of government gun grabbers once more trampling the Constitution.

As Harlon Carter had foreseen, Knox had proven hard to keep buried. His reemergence as a board member on the fundamentalist side of the National Rifle Association, which paralleled that of his alter ego, Tanya Metaksa—who was also becoming increasingly active on the board—meant that Wayne LaPierre would have to sway to the ideological right to maintain his support base in the association. But as always, the story was more complex. Wayne was willing to give Neal and Tanya free rein, provided they defended him from "a handful of dissidents" on the board who questioned his financial management, especially his reliance on ad hoc lucrative payments to consultants. So while Wayne could echo the zealotry coming from the Knox-Metaksa camp, I later learned that he was far more concerned with his personal fortunes than with Second Amendment absolutism.

(Neal Knox and other knowledgeable board members would later condemn the personal greed of the NRA's senior officials. In 1995, Knox charged that Wayne LaPierre's annual compensation had risen to $250,000.)

•   •   •

The political sniping and crossfire sputtered and flared as the siege of Mt. Carmel dragged on past eight weeks. Koresh—aware that he now faced charges of murdering federal officers—refused to negotiate in good faith, claiming he needed time to complete work on his murky apocalyptic prophesies. A handful of children and adults left the compound, but more than eighty Davidians remained loyal to their leader inside the building.

On a county road near the FBI's perimeter, a lanky young Gulf War veteran wearing a "chocolate chip" camouflage army cap watched the progress of the siege as he peddled gun rights bumper stickers neatly stacked on the hood of his car. Several were standard-issue NRA: FEAR THE GOVERNMENT THAT FEARS YOUR GUN, A MAN WITH A GUN IS A CITIZEN, A MAN WITHOUT A GUN IS A SUBJECT. The young veteran's name was Timothy McVeigh. He had left the army embittered after failing to qualify for Special Forces training. Now he seemed to have found a new cause: protecting individual freedom—especially Second Amendment rights—from a rapacious government.

In mid-April, the FBI convinced newly confirmed attorney general Janet Reno to authorize a full "take down" of the Davidian Waco compound, justifying the assault on the pretext that child abuse was still rampant inside the besieged Mt. Carmel complex. The attack began at dawn on April 19, spearheaded by combat engineer vehicles (CEVs) and armored personnel carriers. Using long booms, the CEVs smashed holes in the wood frame structure and pumped CS gas inside. Then the CEVs used their bulldozer blades to rip through doors and walls. No Davidians surrendered. Just after noon, fires broke out in different parts of the building. A whipping prairie wind fed the flames. Within minutes, the structure was blazing.

One woman, her clothes on fire, managed to escape. Eighty-two children and adults did not. The blazing walls and floors collapsed into an incandescent heap as CNN broadcast live images of the ghastly scene.

Timothy McVeigh watched the live television coverage from his brother's farm in Michigan.

In the last week of April, I attended the 1993 NRA meeting in Nashville. As I suspected, the disaster in Waco was the main subject discussed. There were heated but impractical motions from the floor calling for a resolution to disband the BATF, and for President Bill Clinton's resignation, which Wayne LaPierre and his allies crushed. It made no sense for the association to paint itself into a radical corner and risk losing tens of thousands of new members who sought moderate, predictable protection of their Second Amendment rights.

Wayne's allies now included Neal Knox, who, having returned to the NRA's board of directors in 1991, was proceeding to stack it with like-minded acolytes. Although there was no paper trail to prove it, Knox had clearly embarked on a second campaign to wrest control of the National Rifle Association from anyone who would oppose him.

"Neal's got his eye on the prize," Roy Innis said to me, echoing the old civil rights mantra.

"Yeah, he's got his eye on Wayne's job," I said.

For his part, Wayne continued trying to straddle the middle ground at the meeting. Interviewed by the *Washington Post*, Wayne avoided casting the Waco disaster as a Manichean struggle between the forces of Good and Evil. "I don't think we know yet," he said when asked if the Davidians were the type of "law-abiding citizens" for whom the NRA championed Second Amendment protection.

But when Wayne took the rostrum for his stem-winder speech later in the week, he pledged to marshal all the NRA's considerable political force in the coming "fight for freedom."

Noting the ambivalence that many Americans felt after Waco, he said they had been "driven apart" by the most powerful "social tyrant that ever before existed on this planet: the American media."

When in doubt, I thought, *bash the media*.

That always played well to members. And Wayne was careful to keep them on his side. Membership rolls had grown by six hundred thousand under his stewardship as executive vice president, and now again totaled more than 3 million. This figure represented potential contribution and membership renewal income in the tens of millions of dollars. Only a handful of board members and salaried officers knew what Wayne had to gain personally from this revenue stream. His total compensation package was hidden from the membership and from most of the board of directors and never discussed.

Although Wayne and other speakers gave the standard denunciation of the Brady Handgun Violence Prevention Act, the bill was almost certain to be voted into law before the end of the current congressional session. Bill Clinton had come into office with a solid majority in both the House and the Senate and promised to sign the bill, and a Democratic Congress was not about to rebuff its party's new president after twelve years of a Republican White House. The NRA was already planning to use the new law as a fund-raising tool, dunning the membership to fund "repeal" campaigns. But this was a transparent ploy. The bill likely to pass had been amended so that the HCI-backed waiting period would be replaced by a computerized National Instant Criminal Background Check System (NICS) established by the U.S. attorney general within five years.

Both the NRA and my organization were on record as favoring NICS. In fact, during the fall of 1993, in House Judiciary testimony on the Brady Bill, the ASSC "enthusiastically supported" point of purchase background checks as a means of protecting our retail dealers from inadvertent transfers to prohibited persons. Following that testimony, I held my breath fully expecting a broadside of attacks from the "hardcore" gun community.

Unlike the NRA, then, I had no intention of tilting at windmills by lobbying against legislation that was a virtual shoe-in on the Hill.

Less certain was the federal assault weapons ban, which California senator Diane Feinstein and New York congressman Charles Schumer were pushing toward passage. My members were already planning tactics to counter federal bans on "military-style" semiautomatic weapons. If Congress followed the California model and named specific firearms, gun makers could simply move a screw or a cosmetic piece of metal and give the guns another name. If the pending law cited attributes such as external pistol grips or bayonet mounts, the manufacturers could produce guns lacking those specific accessories. Yes, the industry would do its best to prevent the drive-by bayonetings that were causing such havoc everywhere.

The membership of the American Shooting Sports Council had steadily increased to include every major American and European gun maker. (With my board's concurrence, I'd changed the ASSC's name from "Coalition" to "Council" in 1992 when I'd moved my office from Florida to suburban Atlanta. The word "council" sounded more businesslike and had an air of permanency.) We could now justify our logo, "Representing the Firearms Industry."

The fact was that the ASSC was attracting industry members because of its moderate and practical approach to legislative and public relations. Zealotry had long been the NRA's strong suit, but we would never survive if we were in direct competition with them. I also knew that their quest for hegemony would never permit a powerful, independent industry group to encroach on the NRA's traditional turf. But, as the old saw had it, politics was the art of the practical. We would make friends where we could, avoid antagonizing potential enemies, and do our damnedest to keep the industry on a profitable footing.

•   •   •

By 1993, I'd established a growing presence in Washington with Frank Dugan as well as a West Coast operation based in Sacramento headed by Bob Ricker. I maintained the ASSC's headquarters in Atlanta and traveled the country, often with our chairman, Mike Saporito, conferring with our members, putting out brushfires, and courting the media. We were on our way to becoming "the kinder, gentler gun lobby."

The antifirearm sentiment grew more vehement when lone, deranged gunmen committed sporadic multiple killings. On July 1, 1993, for example, Gian Luigi Ferri, 55, a delusional failed entrepreneur, invaded the law offices of Pettit & Martin at 101 California Street in San Francisco. Like the killer at Luby's Cafeteria in Killeen, Texas, Ferri carried multiple weapons. His arsenal included two TEC-9, 9 mm semiautomatic pistols and a .45 caliber handgun. He entered a conference room and began firing, then chased victims down corridors and into offices, randomly shooting some, sparing others. When the police SWAT team arrived, Ferri shot himself through the head. The Pettit & Martin death toll reached eight with six wounded. Ferri's motives were obscure. In a rambling diatribe he listed all those who had ruined his life, including two of the firm's lawyers.

Following the Killeen massacre, antiviolence advocates campaigned for draconian gun control, including universal firearms registration and handgun confiscation—measures of dubious practicality or political possibility. The fact was that there were crazy people in every society and there were about 200 million firearms in the hands of 70 million American gun owners. The specter of confiscation would simply drive a significant number of these weapons underground.

I knew that this was a valid assessment because the ASSC's wholesale distributors and retailers reported robust sales of handguns to what I called the "libertarian, Jeffersonian elements." These were nontraditional gun owners, including "urban dwellers, feminists, and suburban entrepreneurs." They were not hunters or sport shooters. But they felt increased need for self-protection due to an "unreliable and indifferent criminal justice system." They would be more than willing to undergo criminal background checks during the five-day waiting period of the Brady Bill's initial years. Equally, many of these law-abiding citizens might choose semiautomatic "assault"-type weapons to protect their families.

Lacking an absolute ban on private gun ownership (perhaps enforced by a huge force of federal paramilitary agents) these citizens would continue to obtain legal weapons for a variety of reasons. Feminists, I noted, cited the empowerment of gun ownership. To me, this could be summed up by the old slogan, "You can't rape a .38!" I stressed that it was up to the firearms industry to help build a coalition of our natural allies, fearful city dwellers and suburbanites, con- cerned hunters and sport shooters, who could join to "isolate the prohibitionists."

Unlike the NRA, I wasn't asking our members for endless contributions. I needed something more valuable, their cumulative wisdom, business experience and connections, and their collabora- tive hard work.

●   ●   ●

I was hopeful that this approach would ultimately bring a semblance of reason to the firearms industry's role in the national debate on guns. But while I was confident this reasoned, patient approach would accomplish that goal, I saw signs that the National Rifle Association was lurching into one of its tectonic upheavals. Neal Knox and Tanya Metaksa were squeezing their way back into power at the NRA. Furthermore, staid traditional firms like Sturm Ruger, Winchester, Remington, and Beretta— companies that had once felt secure from the messy world of politics within the old Sporting Arms & Ammunition Manufacturers' Institute, Inc. (SAAMI), now distanced themselves from the NRA's fundamentalists and sought comfort in the ASSC's moderate policies.

This was not to say that our group would ever compromise its basic principles on Second Amendment rights, or on the need to protect the industry from legislative or law-enforcement harassment. On those issues, we were just as adamant as the NRA. But the NRA was more focused on its dues-paying membership and hard-core contributors than on the industry's goals. And, the ASSC also diverged sharply from the NRA's more zealous public stances. While recognizing that the Neal Knox–Tanya Metaksa faction had regained considerable influence at the NRA, I still had no basic dispute with the association as an institution—provided its ceaseless pursuit of hegemony would cut us enough slack to accomplish our objectives.

On the federal level, the ASSC lobbied strenuously to protect the firearms industry. Ohio senator Howard Metzenbaum was attempting to add firearms to the jurisdiction of the Consumer Product Safety Commission, and was encouraging the Environmental Protection Agency to consider banning lead ammunition.

Just as I had lobbied previously for the NRA at the statehouse level, I brought together an industry grassroots response by firearms dealers, wholesalers, and manufacturers. We delivered a strong message about jobs, tax revenue, and the economy to key uncommitted legislators. I knew from my NRA northeast district days that New England was not an unassailable monolith of antigun opposition. Liberalism might have been the prevailing political ethos in Connecticut and Massachusetts, but members of Congress were practical. They recognized the importance of highly paid manufacturing jobs and the tax revenue the gun industry generated.

To make sure our industry's message was reaching the right audience on Capitol Hill, I worked with my staff and board in 1993 to begin an annual ASSC "Washington Fly-In." Our members, including most of the CEOs, flew to the capital and met with members of Congress, their staffs, and with various federal agencies that regulated our industry. We resumed the NRA's defunct popular wild game banquet around the presentation of the ASSC's Congressional Leader of the Year award. Quail, pheasant, venison, and an occasional wild boar were a step up from the usual Washington rubber chicken or shoe-leather steak. The event gave legislators and their staff the chance to connect faces with names and to realize that ASSC members were serious, reasonable businesspeople, and not gun-toting fanatics.

Beyond the bonhomie, the fly-ins were a serious exercise in education. Our chairman, retired Judge Michael Saporito, welcomed the guests at the wild game dinner honoring House Judiciary Committee chairman Jack Brooks, a Democrat from Beaumont, Texas. He was our first Congressional Leader of the Year. The menu that night featured marinated venison backstrap, tender enough to cut with a fork.

As he was leaving, Congressman Jack Brooks took me aside. "Feldman," he said with a rich Texas Gulf Coast drawl, "that was delicious. I expect to have the recipe for that venison on my desk in the morning." He grinned. "Otherwise, you're gonna see some pretty serious gun control coming down the pike. You hear me!" (From then on it was Venison à la Brooks at our dinners.) Brooks was known as a strong NRA ally, and had been a featured speaker at their annual meeting several years before. But it was clear that he recognized the ASSC offered a separate perspective on the gun issue.

After the event, Jim Baker called me. "How the fuck did you get Jack Brooks?" he asked, genuinely impressed.

I didn't explain that Frank Dugan had close relations to Brooks. "Hey, Jim," I merely replied. "I've got a *few* connections in this town."

● ● ●

With the elements of education and human contact in mind, the ASSC organized hands-on shooting lessons and firearms demonstrations in June for Capitol Hill staffers. They included legislative aides from both the Senate and House members, as well as from both Judiciary Committees. We met at the patrician Fairfax Rod and Gun Club, a stone's thrown from the Bull Run Civil War Battlefield. Expert industry firearms instructors gave basic classroom lessons on the history of firearms from muzzleloaders to polymer stock machine pistols. We had arrayed on tables more than fifty guns in every imaginable configuration: single-shot .22 caliber rifles like I used to shoot at summer camp; bolt-action big-game rifles; lever-action Wild West carbines; and pump-action and autoloader shotguns. Some of the guns had classic varnished wood stocks, others were encased in black plastic. The handguns ranged from tiny two-shot derringers to double-action revolvers to semiautos in every conceivable caliber and style.

Steve Otway, CEO of Heckler & Koch, USA, led the instruction, keeping the audience enthralled. Probably the most revealing moment was when Steve poured a hefty mound of modern gunpowder into a pan and asked if the staffers had been led to believe that ammunition was inherently explosive. As they were all nodding yes, he dropped a match into the pan. Poof! A flash and a cloud of smoke. So much for the explosion—and another media myth. Modern gunpowder was a propellant; only black powder was explosive, Steve explained. It had to be encased in a cartridge and ignited by a priming cap.

After lunch, we moved the equipment out to the firing range. Weapons expert Charlie Sunderlin from H & K demonstrated the explosive impact of various firearms. Starting with a .22 and finishing with a black-powder muzzleloader, he destroyed a number of water-filled milk jugs. The single-shot muzzleloader was loud and devastating compared to the relatively mild crack from a Hungarian AK-derivative semiauto. Then Sunderlin gave an impressive demonstration with a .38 caliber revolver using four standard police-issue cylindrical speed loaders, which gave the pistol a rate of fire, every bit as fast as a semiautomatic handgun. The message was clear: "A gun is a gun is a gun."

Now we invited the staffers themselves to get "on the line" and fire. Wearing advanced ear protection, they tentatively came forward and lifted the weapons—under the close supervision of Otway or Sunderlin—and began to plink away with the .22s. They moved up to lever-action carbines, and then on to .223 and .308 rifles. Within twenty minutes, even the most reluctant were braced on the shooting stands, squinting downrange as they squeezed the triggers.

To me, one of the most revealing moments that afternoon was when a staffer from Congressman Fortney "Pete" Stark, a well-known gun prohibitionist, fired a full magazine from the AK (which he had earlier called an "assault weapon").

Then he turned to the instructor, "Can I shoot a couple more? I'm just getting the hang of it."

We gave him two more 30-round magazines and he proceeded to blast away. Earlier that year during committee hearings on the Hill, this staffer had advised members to help ban weapons that "sprayed" bullets. Now at the Fairfax Rod and Gun Club he was gaining an understanding based on actual hands-on experience that a semiautomatic rifle fired only one round for each pull of the trigger.

In our analysis of the event, we agreed that the best way to change the hearts and minds of legislative staffers was to offer them the educational and practical shooting experience—in other words, fun—that a day on the range provided. They could then draw their own conclusions. Less than three months later, the ASSC organized another congressional staffer "Firearms Safety and Education" day at the Gun Club, which was even more successful. The range shooting became a very popular regular event with congressional staff members.

● ● ●

As I anticipated, our direct lobbying against the pending federal assault weapons ban was considerably less effective. The votes just weren't there. Ruby Ridge, the Waco disaster, and the massacre at 101 California Street made it very hard for members of Congress to vote for any legislation that might appear soft on guns. It didn't matter that both pending laws were largely symbolic. And in fact Congress was dealing in symbolism not substance. I'd labeled the waiting period bill the "Brady Charade" Act because it was flimflam over substance.

The laws that President Clinton signed on November 30, 1993, and which took effect in the thirty-two states that had no background check system *seemed* far more important than they were. There were two sections to the Act, the interim and the permanent. Both applied to federal firearms licensees. The interim provision would end five years after the law went into effect on February 28, 1994. During that period, sellers would be required to verify the identity of any handgun buyer using a picture ID card issued by a government agency and to obtain a statement similar to the standard Form 4473. Within one day, the dealer had to furnish a copy of the statement to the chief law enforcement officer of the community where the buyer resided. The dealer then had to wait five business days. If a weekend or a holiday occurred, which was likely, the waiting period could be six business days.

But there was a major catch. Despite all the hoopla, police or sheriffs were *not* required to check the buyer's background. So the ostensible purpose of the time-consuming and expensive process was obviated—hence the "charade."

On September 29, 1993, I'd testified about this and other troubling aspects of the Brady Bill before the U.S. House Judiciary Committee's Subcommittee on Crime and Criminal Justice:

"Conceivably under this bill, a felon could acquire a handgun from a licensed dealer after waiting the five business days because there is no mandatory check to snare felons. If accepting a meaningless but politically correct waiting period is the only way we can get a tough reliable criminal dragnet enacted into law, so be it!"

The ASSC was not happy with the bill, but we knew enough to help shape it and to save our political capital for winnable fights.

And we did accept the permanent provisions of the Brady Bill that required the U.S. attorney general to establish a National Instant Criminal Background Check System within five years. The purists wouldn't be pleased, although, if done properly, the law would end much of the legal uncertainty inherent in gun transfers. The NICS would apply to *all* firearms purchases, handguns, and long guns. At the point of purchase, an FFL holder would be required to contact the system in West Virginia to receive a unique approval number for the sale, and also to verify the identity of the buyer using a picture ID. If the dealer did not receive a response within three business days, he could transfer the firearm without the approval number. The NICS would be prohibited from keeping any record of the sale except for the unique number and the date it was used.

The Brady Bill required that multiple sales of firearms be reported to state and local police. The law prohibited "common carriers" such as airlines, buses, trains, and parcel delivery services from demanding that outside firearms tags (an invitation to theft) be placed on luggage and packages. The bill increased FFL fees to $200 for the initial three-year period, and $90 for each three-year renewal. The ASSC cried some crocodile tears about the increased license fees, which would reduce the number of "kitchen-table dealers." But

Bill Bridgewater and his small dealer cohorts were quite pleased, even while the NRA ranted.

And nobody with any knowledge of the real world believed for a minute that criminals would be greatly affected by the Brady provisions. Typically, they did not buy their guns in person over FFL counters. We disparaged the Brady Act as typical Clintonesque "feel-goodism."

During this period, a bitingly sarcastic mock Form 4473 began to circulate in the gun community. Printed on the familiar yellow paper stock and divided into sections and check-off boxes, the form was an acerbic parody. Under gender, for example, the categories "transvestite, transsexual," and "other sexually challenged" categories were listed. "English speaking—southern districts" was a language category. Possible reasons for a dealer refusing to sell a firearm included "Are you presently in deep shit with the law?" "Are you an idiot or a nut?" "Are you a Commie?" "Did you vote for Clinton?" "Do any of your bed sheets have cutouts for eyes?" "Do Girl Scouts sexually excite you?" "Do Boy Scouts sexually arouse you?" "Have you ever had a relationship with any farm animal? (Note—mutual consent is not an issue here.)" Under the form of identification boxes, one was "State inmate identification card," while another was "I used to date his sister." There was a space to write the transferee's name or a check box simply listed "Bubba."

Paraphrasing Jimmy Buffett, I told Mike Saporito, "If we can't laugh, we'll all go insane."

●   ●   ●

Although guns were obviously a major factor in U.S. political life, we suspected that individual attitudes toward firearms, the NRA, and gun control were more complex than one imagined. The NRA operated in the black-and-white universe of pro– or anti–Second Amendment. But the ASSC, whose members had to function in the business world, could not afford to be so inflexible. So in April 1994, the board approved my plan to conduct a nationwide opinion poll that would provide a reliable information base. We retained the Eddie Mahe Company to engage the Tarrance Group, a well-established public opinion research firm, to conduct the survey. They contacted a thousand adults across the country between April 16 and 18, 1994, and produced results with a 95 percent confidence factor (accurate to $+/-$ 3.1 percent) as verified by sophisticated computer analysis.

When asked to list the "Number One problem facing this part of the United States today," 33 percent (by far the largest segment) listed crime. Only 2 percent cited guns, even though most approved of Bill Clinton's job performance. The question on the cause of violent crime in the United States found drugs (21 percent) and the breakdown of families (13 percent) much higher than guns (10 percent), and an overwhelming 57 percent backed reforming the judicial system to provide tougher penalties for criminals. But only 12 percent favored banning gun ownership.

More than 80 percent of those surveyed strongly or "somewhat" agreed that the Constitution guaranteed the right for individuals to own a gun and use it to protect themselves. So, it wasn't surprising that guns were not seen as a threat to children, whereas drugs were considered a threat by a total of 71 percent of respondents. Handgun Control, Inc., and the NRA had almost equally strong and somewhat favorable ratings, each totaling about 50 percent. But when asked specifically about the NRA, 52 percent found it "too extreme," while 35 percent said, "the NRA is right [correct]." An overwhelming 66 percent agreed that banning guns would only allow criminals to obtain firearms illegally. When asked to identify the meaning of the term "assault weapon," most (23 percent) recognized a semiautomatic rifle, but an equal number thought machine guns or "military-type" guns met this definition.

Significantly, the largest percentage (37 percent) favored gun registration. In the seminal question (as the post-9/11 world would show us) whether "you personally [would] be willing to give up some of your basic Constitutional rights . . ." in order to reduce crime and promote security, a surprising 46 percent were willing to do so. Only 28 percent voiced strong opposition to this concept. Yet well over half of those surveyed said having a gun in the house made them and their families feel safer.

What this survey demonstrated was that, while Americans did support the Second Amendment guarantee of private gun ownership, and found that guns provided protection against crime, Americans were more flexible than the NRA. This was especially true when it came to some aspects of the controversial issue of gun registration.

For the ASSC, the Tarrance survey showed that although there were lots of angry voices swirling around the gun issue, the majority of Americans were more balanced. This helped us plan a strategy of moderation and avoid self-defeating extremist positions during the 1990s.

•　•　•

As the Brady legislation moved toward passage, the Democratic-controlled Congress prepared to pass an equally symbolic federal assault weapons ban under the umbrella of a huge $30.2 billion "omnibus" crime bill. In August 1993, President Bill Clinton summarized what he and his party sought in the crime bill: a federal assault weapons ban, funding to hire a hundred thousand new "community police officers," new federal death penalties (aimed at drug kingpins and killers of corrections officers), and a streamlining of the appeals process for death row inmates in the federal system.

In late 1993, Jim Baker resigned as executive director of the NRA's Institute for Legislative Action, effective just before the Brady Act became law in February 1994. He had once been Wayne LaPierre's most effective lieutenant—although insiders realized Wayne had begun to keep him in an increasingly weak position. Wayne did not let Jim appoint his own team at the ILA; his first head of Federal was Patrick Raffaniello, a veteran Hill staffer with connections to Big Oil whose salary was actually higher than his own. From 1991 to 1993, chaotic personnel changes at the ILA saw three Federal directors and three heads of state and local come and go. All Jim Baker ever cared about or seemed to understand was Washington, but the turmoil at the state and local level undercut everything he tried to do on the Hill.

Outside the NRA, Jim's resignation was seen as tantamount to hara-kiri. The full truth was far different: after all the grief he'd taken under his one-time buddy, Wayne LaPierre, Jim did not want to be "in charge" of the association's lobbying when the Brady Bill and possibly the federal assault weapons ban became law. But he stayed close to the NRA, establishing his own lobbying firm with just two clients, the National Rifle Association and the Sporting Arms & Ammunition Manufacturers' Institute (SAAMI).

To the surprise of most of us, Wayne LaPierre chose Tanya Metaksa to replace Jim as head of the ILA. She was the same old bayonet-'em-in-the-guts style lobbyist to those who might cross the NRA. She was the embodiment, the scornful face and gruff voice of the NRA's old sobriquet, "Never Re-Elected Again."

People working at the association's new $17 million glass-cube headquarters off Route I-66 out in Fairfax, Virginia, told me that the NRA kept Jim on a "very generous" six-figure retainer. And SAAMI began to rely on his guidance through the maze of Capitol Hill's corridors. But even as SAAMI's blue-blood American companies were paying for Baker's "inside" advice, a growing number of them were joining the American Shooting Sports Council, thus putting Baker and me in a potentially competitive position. On my almost monthly trips to D.C., I'd stop in to see Jim in his hideaway office on N Street. He'd perk up when I talked about mail-back cards in gun boxes, creating a new mailing list of gun owners outside of the NRA. He seemed bored by not being in the heart of the storm and was waiting for SAAMI to step up his lobbying efforts—it would be a long wait!

After Clinton set his first-term anticrime objectives, Senator Joseph Biden and Congressman Jack Brooks, the chairmen of the Senate and House Judiciary committees, introduced bills based on the White House goals. Biden, an astute Delaware politician, avoided a fight (with the NRA's Metaksa and other pro-gun groups) in his own committee and took the bill directly to the Senate floor. There, the Democratic majority approved his legislation virtually intact, a bill that would authorize more than $22 billion for the community police hiring, enforcement of a ban on certain semiautomatic weapons, harsh new sentencing guidelines, and programs to reduce violence against women. Because his bill had plenty of appealing "pork" in the form of new federal funding for prison construction, it passed by a comfortable bipartisan margin, despite the NRA's vigorous lobbying against it.

The NRA was more effective on the House side and prevailed on Jack Brooks and other leaders to peel off sections of the omnibus bill from the more controversial firearm sections. That fall, Brooks took the more acceptable elements of the bill—grants for police hiring and drug treatment for prison inmates—through his committee and onto the floor where they were passed and were basically held ready to be folded into the larger eventual Senate-House legislation.

When the House reconvened after the winter recess, most of the members had a taste for pork. Everyone knew that a huge bill was going to pass this year and wanted a slice of the package. By April 1994, the crime bill price tag had swollen to $28 billion, which matched most of the Senate bill's provisions, but earmarked twice the funding for crime prevention.

Astute parliamentarian that he was, Jack Brooks managed to shunt the assault weapons ban aside. This was a temporary victory. He also knew which way the wind was blowing in Congress: a separate bill banning the manufacture and sale of a specific list of semiautomatic weapons *did* pass the House on May 5, 1994.

On that day the ASSC's leaders were meeting in Atlanta for a strategy session with our chief political consultant, Eddie Mahe, and his team of corporate political consulting gurus. We were getting regular updates on the assault weapons bill House votes from Carole Bridgewater. When she called to announce, "They've passed the ban," Ron Whitaker, the CEO of Colt's, rose and walked out of the room. "We're finished," he said, his face stony. Indeed the civilian .223 caliber AR-15 semiautomatic rifle was one of Colt's most profitable products.

Representative Jack Brooks had thought that he could hold the Republicans, but Clinton got the Chicago papers to unload on Henry Hyde, and once Hyde jumped ship, all control was lost.

That did not sit well with the antigun control Democrats who were the allies of both the NRA and the ASSC. In an August 11th vote, Brooks marshaled these Democrats to join most of the Republicans in preventing the conference committee report from reaching the House floor. Paul Jannuzzo and I were inside the Capitol, walking past the Democratic cloakroom, when we spotted Jim Pasco, director of congressional affairs for the BATF. "You guys won this one," he called. "But it's not over." Pasco's open political support for the Democrats was a blatant conflict of interest, but so was his ongoing work that helped Sarah Brady write the testimony to be delivered to congressional committees. Obviously, Pasco knew where his interests lay in this administration. During the following days, much closed-door horse-trading ensued, and on August 21, the House adopted a slightly revised conference committee report, which did include the assault weapons ban, by a vote of 235–195.

It would be nice now to claim prescience, but none of us knew at the time that this vote (and the subsequent final Senate vote) would seal the Democrats' fate, triggering an electoral avalanche that buried them that November. For the next twelve years, the Republicans would control both houses of Congress. Jack Brooks and John Dingell (one of ILA's founders) had felt obligated to vote with their party, even though they had opposed the assault weapons ban section. House Speaker Tom Foley, a perennial NRA luminary, even stepped down from the chair to vote for the bill and against gun owners. This would be his political death knell.

Late on the evening of August 25, the Senate finally voted 61–38 to pass the bill.

President Bill Clinton had promised to sign the bill—after all, his White House staff had practically dictated its major provisions. He did so with much flourish on the White House lawn on September 13. At that moment, a ten-year "sunset" provision on the assault weapon sections began to run, leading to its eventual demise immediately prior to the 2004 Bush/Kerry election.

●   ●   ●

We at the ASSC initially saw the semiauto ban as a serious challenge. The revenue streams of several of our members, Colt's Industries, Heckler & Koch, Intratec, and Liberty Arms rested on guns that were banned in the new law. But on closer examination, the omnibus crime bill provided us ample room for maneuver. The final version coming out of Congress required the "restriction on manufacturer, transfer, possession of certain semiautomatic assault weapons." The new amendment "grandfathered" all the weapons lawfully possessed at the time the law became effective, which meant that assault weapons "lawfully held in the inventory" by federal firearms licensees (and individuals) could continue to be "possessed and transferred."

In other words, there was a grace period during which dealers and private buyers could stock up. Clinton signed the bill, which went into effect September 13, 1994. We had recommended early in the summer that our members start manufacturing all that they could as quickly as they could. The "ban" only applied to actual firearms (or copies or duplicates) of weapons "known as . . ." and gave a *specific* list of Norinco, Kalashnikov, UZI, Colt AR-15, Intratec TEC 9 . . . and included a total of nineteen particular weapons.

Further, the ban covered any semiautomatic rifle that could accept a detachable magazine and had at least *two* of the following attributes: a folding or telescoping stock, a pistol grip that protruded conspicuously, a bayonet mount, a flash suppressor, a grenade launcher. Thus you could make guns with multiple variants and they were still legal. Combining variants on the *same* gun was a sin—it was also a felony.

The act also banned "large capacity ammunition feeding devices," but grandfathered in such magazines lawfully possessed before the law was signed. Specifically, newly manufactured magazines that held more than ten rounds would become illegal. Having three clips of ten rounds each was okay, but a single (new) clip with eleven was a big no-no! Sound crazy? It was.

In discussions with our members, I recommended a strategy of adaptation rather than the rigid opposition to the law that the NRA favored. That take-no-prisoners approach had only intensified with Tanya Metaksa in charge of the Institute for Legislative Action. But the ASSC had other ways to operate. Manufacturers could rename their firearms. And they could modify their guns to reduce the number of offending attributes. Thus Colt could remove the bayonet mount and flash suppressor from its AR-15 and introduce an almost identical weapon called the Colt "Sporter." Other semiautomatic rifle makers followed suit. I did not feel ethically compromised by this approach. If the antigun politicians could read English, there were thousands of pages of testimony and academic research that proved semiautomatic rifles were *not* a major contributor to America's crime problem. But, like Governor Jim Florio, the politicians sought the quick, cosmetic fix.

Because of the ban's grandfather clause, I gave the ASSC's manufacturers some unequivocal advice. "Make as many guns and high-capacity magazines as you possibly can. Put your plants on three shifts, seven days a week. You won't get stuck with unsold product." Some of our members took the advice in the spring and by the time of enactment had a ten-year supply of "high cap" magazines that would soon be worth far more money than anyone could have imagined just a few months earlier.

Soon the gun press was advertising "New Pre-Ban" 30-round magazines, many of them military specification imported from NATO or former East Bloc countries. Buyers who were willing to pay up to $2,500 for a quality semiautomatic rifle were eager to lay in a good supply of high-capacity magazines for these weapons at about $40, $50, $60, and up.

If the purpose of the assault weapons ban was to reduce the number of these guns on the street, the bill had exactly the *opposite* effect. But many Democratic politicians stubbornly continued to believe the media myth that semiautomatic rifles were the "weapons of choice" of gang-bangers and drug peddlers, although law-enforcement professionals and academic analysts kept telling them this simply was not true.

Now the United States would have the chance to test the validity of that statement. Because of the assault weapons *ban* there were more semiautomatic rifles in the hands of private citizens than ever before. The following year at SHOT Show we would issue in absentia two "Salesman of the Year Awards," one to Senator Diane Feinstein and one to President Bill Clinton. The law would be in effect for an initial period of ten years. So crime statistics between 1994 and 2004 would answer the question about the impact of the assault weapons ban on violent crime.

●   ●   ●

We all realized that the ban would have a direct impact on the 1994 elections. If the NRA had been praying for a rallying (and fundraising) issue, passage of the omnibus crime bill provided it. The act became law just three weeks before House minority whip Newt Gingrich and his senior colleagues stood on the Capitol steps and announced their "Contract with America," which they described as a blueprint for the "renewal" of the nation. This revolutionary

document listed specific steps for reforming Congress and introduced a series of bills that a new, Republican-controlled Congress
would strive to pass. In the proposed criminal justice legislation
("Taking Back Our Streets"), the contract ridiculed many of the
provisions of the House's Omnibus Crime Bill, (including "hug-a-
thug" benefits, in other words, midnight basketball leagues), which
had been passed "after a crazy weekend session at the end of August."

The ban on "at least 150 semiautomatic weapons" was prominently listed. The bill did *not* call them "assault weapons," nor did it
advocate immediate repeal of the ban. It didn't have to; the entire
tone of the Contract advocated reduced government interference in
citizens' lives. Second Amendment advocates who actually took the
time to read the Contract would realize they would have allies in a
new Republican Congress.

As soon as the assault weapons ban passed on the Hill, a buying
frenzy erupted nationwide. People lined up at gun shops and sporting
goods stores to buy as many "pre-ban" semiautomatic firearms as
they could afford. Many purchasers wanted the guns for their own
use; others saw them as a profitable investment. That fall I was driving
by Adventure Outdoors in Smyrna, Georgia, outside Atlanta, on my
way to see Paul Jannuzzo at the Glock facility. There were two long
lines snaking down the block from the gun store. One was a customer
line waiting to buy UZIs, Norincos (or much cheaper imported East
Bloc SKSs), and high-capacity magazines. The other line was men
and women signing up to work as volunteers for Republican chal-
lenger Bob Barr, a pro-gun congressional candidate who had wisely
put a sign-up table near the store.

Guns and Votes, I thought, *Votes and Guns*, wondering if the
Democrats in Washington had any clue of what was happening.

It became clear that Representative Jack Brooks, the longest
serving member of the House, who had been in Congress forty-two
years, saw ominous signs when the NRA membership in his district
began supporting Brooks's opponent—a Republican lightweight
named Steve Stockman—after the crime bill passed. The most
menacing development for Brooks was the NRA/ILA's tepid support
for the chairman, the man who led the floor fight to prevent the
assault weapons legislation. This was Tanya Metaksa's payback for
Jack's vote for the crime bill that contained the assault weapons ban.

Brooks was one of the NRA's oldest and closest congressional allies, and his seniority among Democrats made him invaluable—even if control of the House shifted to the Republicans. But Tanya took no prisoners. Almost as a cruel taunt, she sent a "Dear Fellow NRA Member" letter in which she damned Brooks with the faintest possible praise. After noting that Brooks had earlier "led the fight against the ill-conceived assault weapons ban," she stressed that he had "handed Clinton a late August victory" by supporting the crime bill. Tanya gave lip service to the specter of a Congress without Jack Brooks, which she said would be "more hostile" to gun rights. "In the Ninth District of Texas," she concluded, "we have a situation, where on the one hand, the Republican candidate has enunciated strong support for our Second Amendment rights and on the other, the Democrat has been one of our staunchest allies in Congress. The choice is up to you."

"(Jack) . . . has been one of our staunchest allies," I read when the letter crossed my desk in mid-October. In other words, the NRA was throwing Brooks to the wolves. Brooks's campaign tried ineffectively to use this letter, but its hollow core was obvious.

When I saw what was happening in Jack Brooks's race and realized the decisive role that the mobilized NRA activists would no doubt play, I decided I had to personally help him.

"Mr. Chairman," I telephoned Brooks, "I'm coming out there and work on your campaign."

Before I flew to Beaumont, I drafted a strong letter of support for Jack Brooks that the ASSC leaders Alan Mossberg, president of Mossberg & Sons; Ron Whitaker, president of Colt's; and Ed Shultz, president of Smith & Wesson signed. They represented three of America's oldest, most stable gun makers. "Simply put," the letter stated, "you have done more to protect and preserve the firearm civil rights of all Americans than anyone else in Washington, D.C." The letter called Brooks the "Leader of the Century" for defending the right of the American people to keep and bear arms. We also chided "those uninformed or misinformed organizations that have raised questions about your final vote on the 1994 Crime Bill."

Take that, Tanya, I thought when I sent the signed letter to Jack, knowing his campaign would run it as a full-page ad in the *Beaumont Enterprise* and the *Houston Chronicle*.

In Beaumont, the impact of Jack Brooks's long congressional tenure was clear when you drove past the Jack Brooks U.S. Post Office and other public buildings. Meeting with Brooks and his judiciary committee staff director, Jonathon Yarowsky, I asked the congressman if he'd ever used the venison backstrap recipe I'd provided.

He chuckled. "Feldman, for a Yankee, you're okay."

The banter was all well and good, but there were serious issues involved in this tight race. I managed to get on a Beaumont talk show ("Redneck Radio") and spoke for one hour in strong support of Brooks. It was easy to recognize the "prepped" gun activists who called in because they all fell back on the same script—Brooks was a gun grabber at heart. "No, my friend," I replied. "Jack Brooks has been the best friend you and gun owners across America have ever had."

But at the end of the day, Jack Brooks lost to Republican Steve Stockman by a margin of 52 to 48 percent of the vote.

Part of this defeat could be attributed to the national clamor for term limits. But most of the fault lay in the NRA's largely abandoning its old ally. This same tactic was more properly used against House Speaker Tom Foley, with the NRA churning up the political wrath of activists in Foley's Washington state district. (Foley's loss was the first time a sitting Speaker of the House had been defeated in 130 years.)

Beginning in September 1994, the *American Rifleman* had launched focused, hard-hitting pro-Republican, anti-Democratic articles leading up to the November election. The cover of the September issue showed a shirtless, blow-dried politician with a yellow band down his backbone. "You Trusted Them With Your Freedom And Now . . . Too Many Politicians Show Their Stripes." Tanya Metaksa wrote the lead feature, "I knew that many politicians would find the cover offensive. I knew they'd be outraged that I would portray many of them as downright cowards," and she proceeded to lambaste all those who had sided with the White House and voted for the crime bill. The cover of the October issue, which contained the 1994 election guide, was even more corrosive. In an almost pornographic and realistic painting, Lady Liberty was being assaulted from behind by the same politician. This time, he wore a dark suit and a striped power tie. The female icon of American freedom struggled against her assailant, but he had one hand covering her mouth and the other ripping down her flowing robe, so that her left shoulder and part of her breast were exposed. The politician's hands were muscular; Liberty's were slender and weak. In case the members missed the message, the cover spelled it out: "Stop The Rape Of Liberty."

Inside, the text railed against the Brady Act and the assault weapons ban calling them "the largest step ever toward the disarmament of American citizens." Tanya Metaksa introduced the election report, which was tailored as an insert for each state. "It's Payback Time!" her Dear NRA Member letter was headlined, "Time to reward our friends, and punish our enemies. November 8, election day, is the turning point—the day when, if gun owners don't stick together, your rights could be lost forever." Her message went on to call for support of the NRA's Democratic allies who had bravely stood by gun owners and defied their own president.

Republican candidate Bob Barr, a former U.S. attorney, was the ASSC's favorite in the 7th District around Atlanta. I was at Barr's victory party at the Cobb County Convention Center on the night of November 8 when the votes began rolling in. It was clear he stood to defeat Democrat Buddy Darden, who had tried to straddle the fence on the gun issue, but had ended up voting for the assault weapons ban in the final crime bill. Paul Jannuzzo and I strolled over to Newt Gingrich's party in an adjoining ballroom, where the scope of the Republican groundswell was just becoming apparent.

"Congratulations, Mr. Speaker," I said.

Gingrich seemed pleased but wary of speaking too quickly. "We'll just have to wait and see on that one."

By the next morning, the whole country saw.

●   ●   ●

Nationwide, the 1994 midterm elections were a disaster for the Democrats who lost fifty-four seats in the House and eight in the Senate. The last time the Republicans had controlled the House was in 1954, and they hadn't had a majority in the Senate since 1986. Although many pundits attributed the GOP victories (and the Democratic losses) to various congressional scandals or to discontent with the Clinton White House, few mainstream (nongun issue) observers realized what a critical role guns had played in the 1994 Republican landslide.

It wasn't that the NRA dumped "millions" of PAC dollars from its Political Victory Fund supporting Republicans and pro–Second Amendment Democrats. Spending during the campaign was not exceptional. But grassroots activism to get out the vote was. Midterm elections traditionally draw many fewer voters than presidential contests. But the polls were crowded across the country on November 8, 1994. When I later asked Congressman Bob Barr about the election, he told me, "Guns were the pivotal issue in my district. That, along with Bill Clinton, who epitomized what was wrong with big government." The gun issue "crystallized the anger of so many Americans who were asking, 'If the federal government can take away a right expressly guaranteed in the Constitution, what's next?'"

President Bill Clinton was more direct. He told the *Cleveland Plain Dealer*, "The NRA is the reason the Republicans control the House."

●　●　●

Even before the election, the media was calling 1994 "the Year of the Angry White Man." For Second Amendment zealots, anger about Ruby Ridge and Waco came to a head with the Brady Act and the assault weapons ban. Although most Americans still trusted their government, tens of thousands came to embrace conspiracy theories that the Clinton White House was plotting with the United Nations to impose a totalitarian New World Order on U.S. soil. Reports of unmarked black helicopters fed a growing urban (and rural) legend that "foreign speaking" U.N. troops were landing in the southwestern desert or the Rockies (or Appalachia) to set up secret bases and/or concentration camps, usually called gulags.

Fears of federal gun confiscation began to spread. And articles appeared in gun publications on how to hide semiautomatic weapons (or even your hunting rifles). The favored, and most practical means, was to construct simple, waterproof gun containers out of polyvinyl chloride drain pipe, glue a PVC cap on one end, place the weapon or weapons inside (with ammunition), and seal the other end with another cap. The tube could then be safely buried. The clandestine nature of this activity appealed to men whose Rust Belt factories had exported their jobs to China or India; men who fondly remembered the paranoid 1980s movie *Red Dawn* in which a small band of resistance guerrillas had overcome Communist occupiers in the Rockies. John Milius who directed and co-wrote *Red Dawn* has served on the NRA board for more than ten years.

After Ruby Ridge and Waco, resistance did not seem so paranoid to many who began to form militia groups, which quickly spread through the Midwest and the plains states, and in rural counties in the South. Most militia units practiced military tactics on private land with members dressed in surplus camouflage uniforms and boots. Firearms, including fully automatic weapons in a few cases, as well as tactical marksmanship, were the hallmark of the movement, just as fascination with guns and explosives was a common denominator. The Second Amendment right to keep and bear arms was a unifying article of faith to the militias. Some groups like the Michigan "Wolverine" Militia (which was also the name of the guerrilla unit in *Red Dawn*) had a relatively formal command structure. Others were loose, shifting bands.

Driving through crumbling blue-collar neighborhoods in the Northeast, I saw the kind of anger and frustration that fueled the militia movement. On one stretch of highway, a cheap motel proudly proclaimed, AMERICAN OWNED AND OPERATED in defiance of the Hindu immigrants who had bought up the larger nearby chain franchise. One diner up the road had a sign on the door, ENGLISH ONLY SPOKEN HERE.

The unwritten message was that you could push a man only so far. Country singer Lee Greenwood's "God Bless the U.S.A." became the anthem of this groundswell of discontent:

> I'm proud to be an American where at least I know I'm free.
> And I won't forget the men who died, who gave that right to me.
> And I'd gladly stand up next to you and defend her still today.

But there was a darker side. Among the more disturbing aspects of the militia movement were the anti-Semitic and white supremacist nature of several groups. It was easy for members who were convinced that U.N. troops were dropping from the night sky in black helicopters to believe that the "Zionist Occupation Government (ZOG)" was actively abetting this hidden takeover. The BATF's gun-grabbing, black-clad storm troopers were seen as the foot soldiers of the ZOG. When you stirred in conspiratorial fears about Freemasons, a cabal of international financiers, and liberal religious groups you ended up with frightened, heavily armed men—there were few women in the "combat" branches of the militias—eager to reclaim their precious heritage as free-born Americans. They passed cryptic messages on computer bulletin boards or by unlicensed short wave radio in order to avoid government wiretaps. Face-to-face contact often occurred at gun shows.

●   ●   ●

Although liberal sophisticates dismissed the militias as so many shambling Bubbas—David Letterman had an ongoing shtick about them on his show—the NRA recognized the potential these groups represented. The association's membership had fallen by more than three hundred thousand after the assault weapons ban, the decline due in part to the NRA's failure to protect Second Amendment rights, but also to the unwise decision to raise annual fees from $25 to $35.

So the NRA cautiously began to court the militias and their far-right allies. Board member Robert Brown ran a laudatory cover-story article on the Michigan militia in *Soldier of Fortune*. In a column he wrote for the December 1994 issue of *Shotgun News*, Neal Knox insinuated that the assassinations of John and Robert Kennedy and Dr. Martin Luther King Jr., as well as the 1989 Stockton massacre and other mass killings might have been the result of conspiracies against the Second Amendment. "Is it possible that some of those incidents could have been created for the purpose of disarming the people of the free world? With drugs and evil intent, it's possible. Rampant paranoia on my part? Maybe. But there have been far too many coincidences to ignore."

After that, Tanya Metaksa met members of the Michigan Militia while traveling through Lansing. (She later denied that anything of substance had been discussed.) Probably the National Rifle

Association's most blatant gambit to the paranoid right was a flamboyant Ackerman-McQueen advertisement attacking the BATF (and the Clinton White House) that appeared in national publications in March 1995.

The full-page ad featured federal agents dressed in black SWAT uniforms and helmets, brandishing submachine guns, as they burst into a home. The headline across the lurid staged photo proclaimed, TELL THE CLINTON WHITE HOUSE TO STAY OUT OF YOUR HOUSE. The subhead attacked the BATF, which DESERVES PUBLIC CONTEMPT. The text cited the threat to civil liberties that "is compounded by the President's proven willingness to condone warrantless search and seizure and by the Attorney General's proven willingness to use lethal force against innocents." The Clinton crime bill, the ad warned, could lead the BATF "to intensify its reign of storm-trooper tactics." As if playing directly to the paranoid right-wing fringe (and its rich potential lode of members), the text described the BATF as a "bureaucracy whose mission is to make gun ownership by definition a suspicious act, and gun owners by class suspected criminals. If the Clinton Administration did not rein in this rogue agency, Congress should step in and abolish it altogether." The advertisement ran prominently in the *Washington Post* and *USA Today* in the first week of March 1995.

In a widely distributed fund-raising letter during this period, Wayne LaPierre noted that the Clinton administration's "semiauto ban gives jack-booted government thugs more power to take away our Constitutional rights, break in our doors, seize our guns, destroy our property, and even injure or kill us."

Wayne was borrowing the epithet about "jack-booted government thugs" from veteran congressman John Dingell (D-Michigan), a longtime critic of the BATF, who first used it in 1980.

In the same fund solicitation that bore his signature, Wayne added, "Not too long ago, it was unthinkable for federal agents wearing Nazi bucket helmets and black storm trooper uniforms to attack law-abiding citizens. Not today."

The advertisement and Wayne's harsh words were poorly timed. Just after nine on the morning of April 19, 1995, Timothy McVeigh—who had kept vigil at the Branch Davidians Mt. Carmel compound—parked a yellow Ryder rental truck on the north side of the Alfred P. Murrah Federal Building in downtown Oklahoma City, which housed several government agencies, including FBI and BATF offices. The truck was a massive bomb. Plastic tubs contained about five thousand pounds of ammonium nitrate farm fertilizer mixed with nitro-methane, normally used to fuel racing cars.

McVeigh intended to strike a blow against the oppressive U.S. government, exactly two years after the holocaust that had swept the Mt. Carmel compound. He tripped a time fuse and walked away. The resulting blast was so powerful it could be heard thirty miles away. The entire northern face of the multistory building was ripped away. A total of 168 people, including many small children from the building's day-care center, were killed. More than 800 people were wounded, some with maiming injuries.

Within twelve hours, McVeigh was under arrest, having been stopped for a routine traffic violation. He freely admitted his anti-government obsession and voiced his sympathy for the militia move-ment—although he himself, a Gulf War combat veteran, had never trained with the Michigan Militia as some later claimed. Even though there were no guns used in Oklahoma City, somehow the debate in the media focused on guns, and NRA spokespeople were everywhere defending gun rights—although they came across as defending the militias. When McVeigh was arrested, he had a Glock under the seat, and the trace on this gun led directly back to Kingman, Arizona, where his friend Michael Fortier was subsequently arrested.

(Neal Knox proceeded to muddy the militia issue further by refusing to distance himself from the movement: "Unless those people have committed a violation of the law, I'm not going to say we can't have anything to do with those people." He added that there had been a secret orchestrated effort to unfairly link militias to the bombing. Neal's sense of conspiracy was unchecked.)

Instead, it developed that McVeigh had planned and executed the attack with a malleable accomplice, an old army buddy named Terry Nichols. The two had become drifters and small-scale metham-phetamine peddlers who sold weapons on the gun show circuit.

When the news media began to connect the dots between the bombing and Wayne LaPierre's fund-raising diatribes against the BATF, membership in the association slipped once again. Wayne LaPierre conceded that the NRA's arguments had sometimes been "strong and overblown." However, he insisted that the abuses the

FBI and the NRA committed had to be stopped "if we're to get a handle on the paranoia that's sweeping the country, especially in the gun ranks." In other words, Oklahoma City was a shame, but the NRA was justified in its harsh rhetoric. Wayne learned an important lesson with his backpedaling—never apologize. If you do, your enemies want more and your supporters view you as weak.

Former president George H. W. Bush strongly disagreed. He wrote NRA president Tom Washington a widely circulated letter on May 3, 1995, in which Bush resigned his life membership in the association. He was "outraged" that "even in the wake of the Oklahoma City tragedy," Wayne LaPierre defended his attack on brave and dedicated federal law-enforcement officers. Bush wrote of Al Wicher who had served on the president's Secret Service detail and had later been killed in the Oklahoma City bombing. "He was no Nazi," Bush emphasized. "[The NRA's] broadside against Federal agents deeply offends my own sense of decency and honor; and it offends my concept of service to country."

Wayne LaPierre felt forced to give a mealy mouthed apology: "I really feel bad about the fact that the words in that letter have been interpreted to apply to all federal law enforcement officers. If anyone thought the intention was to paint all federal law enforcement officials with the same broad brush, I'm sorry, and I apologize."

President Clinton scoffed at Wayne LaPierre's contrite statement and called on the NRA to return "the ill-gotten gains from their bogus fund-raising letter."

That wasn't about to happen. The NRA's deficit had grown from $10 million when Wayne took over in 1991, to $34 million in 1992, and soared to $59 million in 1995. "The NRA was decaying and was in danger of dying," as it consumed its endowment, Wayne later admitted.

That unpleasant confrontation with reality didn't initially seem to bother Neal Knox or Tanya Metaksa and their true-believer allies on the board. For Wayne's part, no one apparently recommended that his salary and bonuses be cut.

I became enmeshed in the dispute when the *Atlanta Journal-Constitution* interviewed me that May. "The current board of the National Rifle Association does not represent the mainstream NRA member, let alone the mainstream gun owner," I said. "I think their rhetoric's too extreme." From the NRA's point of view, the American Shooting Sports Council had just thrown a big hunk of fat into the fire.

But the NRA was forced to backpedal on the issue of militias. In June 1995, NRA president Tom Washington publicly reaffirmed the "NRA's pre-existing policies and position" on militias: "The NRA vehemently disavows any connection with, or tacit approval of, any club or individual which advocates (1) the overthrow of duly con-stituted government authority, (2) subversive activities directed at any government, (3) the establishment or maintenance of private armies or group violence."

The statement reaffirmed the Second Amendment right of all citizens to keep and bear arms, which, it stressed, guaranteed "the right of citizens to participate in militias for proper, lawful and Constitutional purposes."

I'm a lawyer, but I had a hell of a hard time parsing that language to discover the NRA's true position on militias. Is it possible that's what they intended?

●   ●   ●

For about a year, I had been working with the ASSC's manufacturers, wholesalers, and retailers, and the Bureau of Alcohol, Tobacco, and Firearms on streamlining the system employed in tracing guns used in crimes. Under the old procedure, when a gun was recovered at a crime scene, local law-enforcement officers called the BATF with a serial number and asked the bureau for a trace. A time-consuming search of the paper trail ensued. For example, the BATF would call the manufacturer, Smith & Wesson, which had to dig into its paper files to find the wholesale dealer to whom that particular gun had been shipped. Next, the wholesaler had to repeat the process, and maybe three or four days into the trace, authorities might discover which gun shop had ultimately sold the firearm. Then a burdensome hunt through the filed copies of the Form 4473 at the retailer was required to identify the individual who bought the gun. By now, a full week could have passed between the crime and the trace. And our retailers, wholesalers, and manufacturers would have lost a lot of time, in other words, money. This "quill pen" process was clearly obsolete.

I went to the BATF's Washington offices—the Belly of the Beast to the NRA—to work on procedures that would bring gun traces into the Information Age. Working with BATF's Bill Earle, Terry Cates, Wally Nelson, and Gerald Nunziato, we developed a system that would streamline the process while assuring privacy protection for gun owners. Each manufacturer, led by Robin Sharpless of Harrington & Richardson, would convert its shipping records to digital form and keep them on "stand-alone" computers that could only be accessed by the BATF's National Tracing Center in West Virginia. The wholesalers, led by Mike Saporito at RSR, duplicated this procedure. After a year, the hardware was up and running. Our manufacturers and wholesalers were no longer obliged to assign employees to conduct detailed paper record searches. The average time for a completed trace had fallen from as long as a week or more to just thirty minutes.

But, predictably, the NRA and Tanya Metaksa hated this "compromising" innovation. The ASSC was "in bed" with the gun-grabbing "Great Satan."

For my part, I found the BATF officials with whom I dealt, in particular the new director, John Magaw, practical and friendly. As the project neared completion, my frequent visits to the BATF's headquarters no longer required regular doses of Valium. In October 1995, Director Magaw publicly thanked federal firearms licensees for helping to make the new system a success. He also cited "unprecedented" cooperation with firearms industry members in cutting red tape.

• • •

At the April 1995 NRA convention in Phoenix, I was awarded the Shooting Industry Award for the period 1994–1995 by its Academy of Excellence. The award cited my "untiring dedication to the industry," noting that I had "traveled throughout the country to counter antigun movements, repeatedly met with congressmen and government officials, and become a familiar pro-gun spokesman on television." That year, a separate Excellence in Marketing & Promotion award went to the ASSC. "During the volatile anti-gun battles of 1994, the American Shooting Sports Council carried the pro-gun banner . . .

representing the entire shooting industry. The ASSC took on antigun forces on all fronts, including in the halls of Congress."

What these awards did not note was that the ASSC, through our policy of cooperation, had helped soften the blow of antigun legislation like the Brady Act and the assault weapons ban. I knew that the NRA, in particular Tanya Metaksa, would be seething as we accepted our awards, which were a direct challenge to the association's hegemony.

That challenge only became more visible when the industry invited the BATF's director to be the keynote speaker at the National Association of Sporting Goods Wholesalers' hunting show in November 1996. Magaw again praised the industry for its cooperation on establishing the computerized crime-gun trace system, which he said had been established "without compromising the integrity of the law, our commitments to Congress, or the very important Second Amendment."

When both Tanya Metaksa and I testified before the U.S. House Appropriations Subcommittee responsible for the BATF's budget, I had already met with Pete Gagliardi, the bureau's head of congressional affairs to discuss my testimony. Pete ushered me into the committee room when Capitol police tried to keep me waiting in line in the corridor. "He's with us," Pete explained.

The ASSC had now developed excellent relations with the BATF, and we backed a budget increase that would allow expansion of the online tracing system, which, I said, was "considerably more efficient for law enforcement and substantially more cost-effective for our industry." As I testified, Tanya sat at my right elbow, her lips curled in contempt. I might just as well been advocating federal funding for child abusers. Suffice it to say that her testimony was less generous.

Although Tanya was a lost cause, I wanted to maintain working relations with the NRA, and I still considered Jim Baker a friend. Even the ostensible hardliner Bob Brown had asked me to run for the NRA board of directors. I had to say no because it was best to keep the industry a separate entity from the association. I was having a difficult time defending NRA heavy-handed nonsensicality as an outsider, why be on the inside and be even more hobbled?

● ● ●

At the NRA's September 1996 board meeting, ripples of dissatisfaction about the senior staff's mismanagement and the looming financial crisis began and would eventually grow into a storm of discontent. The criticism focused on Wayne LaPierre, Tanya Metaksa, and Marion Hammer, the "pistol packin' grandma" from Florida who'd become the association's president in 1995. This censure was not surprising, given the association's potential bankruptcy. But the leader of this revolt *was* unexpected: Neal Knox, who had long been Tanya's closest ally.

Commenting a few years later about this "mutiny at the NRA," Knox criticized "the paid staff, led by the executive vice president and financially supported by contractors [i.e., Ackerman-McQueen] who were growing wealthy" at the expense of the association and its members. Once Knox decided to exert his independence, he began to hang out a great deal of dirty linen for the membership (and the American public) to see. Knox revealed just how cynical Wayne LaPierre had become.

After a 1996 finance committee meeting, Knox wrote that Wayne told Second Vice President Albert Ross that a proposed resolution could destroy "the greatest fund-raising organization this country has ever known. Albert was appalled, for NRA's duty is to defend gun rights and provide services to the members, not milk them." Knox acknowledged that contributions had increased from $13 million in 1991 to $36.4 million in 1995, but he stressed that members were tired of it, in particular the obsequious certified mail fund-raising letters and ersatz priority overnight mail. Despite the surging contributions, Knox noted, the NRA's net worth had declined more than $60 million by 1996. That year, a management audit that Knox had helped ramrod revealed that millions had been spent on work without written contracts, in violation of fundamental board policies.

Neal Knox was reportedly maneuvering to undercut Wayne LaPierre, Tanya Metaksa, and Marion Hammer. But he refrained from making his move because the 1996 national presidential elections were just six weeks away. He waited until the winter board meeting at the Marriott Key Bridge in Arlington, Virginia. In delaying his planned revolt, he gave Wayne LaPierre and his allies the needed time to plant stories in the *National Journal* and the *Washington Times* that Neal's "faction" was planning a coup. With the help of

Ackerman-McQueen, Wayne accused Knox of right-wing "extremism" and claimed his majority board members wanted to turn the NRA into a "militia-type organization." Continuing to sandbag Knox, Wayne and his supporters managed to place a full-page ad in the board election issues of the NRA magazines—well past normal submission deadlines. Urging members to "Support the Winning Team," the ad contained flattering pictures of Marion Hammer, Wayne LaPierre, and Tanya Metaksa. It called on members to vote against nine director candidates, including vice presidents Neal Knox and Al Ross, as well as Finance Committee Chairman Rick Carone (who had detailed the fiduciary incompetence, or malfeasance, of the Winning Team).

The ad was effective, and five of the nine targeted members were defeated. The balance of power on the board shifted away from Knox's faction.

At the May 1997 NRA annual meeting held in Seattle, Tony Makris (of Old Towne Armory fame), the head of the Mercury Group, a wholly owned subsidiary of Ackerman-McQueen, maneuvered to win a one-year seat on the board of directors for his close friend Charlton Heston. Makris had convinced Heston that the celebrity was needed to save Wayne and defeat Knox. (Ack-Mac was also determined to keep its cost-plus monthly retainer sweetheart deal with the NRA.) Heston was easily elected to the board. On the Monday following the members' meeting, Heston won a close race against Knox for the first vice presidency, and Al Ross was defeated in his bid to remain second vice president. (Ackerman-McQueen retained its lucrative arrangement with the NRA.) Heston was now in position to assume the presidency when Marion Hammer's term expired.

I was at the Seattle meeting when this maneuvering, largely out of sight to the members, took place. Neal Knox, old warhorse that he was, had been outmaneuvered. I thought of the crude adage that it was better to have your enemy inside the tent pissing out than outside pissing in. I also thought of Harlon Carter, who had died of cancer in 1991. I wondered what he would have thought of the still-defiant Knox. This time, it seemed, Knox really did have the best interests of the Second Amendment and the National Rifle Association membership, if not its leadership, at heart.

•   •   •

In the spring of 1997, Wisconsin democratic Senator Herb
Kohl began pushing for legislation that would have made it mandatory for all firearms dealers to include "trigger locks" on every
gun they sold. Both the NRA and the ASSC lobbied against this
legislation. Although the Kohl bill cited accidental deaths
among children playing with loaded guns—about 180 a year, many
fewer than bicycle-accident deaths—the solution of a practical
trigger-locking device was not adequately addressed. And when it
came to firearms, one size (or type) of trigger lock definitely did not
fit all.

But Kohl was a clever politician. He quickly adapted the trigger
lock proposal into a call for mandatory "child-safety locks." The
trouble with that concept was that his proposed legislation offered no
technical specification. Also, it was directed to the wrong level of the
industry, the dealer, not the manufacturer. If the law were to pass, the
childproof devices might include anything from a simple cable-type
bicycle lock through the gun's action all the way up to a high-quality
alloy insert in the trigger housing that could only be opened by
combination. Some of these locks would prohibitively raise the cost of
an otherwise inexpensive gun—while providing a false sense of
security at best.

In a meeting of the Senate Judiciary Committee staff, the NRA
suggested that dealers should offer for sale a locking device. This
pissed me off. Why put the onus on the dealer and not the manufacturer? Why fight this provision when it was going to happen
anyway? This was just the NRA maneuvering for a conflict, but a
fight that our friends on the Hill would look silly defending—even if it
brought in more dollars to the NRA's war chest.

That May, much to the displeasure of the NRA, Ed Shultz of
Smith & Wesson took preemptive action by announcing that his
company would henceforth ship all of its new handguns with simple
child-safety locks.

(The Kohl bill was never defeated; it lingered and Bill Clinton
eventually pulled his support after the industry took proactive action
through the ASSC.) But Shultz's action wasn't the end of the story. In
early September 1997, I learned that the Clinton White House was

planning to reopen the issue by requiring child-safety locks on all weapons belonging to federal law-enforcement officers.

"That's the first foot in the door of mandatory locks unless we derail it into safer territory," I told Bob Ricker who was now in charge of our Washington office.

On September 22, I had a telephone conference with Bob Delfay of SAAMI and Ed Shultz to discuss a meeting with Clinton's chief Domestic Affairs Advisor Rahm Emanuel concerning White House plans for child-safety locks on handguns. We agreed that a meeting could be productive provided it was kept strictly confidential. Two days later, I ran into Bob Delfay and Jim Baker at the annual Congressional Sportsman's Foundation Dinner. Jim wondered whether it was a "good idea" to meet with a White House official, and then came right out and voiced his opposition. Bob Ricker asked what harm could come from hearing what Emanuel had to say. The next morning, Ricker and I met Delfay, Baker, and Art Wheaton, chief operations officer of Remington Arms and president of SAAMI, to discuss an agenda for the initial White House meeting.

"Let's stay flexible on this and not paint ourselves into any narrow corners," I recommended.

At 9 a.m., we met Emanuel at the Park Terrace Hotel. He proposed a voluntary, industry-wide "trigger-lock" program similar to Clinton's agreement with the television networks regarding program ratings. Emanuel also advised us that the President planned to announce on October 15 that all federal law-enforcement agencies were "in compliance" with his directive on childproof safety devices for firearms. In other words, we had better get ahead of the ball or get run over.

Just to clarify the issue, Emanuel added, "This is a priority to the President and he prefers to handle the issue on an industry-wide *voluntary* basis." He put down his cup of coffee and looked at each of us in turn. "However," Rahm said, "the President will actively push for passage of the Kohl bill if necessary." It was heads he won, tails we lose.

We all agreed to respond to the White House proposal within two weeks.

After Rohm left, Baker and Delfay agreed to speak with the SAAMI members with Ricker and me talking with the broader ASSC handgun membership.

Bob Ricker and I recognized that Clinton would intensify White House pressure on Congress for "mandatory trigger locks" in his October 15 announcement if the industry did not devise some way to triangulate the White House.

"No way around it, Bob," I said. "We've got to come up with a strategy that makes us look like the responsible industry. We can't appear to be obstructionist naysayers just because it's good for strategic political wedge building—that's the NRA's role."

The plan would have to involve Republican congressional participation and "page dominant" newspaper advertisements to run before October 15.

"We've got a limited window of opportunity for the industry to become proactive, help our friends in Congress, and look like the good guys that we are in the press," I said.

●   ●   ●

Following that meeting, Bob Ricker and I made a quick trip to Denver to show the ASSC flag at the annual Gun Rights Policy Conference. The delegates stayed at the Holiday Inn near the defunct Stapleton Airport to save money. Ricker had been in secret contact with California governor Peter Wilson's staff, working on a plan to veto the latest cockamamie gun control measure in Sacramento: a provision in a larger gun control bill to verify the "melting point" temperature of the metal in inexpensive handguns. This was another sounds-good-won't-work concept that would have hurt several of our members. I thought it funny that California would ban a gun whose metal alloy would melt a hundred degrees or so after the skin on the shooter had melted, but no idea was too silly for the antigunners on the left coast! The NRA opposed the entire bill and hated amending out any of the more outrageous provisions that arguably made passage easier. But when Tanya Metaksa came breezing into the hotel lobby surrounded by her royal court that afternoon, the desk clerk handed her a fax from California.

"Hey, Tanya," Bob Ricker called, "look's like good news from the governor, huh?" Of course we all knew what the message said.

She graced us with her trademark scowl. "No thanks to any of *you*."

"Tanya," I retorted loudly for all the assembled activists to hear, "your arrogance is exceeded only by your ignorance."

•   •   •

On October 1, 1997, our board unanimously approved the ASSC's child-safety lock initiative. We called senior Republican congressional staffer Paul Larkin, Counsel to the Senate Judiciary Committee, and requested a meeting. Two days later, Bob Ricker, Larkin, and I met in the Capitol office of Randy Scheunemann, a senior staff member to Majority Leader senator Trent Lott.

Both Larkin and Scheunemann liked the plan and acknowledged the "political necessity" of moving ahead with an announcement before the president stole the thunder on October 15. We set a tentative date, time, and location for the event: 10 a.m., October 9, in the pressroom of the Capitol. Larkin and Scheunemann were confident that Republican senators Lott, Nichols, Craig, and Hatch would host the press conference. Bob Ricker and I stressed that we'd be obliged to give the White House prior notice before beginning the ad campaign. But Scheunemann requested that we not discuss the press conference with the White House until Wednesday, October 8, when the Senate leadership would invite select Democrats to participate—Senator Joe Lieberman was the guy we all wanted. I said I would contact SAAMI before our next meeting.

Ricker and I then dashed over to our political consultant, Eddie Mahe, to discuss the two Senate staffers' recommendations. I called the ASSC officers, to report progress. That evening, I received a fax notice from Bob Delfay that SAAMI would meet in Connecticut on October 20 to discuss "timely regulatory proposals [child-safety locks]." In other words, SAAMI would not commit. October 20 was five days *after* the planned White House announcement. Waiting until then would undercut any proactive effectiveness. It was just like SAAMI. If we bury our heads in the sand long enough and deep enough the wave will pass over without harming us—yeah—except I wasn't prepared to let our members drown in the tidal interval.

During an October 6, 1997 conference call, the leaders of ASSC and SAAMI discussed the merits of moving ahead. Jim Baker, who represented SAAMI and had promised to stay in close touch during

sensitive White House negotiations, was mysteriously "incommuni-
cado," hunting in Alaska, and Bob Delfay was also unavailable. The
two of them had never bothered to contact the SAAMI handgun
members, but I had, since all but one were also ASSC members. "It's
a dangerous strategy not to respond to the White House as we
promised," I said. Clinton was known to be vindictive, and he was
still smarting from the 1994 election upsets, which the 1996 election
had failed to reverse.

Later that day, the ASSC staff began making calls to all our major
handgun manufacturers and discussed plans for the news conference. When Bob Ricker contacted the Republican senators' offices,
he found that Scheunemann had not yet briefed them on pending
developments. They would just have to play catch up. Our Atlanta
office began faxing draft ad copy to all the ASSC's handgun manufacturers for their approval. We faxed Scheunemann the same
material and noted that at least eight major handgun manufacturers
had consented to participate in the press conference.

But that night, Frank Dugan called Ricker at home to announce
that Paul Larkin had informed him that the Republicans would
probably "pull the plug" on the event because of the NRA's opposition. Inviting Baker to the meetings had alerted the NRA to the
negotiations since he still worked under contract for both the NRA
and industry—talk about a conflict of interest! The next morning at
Scheunemann's office, we learned that SAAMI was opposed to the
press conference. Before we left, Ricker turned to Scheunemann.
"You realize that the ASSC will have to fulfill its commitment
to the White House and respond to Clinton's request within a few
days."

"If we don't," I added, "the White House could try to use Smith &
Wesson as a wedge to divide the industry by holding them up as a
good company and attacking all the others as bad actors."

Disappointed in the Republicans lack of fortitude, we returned to
our ASSC Capitol Hill office. That evening I faxed Rahm Emanuel
the ad copy, which was scheduled to appear in the *Washington Times*
and the Capitol Hill newspaper *Roll Call*. He immediately called me
and asked, "Can you come see me tomorrow morning at the White
House?"

"We'll be there for sure," I said.

At 11 a.m., Wednesday, October 8, 1997, Bob Ricker and I met Emanuel in his West Wing office. "The President would like to get the manufacturers in here for the announcement," adding that Clinton would prefer bringing the firearms industry executives to the White House during the next day's annual "Top Cop" awards ceremony.

Was Bill Clinton trying to co-opt us, steal our thunder, or sincerely cooperate? It didn't matter which. Since we were going to announce the industry initiative in any event, we might as well use some of the White House's bully pulpit to do so.

Although the timing would be extremely tight, I told him we would get back to him by 1 p.m. to confirm. Ricker and I jumped in a taxi and rushed to Eddie Mahe's office.

"Holy shit," I said. "This is going to make some waves."

Eddie's staff, including my old state and local partner in New Jersey, Rick Manning, quickly and efficiently contacted all the major manufacturer executives who agreed to come to Washington. We scrambled to book airline reservations and hotel rooms. I had canceled the rooms one day before and now had to slip the front desk manager a C-note to bump others so we could all be at the Park Terrace for evening and morning meetings. At exactly 1 p.m. I called Emanuel. "All our major members will be there."

I then asked if Republican senators Trent Lott and Orin Hatch could participate. "Only if Senators Feinstein and Kohl are also invited," he said.

"No," I answered. "That wouldn't be appropriate."

That evening, the ASSC's board of directors began arriving at the Doubletree Hotel. At 9 p.m., Ricker called Tanya Metaksa to read her our ad copy—due to be published in *Roll Call*—as a courtesy. "I hope you know what you're doing," Metaksa said.

Later that night, SAAMI's Bob Delfay faxed a letter to Smith & Wesson's Ed Shultz and me requesting that all parties "reconsider their timetable," cancel the White House announcement, and use their organization's Center for Firearm Safety and Responsibility as the venue for the industry's child-safety lock announcement. We declined.

At 7:30 a.m. on Thursday, October 9, 1997, Bob Ricker arrived at the Park Terrace just as his pager buzzed. It was Jim Baker returning from Alaska. Baker was livid. "Feldman has deliberately done this to me," he shouted over the phone. "And I am going to do *everything in my power* in the next three hours to undo what you have done."

Apparently, Baker got through to the White House because Rahm Emanuel called just thirty minutes later to ask if "an industry problem" had developed. "No," I said. "We'll be there."

We met Bill Clinton in the Oval Office. If ever there was a natural-born charmer of a politician, it was he. Some of our members present might have been cursing him months or weeks before, but now they smiled as the youthful Clinton shook hands and joshed.

"I want to thank your staff, Mr. President," I told him, "for offering to find me a spot in the witness protection program."

He laughed convincingly.

Outside on the terrace above the Rose Garden where the ASSC members sat in the baking October sun, I made my brief comments. After joining in the salute to the "esteemed police heroes" assembled behind us, I reiterated "our long-standing policy of promoting safe and responsible firearm ownership, storage, and use." To enhance safe storage, I announced, "within the coming year, most major handgun manufacturers will institute company policies of providing safety devices with all handguns shipped in the United States."

Clinton, a speed-reader, had probably digested my brief remarks for their political content in about three seconds before the presentation. In a few words, we had preempted his planned October 15 child-safety lock announcement. The headline coming out of this event would be that the industry—not the White House—had voluntarily taken this bold step.

"Mr. President," I concluded, "we are all Americans. And by our being here today we demonstrate that there are issues on which we can all agree and work together."

In his comments, Bill Clinton emphasized "the importance of the breakthrough we are announcing today in our efforts to protect children from gun violence." He cited each of the participating companies and asked their representatives to stand and be acknowledged.

As I joined in the applause, I saw the blinking red light on the nearby White House video camera. C-SPAN would broadcast these comments live, and I knew that there would be an interested audience out in the NRA's northern Virginia headquarters.

As we walked out of the West Wing where all the reporters were gathered, for additional comments, I recognized the same befuddled look on their faces, a look I hadn't seen since my Bernie Goetz news conference twelve years earlier. This was a man-bites-dog story.

It didn't take long for the other shoe to drop at the NRA. One day later, Wayne LaPierre sent a bitter accusatory letter to the chief executives of every company that had participated in the event. "Firearms safety—as it's being pressed by the Administration—is a phony. It is simply a stalking horse for gun bans." In his harsh conclusion, Wayne wrote, "You are not selling firearms to Bill Clinton and Janet Reno. And he is not selling firearms safety to the public. He is selling a means to an end. Your end . . . You have made a grievous error. It is now left to others—your customers, all peaceable gun owners—to keep it from being a fatal error."

Appearing before the House Judiciary Committee on May 27, 1999, Wayne LaPierre would testify, "For a century we've taught it's not just reasonable but essential to use safety locks, trigger locks, gun safes or any other voluntary means appropriate to keep firearms out of the wrong hands." I guess the industry and the ASSC hadn't "destroyed" the Second Amendment after all, but back on Thursday, October 9, we were apparently poised to challenge the NRA's hegemony over any discussions relating to guns in America.

Most of our manufacturers shrugged off the vitriol of Wayne's letter. But not Paul Jannuzzo. As Glock's vice president and general counsel, he lit into Wayne and defended our proactive measure, which had completely bypassed the stratagems of the NRA. In a faxed letter, Paul chided LaPierre for the public relations gaffes in his jackbooted thugs ads and fund-raisers.

"Finally," Paul concluded, "if you ever again feel the need to speak to me in such a condescending manner, have the spine to do it in person, but be prepared to have your head slapped."

The NRA responded by waving the law book at Jannuzzo, pompously claiming that he had threatened Wayne LaPierre. Although Paul laughed that off, I knew he would happily indulge himself with a little head slapping should the opportunity arise.

The only problem was that it was always hard to identify the head on an amoeba.

10

THE END GAME

fter the Rose Garden ceremony, the news media lauded the American Shooting Sports Council for our "moderate" approach to firearms safety. In other words, unlike the NRA, the ASSC didn't pounce on every gun issue and try to use it as a political wedge or a fund-raising tool. We were determined to win the war for the "hearts and minds," not fight a costly battle because it provided more direct mail fund-raising opportunities.

The reaction of the *Dallas Morning News* was typical of this positive coverage. "Hot as a Pistol," the paper's front-page article was headlined. "Increasingly prominent gun trade group wins praise for conciliatory attitude behind safety-lock agreement," the subhead read. "There is a new sound to the American gun debate. It is the voice of compromise and moderation coming from the Atlanta-based American Shooting Sports Council." I could almost hear steam hissing out of the windows at the NRA's headquarters. Noting that the ASSC's approach was winning us "friends and influence" on Capitol Hill at the expense of the NRA, the story quoted Dave Tinker, editor of *Firearms Business*: "Maybe it's the coming of age of the gun lobby." Now, I knew, the steam wasn't just hissing. The boiler was in danger of blowing. Anytime you're accused of "moderation" on the gun issue, it was clear the road ahead would be rocky.

To make the NRA's position quite clear, the NRA's board member Bob Brown used the "Command Guidance" column inside his *Soldier of Fortune* magazine to rip into the ASSC and me. "One Richard Feldman," he wrote, explaining that I was a former NRA lobbyist, "who now purports to 'represent the firearms industry' . . . floundered frenetically around Washington" before appearing with Bill Clinton and the "standard backdrop of 'bleacher cops' [in the Rose Garden] at 1030 hours on 9 Oct." (Not only did Brown favor alliteration worthy of Spiro Agnew, he also laced his text with military jargon whenever possible, pandering to his wannabe mercenary readers.) What was especially hypocritical was that Bob Brown knew exactly who I was. In 1995, he had personally urged me to run in the next year's NRA board elections, in recognition of my success as a lobbyist representing the firearms industry. I'd politely declined the invitation because it was better in my opinion to keep the industry and the NRA separate entities. Now, apparently, I was fair game because I had run to "the enemy."

The whole column smacked of Jim Baker, and I figured Brown must have had Jim vet the text before publishing it in the magazine. I'd heard that Jim had practically chewed his trademark outdoorsman's leather vest in frustrated rage after the Rose Garden event.

I could certainly live with Brown's ad hominem attack, but there was some unanticipated *praise* that had me worried if news of it spread.

That October, Philadelphia mayor Ed Rendell called to congratulate me on the safety lock initiative. Rendell, an outspoken antigun politician, and the ASSC had been in contact since late July. I'd opened communications with him because I was alarmed to read in the *Philadelphia Inquirer* that he was considering suing the entire "firearms industry" to reclaim costs to the city caused by what he called "gun crime." (We preferred the term, "criminal misuse of firearms.") Our negotiations were making slow but steady progress— Rendell hadn't started a suit yet—but I didn't want every phase of our discussions played out in the media.

Our first face-to-face meeting had been in August 1997 at the mayor's city hall office. Bob Ricker, Paul Jannuzzo, and I represented the ASSC. The mayor's office was tastefully decorated with mementos of America's most historic city. A deputy mayor and Deputy Police Chief Richard Zappelli, in charge of youth violence, sat beside Rendell, studying us coolly. But it was the mayor himself who forcefully handled the substantive side of the discussion. As a former Philadelphia district attorney, he engaged in some obligatory hyperbole, probably in the hope he could bully us toward a settlement. But his argument was specious. He contended that the firearms industry was "flooding the streets" with guns by intentionally "advertising to criminals," and "shipping guns to areas with the most criminal activity."

"Excuse me, Your Honor," I interrupted, "but that's just not true."

"It's not, huh?" he said, turning to an aide. "I've *got* that ad."

Rendell rose impatiently and then returned with some papers, not a gun ad, but a fund-raiser from Handgun Control, Inc., that condemned an advertisement for Intratec's TEC-9, which was said to be "fingerprint resistant."

The mayor scowled. "Who *but* a criminal would need a 'fingerprint resistant' gun, Mr. Feldman?" Rendell fluttered the papers theatrically, in his best courtroom manner.

We had anticipated this attack. I handed Mayor Rendell the original Intratec ad, not HCI's distortion of it. The advertisement, which had appeared in six-point type in the trade press, was for the company's TEC-KOTE metallic finish, which "provides natural lubricity to increase bullet velocities, excellent resistance to fingerprints, sweat rust, petroleum distillates of all types, gun solvents, gun cleaners, and all power residues."

The technical list of TEC-KOTE's attributes continued, but Rendell had seen enough to realize the Handgun Control, Inc., interpretation was palpably misleading. He'd never be able to use the ad as evidence in a lawsuit against the industry.

"You know," he said, giving me back the page, "in this context, the ad doesn't have the impact they say it does."

We've got our foot in the door, I thought.

But Rendell hastened to announce, "Well, I am still considering a major lawsuit." He confidently lifted a bound legal document on his desk and let it drop to demonstrate its sheer weight.

We knew who had encouraged him. David Kairys, a professor at Temple University Law School, had served on a group of experts that Rendell had established the previous year to investigate the growing problem of gun violence on Philadelphia streets. Kairys, who was familiar with state government lawsuits against the tobacco industry, proposed that a city like Philadelphia could possibly sue gun manufacturers.

To date, almost every lawsuit against a gun maker had been an individual tort, usually based on a claim of a design or manufacturing defect. But Kairys put forward the idea that the industry was intentionally "feeding the criminal element" with handguns. And it was the city that bore the cost of this alleged malfeasance through increased police budgets, ambulance, and hospital services "all the way to the support of a child who might be orphaned as the result of gun violence."

Potentially, he was talking about tens or even hundreds of millions of dollars in civil liability damages in Philadelphia alone.

Kairys's legal theories were novel. He recognized that traditional product liability didn't provide a foundation for a municipal or state lawsuit (handguns, he said, were a problem because they worked too well). So he tried to adapt standard aspects of tort law—public nuisance and negligence—to new legal circumstances. He wrote a memo on his concept and presented it to the mayor that spring. Apparently, that was part of the larger document on Rendell's desk. The mayor gave Kairys and the city's law enforcement and legal officials' authorization to proceed—supposedly on a confidential basis. But by midsummer, either the Philadelphia police or city hall had leaked the story to the news media. That's when I took notice.

I didn't think much of Kairys's legal theory because I knew it would be hard to prove that the industry had knowingly engaged in a public nuisance or negligence by manufacturing and selling a highly regulated, legal product. But I also knew from my days running the Coalition of Americans to Protect Sports that the lawyers involved on both sides were usually the only people who won in protracted tort litigation.

One thing for sure was that the firearms industry had very shallow pockets when compared to tobacco companies. Big Tobacco was about to settle with the states for a reported $246 billion to be disbursed over a period of twenty-five years. Firms like Phillip Morris and R. J. Reynolds could afford such a settlement. The members of the ASSC could not. The entire industry—manufacturers, wholesalers, and retailers, as well as the specialized gun press—generated about $2 billion of revenue annually. Many of the companies were small, privately held firms. Prolonged litigation would bankrupt a number of them, not to mention the trade associations.

So the ASSC and its board firmly believed that it was vital to talk sense to Rendell. Before we left the mayor's office, the palpable tension had dissolved and Rendell asked in a very friendly manner, "Can I have the opportunity to meet with the gun industry?"

"We can make that happen," I said. When you're talking, you're not suing.

•   •   •

Following the Rose Garden ceremony, I'd made sure that Ed Rendell received all the material we had on child-safety devices for firearms, which included a variety of lock boxes, as well as different types of trigger locks. He asked to be our breakfast speaker at the spring 1998 Industry Summit Fly-In in Washington, and we agreed. Before he came, Rendell informed me that rather than file a lawsuit, he planned to head a committee of the U.S. Conference of Mayors on gun violence and invited me to participate as the industry's representative.

Rendell did come to the Washington Industry Summit, and he did speak. But his tough guy D.A. persona dominated the tone of the speech. He gruffly called the assembled CEOs "you people" and assailed them for profiting from "gun violence." Clearly, he was keeping the implied threat of lawsuits in reserve to wrest some concessions from the ASSC and the industry. His posturing was intended to score political points both at home and on the national stage, not with my members, and he wasn't about to cut us any slack.

I next met with Rendell on the Monday after the June 1998 NRA meeting, which, ironically, was held that year in Philadelphia. I'm not especially prone to paranoia, but I did have the distinct impression that there were unfriendly association eyes watching us. To the unrepentant Second Amendment zealots, my sitting down to talk with a well-known gun grabber like Ed Rendell was yet more evidence of treason (or maybe blasphemy) on my part. But the lingering hard-right fringe of the NRA's ranks might have harbored even darker suspicions. Ed Rendell was originally from New York; so was I. He was a lawyer; so was I. He was Jewish; so was I. Could it be that we were both agents of the dreaded Zionist Occupation Government? I could only hope that some of those Neanderthals weren't packing heat and didn't know what hotel I was staying in.

As expected, at that 1998 NRA meeting in Philadelphia, Charlton Heston assumed the mantle of the presidency, for which Ackerman-McQueen and Wayne LaPierre had prepared the ground the year before. And Ack-Mac wrote Heston some great lines to read to the cheering throngs in the convention hall. "Mr. Clinton, sir," he proclaimed in his stentorian Moses voice, "America didn't trust you with gays in the military. America doesn't trust you with our 21-year-old daughters, and we sure, *Lord*, don't trust you with our guns."

But just as the NRA was closing ranks, it seemed to me that the gun industry might be beginning to fragment. Although Jannuzzo, Saporito, and the rest of the ASSC board backed my continuing contact with Rendell, some member companies were getting nervous after hearing rumors that other cities were considering lawsuits based on David Kairys's legal theories. But I tried to reassure them that Rendell had a lot of influence with the U.S. Conference of Mayors, and we were making progress (or at least buying time) with him.

That June in Philadelphia, I spoke with Rendell and with representatives of the U.S. Conference of Mayors, the National League of Cities, and the National Association of Counties. I expressed the ASSC's "earnest desire" to work toward "realistic, practical solutions" to reduce firearm violence nationwide. In an update letter to the ASSC membership on these negotiations, I reported on the demands that Rendell was still seeking. They included: a limit on gun purchases to one per month; a ban on inexpensive handguns; a halt to manufacturing firearms that could accept "high-capacity" magazines; and adoption of "personalized" firearm technology (computer-controlled "smart guns" that could only be fired by an authorized user). Most of these matters concerned law enforcement, state government, or Congress, not the industry.

"It's the same old song," I wrote. "Go after the gun, rather than its illegal use and illegal user." Criminologists and sociologists had repeatedly debunked this "instrumentality theory" that the widespread availability of guns caused crime, I added.

It was at the June meeting with Rendell that the issue of "straw-man" gun purchases first arose. I freely admitted that this was a problem that everyone involved with gun violence had to address. A straw-man purchase involved a felon (or other disqualified gun buyer) using a person with a clean criminal record to buy a gun. This act itself was a felony for both parties. But we knew that the BATF didn't have the resources, and that local law-enforcement in many jurisdictions was not diligent enough to control it. In our eyes, this was more a law-enforcement matter than it was an issue of industry policy. But Rendell still held to his "flooding our streets with guns" view of the industry. So for the moment, we would have to agree to disagree about the problem of straw-man purchases.

Later that month, the BATF's Philadelphia special agent in charge Lawrence Duchnowski wrote Mayor Rendell, commending the American Shooting Sports Council for "working closely" with his agency. Duchnowski stressed that we had maintained "open communication," developed security standards for gun dealers to help curtail firearm thefts, and added that the joint online gun-tracing system we had implemented had been a "tremendous breakthrough" for the BATF. Even someone as politically motivated as Rendell had to take notice of this information. As a result of our negotiations (and the BATF endorsement), Rendell invited the ASSC to join a national joint task force on gun violence that he was forming.

Rendell asked me to address the U.S. Conference of Mayors in Reno at the end of June. There, Ed Rendell and I chaired a panel discussion on the issues of handgun violence and safety, which stressed adequate funding for law enforcement, gun safety, and crime prevention. I challenged the mayors to "drop the sloganeering, forget the ten-second sound bites, and stop the political posturing" if we were to work together on creative, cooperative solutions to the problem of firearms violence and juvenile crime. I repeated that the industry sincerely desired to develop a "comprehensive action plan" with law enforcement and government leaders at all levels. "We must begin thinking outside the box," I stressed.

The mayors at the conference adopted a unanimous resolution to work with the firearms industry on the action plan that the ASSC had proposed. The U.S. Conference of Mayors also applauded the firearm manufacturers who had joined the child-safety-lock initiative that Bill Clinton had announced in the Rose Garden ceremony. But the best news coming out of the Reno conference was Ed Rendell's official announcement that he had shelved his plans for any legal action and preferred instead to pursue common ground with the industry.

During my Reno presentation, I had told the mayors that "lawsuits cost millions of dollars—they cost millions of dollars for cities, and they cost millions of dollars for our industry. That's millions of dollars that won't be spent on child-safety locks, that won't be spent on new technology." All lawsuits accomplished, I stressed, was "to put money in the hands of attorneys." I knew that from my days at CAPS, tilting at tort reform windmills.

Several big-city mayors, including Sharpe James of Newark, New Jersey, agreed. "It makes a good sound bite to say we should sue gun makers," he said, "but I don't think it's practical." St. Louis mayor Clarence Harmon added that "vitriolic rhetoric on either side has not been productive." He called the conference a "momentous occasion" because the ASSC had attended.

Once more the news media, now led by the *New York Times*, complimented the obvious shift toward moderation and accommodation on the part of the American Shooting Sports Council.

I figured that we were on a roll. So I was happy to join Ed Rendell in signing a letter to President Bill Clinton announcing the formation of our joint task force seeking to reduce the level of gun violence in America. We had just met in St. Louis to thrash through some specific issues, including straw-man purchases and the "gun show loophole" (nonlicensees selling guns without benefit of a Form 4473 at gun shows and flea markets). Rendell's proposed solution to these problems originally was a disingenuous mandatory "one gun a month" rule. Policing such a measure would be counterproductive, at least to law enforcement.

So after consulting our board, I wrote to Rendell to explain how his proposal would interfere with the BATF's multiple sales form, which *had* proven to be "the single best investigative lead producer" for gun-running, according to Pete Gagliardi at the BATF. Under this system, a person selling more than one hand-gun had to send notification of that "multiple sale" to the chief law-enforcement officer in the county where the dealer was located *and* also to the BATF's tracing center in West Virginia. Trying to limit sales to one gun a month per buyer would have simply steered those with criminal intent to virtually untraceable single-purchase straw-man transactions, usually by the gangbangers' girlfriends.

In our proposed solution to the problem, we recommended revising the BATF's multiple sales form to include a statement requiring the purchaser's signature swearing under oath that the firearms being purchased were for the buyer personally and not for the subsequent transfer to a third party. The form would also prominently notify the buyer that it was a federal felony to transfer any firearm to someone that the purchaser knows or suspects to be prohibited by law from possessing a gun. Additionally, the dealer would be required to *immediately* notify the chief law-enforcement officer of the jurisdiction where the purchaser lived (before the buyer left the gun store) and to inform him or her of that notification. A potential straw-man buyer with a clean criminal record would not want to face federal felony charges. Moreover, the prosecutors had to be prepared to "nail" the straw purchasers, and not just the trigger-men.

We also proposed the creation of a new gun show license to be held by the promoters of these events. That license holder would be required to clear each transaction at their show through the National Instant Criminal Background Check System if it involved a non-licensed seller transferring to a purchaser.

It had been a successful year and we had our plate more than full. The *Hartford Courant* called our efforts, "a very good start and deserves enthusiastic public support." The rabidly antigun *Atlanta Journal-Constitution* had editorialized that our initiatives, "to make guns safer shows how things get done." We had succeeded in carving out a presence for the industry in the political/legislative and public policy arenas. We had our own voice and our destiny was now in our own hands. I didn't know it at the time, but the summer of 1998 was the high-water mark of the ASSC as an organization and of Richard J. Feldman as its executive director.

• • •

On Wednesday, October 8, 1998, Tanya Metaksa announced her resignation as the executive director of the NRA's Institute for Legislative Action and walked out the door, reportedly strapping on a golden parachute.

The next day, Wayne LaPierre announced that Jim Baker was returning to his former position as head of the ILA. Wayne praised Jim's "incredible wealth of experience and expertise as an aggressive defender of our Second Amendment freedoms." This was not good news before lunch for Richard Feldman. What Wayne left unsaid was that Jim Baker's unrestrained desire for power had cost the industry dearly. Smith & Wesson even resigned from SAAMI over Baker's actions post–Rose Garden announcement. To his credit, he knew how to cut deals on Capitol Hill and avoided Tanya's paint-scraper lobbying tactics. By the time she left, Tanya had pissed off so many members and staffers that she really had become a detriment to the NRA. This was not to say that Jim Baker was any kind of softy. But generally, he knew when to fight and when to bargain.

I recognized, however, that Jim also had a big ego better suited to a congressional chairman and didn't easily forgive perceived insults or challenges to his authority. And it was pretty clear that he saw the ASSC and me as such a challenge. The morning of the Rose Garden event almost a year before, Jim had vowed revenge for betraying him. Now he would be in a position to carry out that threat.

But I thought it was better to mend fences than to keep a grudge brewing. So that week I wrote to Jim to congratulate him on his appointment. "While we have had a vigorous disagreement over events of the last year," I wrote, "I hope we can put aside those issues and work for the good of the firearms community."

I never received an answer. I'm still waiting.

• • •

My anxiety about what Jim Baker might be planning was quickly overwhelmed by a more immediate threat. In late October, we learned that New Orleans mayor Marc Morial was about to file a lawsuit against the firearms industry based on Professor David

Kairys's legal theories. In principle, this suit would be no more dangerous than the legal action Ed Rendell had contemplated. But the National Center to Prevent Handgun Violence (an affiliate of Handgun Control, Inc.) had turned to the Castano Group—a consortium of sixty law firms named for a plaintiff who had sued Big Tobacco—to lead the litigation. With this war chest the Castano Group certainly had the power and wealth to cause real trouble for the firearms industry.

The most prominent attorney in the Castano Group was John Coale. He was a large, shuffling man in his fifties who wore his expensive suits badly and proudly referred to himself as an "ambulance chaser" and a "pirate." The *Washington Post* once rhetorically asked, "Is John Coale really the sleaziest lawyer in America?"

In 1984, Coale had literally descended on the blighted Indian industrial city of Bhopal soon after a poison gas leak from a Union Carbide plant had killed more than two thousand people. Frantically scrambling for plane seats, Coale and his team reached Bhopal just ahead of his competition, ace litigator Melvin Belli. Coale managed to sign up thousands of survivors on retainer forms that most of them undoubtedly could not read. But in the end, the Indian government removed the case from U.S. legal jurisdiction and thus undercut Coale's financial incentive. But it was in Bhopal that he met several future partners, including New Orleans plaintiffs' lawyer Wendell Gauthier, who would later join him in the lawsuits against Big Tobacco and the gun industry. Coale was married to CNN's resident on-screen legal expert Greta Van Susteren. They were both Scientologists, which only increased the offbeat nature of Coale's persona.

The tobacco settlement had made Coale and Gauthier formidable opponents. If they managed to advance their case against gun manufacturers into extended litigation, the industry's legal fees would be catastrophic, especially for the smaller companies.

The case the Castano Group was preparing for New Orleans would be filed against fifteen large and small handgun manufacturers. It would include such major companies as Glock, Colt's, Beretta, and SigArms. It would also name five local gun dealers, and the industry's three trade associations—the ASSC, SAAMI, and the NSSF. New Orleans as the plaintiff would seek reimbursement compensation for the cost of extraordinary police (hiring more officers, overtime pay, etc.) and emergency services stemming from gun violence.

Attorney Dennis Hennigan of the Center to Prevent Handgun Violence was providing legal and technical advice in the suit. Ultra-safe firearms were his particular Utopian passion du jour. "If we can childproof medicine bottles," he told CNN, "why can't we childproof guns?" That was *less* than a ten-second sound bite. As he tried to remove a sample locking device for the camera, he fumbled. All I could think was, *"Bang, you're dead!"*

John Coale told the media that the alliance of attorneys would also help other unidentified cities sue the industry. They were going to do, "what we did to tobacco," Coale said. "It's going to be a very large war."

It might prove to be a lucrative conflict for the plaintiff bar as well. Wendell Gauthier announced that the lawyers involved had agreed that they would receive 20 percent of any settlement, or 30 percent of any damages award. So they would be going for maximum amounts, even if it meant driving the smaller companies into bank-ruptcy, to encourage the better-endowed gun makers to pay one way or another.

We had heard that the city of Chicago was considering lawsuits against gun dealers in neighboring suburbs, alleging an intentional pattern of illegally selling firearms to ineligible buyers, often steering them to the most dangerous weapons. But news of the pending New Orleans suit blindsided us. In a November 4, Fox Butterfield article in the *New York Times*, Mayor Ed Rendell announced that "thirty to sixty cities might file suit in their state courts, all on the same day at some point next year." This came relatively soon after Rendell himself had renounced lawsuits at the U.S. Conference of Mayors. So I felt like I'd been kicked in the guts by a politician's wingtip. *Imagine that*, I thought, *politicians speaking with forked tongues.* "The impact of so many cities filing suit all at once would be monumental for gun manufacturers," Rendell told Butterfield. "They don't have the deep pockets of the tobacco industry, and it could bring them to the negotiating table a lot sooner." He justified his flip-flop by claiming that he had merely put his pending lawsuit on hold while he negotiated with the ASSC. Rendell told Butterfield that he had hoped those negotiations would bring quick results, but added that the industry had refused to support his pet provision of limiting buyers to one gun a month. "That was the seminal test," Rendell said, "and they failed it. Instead the ASSC had merely offered the usual excuses."

When Butterfield interviewed me about the New Orleans suit, I called it "just inevitable, too tempting when you have a bunch of plaintiffs' lawyers sitting on fat settlements from the tobacco industry."

The *Times* estimated that the Philadelphia suit alone could cost the industry $58 million a year, the amount that Rendell claimed Philadelphia paid for gun violence. In New Orleans, Mayor Morial launched his lawsuit in a grandiose manner. "Today is a day for atonement," he said, speaking at a city hall press conference—"This suit is about holding that very successful industry accountable."

●   ●   ●

While I was trying to maintain an optimistic front, the cities' legal offensive had me deeply worried. My experience with CAPS had taught me that the established plaintiffs' bar could wear down most defendants. Just as diving boards had disappeared from almost all public swimming pools, a number of smaller gun makers would be forced out of business if the lawsuits went forward. It didn't matter that the "cities are on shaky legal ground," as an *Investor's Business Daily* editorial stated. The cost of defending multiple suits would be prohibitive for most gun makers that operated on very slim profit margins generated by static annual sales. The suits are "intended to bring the gun industry to its knees," the editorial concluded.

The *Atlanta Journal-Constitution* mocked the cities' rush to jump on the lawsuit bandwagon. If the cities succeeded, "Fatback makers could be held liable for clogged arteries; makers of butter, cheese and eggs responsible for billions of dollars in heart bypass surgery."

Preposterous? Definitely. But I also realized that the newspaper's list of potential defendants in the food industry might be of great interest to the Castano Group.

It made me feel better that a *Wall Street Journal* op-ed titled "Courtroom Cowboys" also lambasted the cities and the "tort sharks" like Wendell Gauthier and John Coale. The *Journal* stressed that, "guns are not the political sitting duck that tobacco once seemed. Gun owners, unlike smokers, are not ashamed of their habit or shy about asserting their rights. The NRA unapologetically defends the interests of its unapologetic members—and does so by marshalling real votes at the ballot box. Polls show 80 percent of citizens support gun-owner rights outside the major metropolitan areas. Those folks elect a lot of senators." (One of those polls was the latest ASSC Tarrance Group survey.) But to me the most promising part of the op-ed was its conclusion: "Trying to sidestep the democratic process and manipulate the courts to fleece an unpopular constituency is no solution to the crime and poverty problems of cities like New Orleans. The mayors may be surprised to discover their lawsuits aren't much of a political winner either."

For the next few weeks, Paul Jannuzzo, Mike Saporito, Bob Ricker, and I searched for practical solutions to the lawsuits that New Orleans and Chicago had now filed. We consulted attorney Ralph Boyd Jr., who had experience both in municipal firearms issues and as a defense counsel in the tobacco litigation. I thought Boyd was the ideal representative. He had spearheaded the federally sponsored Boston Gun Project as an assistant U.S. attorney in the Clinton Justice Department. The project had been hailed as a national model for reducing youth street violence. The key reason for Boyd's success in advising on the project was that he understood that coddling gangbangers and gunrunners was simply ineffective, but they did understand swift and uncompromising judicial intervention.

The program had three major features. First, it built a practical coalition of criminal justice professionals, local clergy, other community leaders, and academics who had worked together designing and implementing the project. Second, the project offered juvenile offenders both carrots and sticks, balancing job training and drug treatment with much stricter enforcement of parole and probation violations. Finally, the Boston Gun Project was flexible, not static.

We saw the program as a possible model that the industry could offer other cities as an alternative to their pending lawsuits. Even if they were seeking quick sound-bite political fixes and not real solutions, I was confident that the news media would react favorably to our proposal. So I hoped to hire Ralph Boyd to represent the industry as a whole through the ASSC and invited him to a November 1998 meeting of key industry executives and their lawyers in Washington, D.C. We gathered in a large conference room across from the AFL-CIO's headquarters on 16th Street, just up from Lafayette Park and the White House. Boyd was a persuasive figure, in no small part because he was the only attorney I knew of who had won any case for the tobacco industry. To me, this success and his Boston Gun Project experience made him an ideal lead partner.

His presentation in Washington was quite impressive. But I'm afraid it didn't impress the outside counsel that a number of firearms firms had retained. What Ralph Boyd was proposing was a definite threat to these defense attorneys' lunch boxes. If there were no lawsuits, the defense lawyers would not rack up the billable hours. This was counterintuitive to many nonattorneys, but the fact was that defense lawyers made their money in protracted litigation, not by avoiding lawsuits or quickly winning the cases for their clients. Many defense lawyers wanted to delay, "clarify issues" (in other words, obfuscate), research, review, meet, consult, reappraise, and reflect— all the while keeping the clock ticking on their billable hours.

I called these outside defense attorneys the "outhouse lawyers" because their legal specialty stank. In my opinion, they represented the worst aspect of the civil justice system.

After Ralph Boyd finished his presentation, Taurus USA's outside counsel Timothy Bumann, a smooth Atlanta product-liability litigator, rudely drawled, "Well, *that* dog won't hunt."

This seemed an open expression of racism expressed by an arrogant southerner toward the only black (Boyd) in the room.

But, racist or not, I realized, most of the lawyers meeting in Washington that day shared Bumann's opinion.

●   ●   ●

My next attempt to steer the industry away from the litigation quicksand involved retaining former Virginia attorney general Andrew Miller. He was a distinguished, white-haired lawyer with considerable influence within the National Association of Attorneys

General. Like Ralph Boyd, Andy Miller had extensive experience in the hard-fought tobacco lawsuits. He recognized the complexity of our predicament and urged the industry representatives to coordinate their legal strategy more closely and to seek representation from attorneys with experience in intricate multijurisdictional litigation— the tobacco and asbestos suits, for example.

I asked Miller to address about two hundred company owners, CEOs, and their attorneys at a private gathering in Tampa in December 1998 during the National Association of Sporting Goods Wholesalers meeting. Miller made a reasoned proposal, trying to impress the owners and executives that in effect they had to hang together—in other words, join forces—or hang separately. And he wasn't shy about stressing the need for experienced counsel. Although he himself was not a candidate for the job, he had many former colleagues that he could recommend.

He may as well have accused the outhouse lawyers in the audience of gross incompetence. Several of them, led by Ruger's Jim Doar from Chicago, jumped up and strode angrily out of the room, slamming the metal doors loudly behind them.

The companies weren't about to seek a cooperative approach in defending against the lawsuits.

This was an unfortunate attitude. Only two weeks before, in a memo to the ASSC membership titled, "The Future of Our Industry," I had told the companies in frank terms that the "litigation tyranny" was coming and that every gun maker, distributor, retailer, magazine publisher, and salesman was at risk. We had to band together for survival and "demonstrate to our opponents that they are in for one hell of a fight. There really is no other choice." Now, it appeared, few if any ASSC members had heeded that warning.

"Too many people in this industry," I told the *Wall Street Journal*'s Paul Barrett, "would prefer to stick their heads in the sand and hope that this will go away. It won't go away."

The industry attorneys' attitude reminded me of bulldogs guarding their bones. It was shortsighted and ultimately counterproductive for their clients.

While the bitterness and recriminations swirled at Tampa that November, I began to hear disquieting rumors that Feldman was being set up as the scapegoat. The reasoning was false, but had a plausible ring. If I had not negotiated with Ed Rendell in good faith (which he abused), the firearms industry wouldn't have been in this mess.

"The long knives are out," I told Barrett.

On the short flight back to Atlanta, a cloak of depression weighed me down. The Tampa meeting had been a disaster. My attempt to act boldly and solve the problem had merely pissed off the attorneys. The outhouse lawyers had now virtually taken over the companies and the run-up to the lawsuits was being tried in the news media and the court of public opinion.

What the hell am I doing working for these people? I thought. Only a little over a year before I had out-triangulated Bill Clinton (the Great Triangulator himself) and given the American Shooting Sports Council and the industry it represented instant nationwide credibility. Now the industry was fractured, with each company or subassociation scrambling to protect its flanks. There was strength in unity, I knew. But the American Firearms Industry was more *dis*-united than I'd ever seen it.

This situation gave the National Rifle Association an opening to reach a goal it had long sought: spreading its hegemony throughout the industry. With the manufacturers, importers, wholesalers, and retailers so badly divided, they might well see the NRA as the knight on a white charger who could ride up and solve their problems. The most obvious way the NRA could accomplish this was by lobbying for state and federal legislation that would prevent the type of lawsuits we were facing, in particular those that did not involve criminal misconduct, but were instead based on bizarre legal theories.

The first success of this approach came soon in Georgia when the state legislature passed a bill banning such lawsuits, for which the NRA had lobbied hard.

• • •

Optimist that I was, I thought I still had some breathing room, maybe six months. So, at the end of February 1999, after consulting Mike Saporito and several other board members, I authorized Bob Ricker to "make preliminary contact" with John Coale in Washington to discuss the status of the New Orleans lawsuit. A phone conversation led Ricker to a brief meeting at Coale's office, which was highly tentative and consisted only of agreeing to determine if further talks might be mutually advantageous. The ASSC kept the contact confidential. Apparently Coale's office did not.

The next day, the *Wall Street Journal* ran a Paul Barrett story, "Gun Firms Discuss Possible Settlement." Talk about waving a red flag at a bull. The outhouse lawyers went into orbit. And the NRA wasn't far behind them on the launchpad. Jim Baker told Barrett the following day that there was "no chance of settlement of these city suits based on conversations I've had with industry CEOs." And the NRA, he emphasized, "will not agree to more regulation legislatively."

Privately, I heard that the NRA was leaning hard on the industry to bring them my head on a platter. What I did not realize was that Jim Baker was exerting much of that pressure through the creation of a new "unified" industry group, the Hunting and Shooting Sports Heritage Fund, which would merge the ASSC, SAAMI, and the National Shooting Sports Foundation. This umbrella organization had been under discussion for months, but I wasn't fully aware of how far those discussions had advanced. I was also unaware that a sole executive would head the Heritage Fund. And that person would definitely not be Richard J. Feldman, Esq.

The Hunting and Shooting Sports Heritage Fund had its first meeting in Phoenix the last weekend of February. I was not invited. Jim Baker, as executive director of the National Rifle Association's ILA, was. So much for separation of interests between the NRA and the firearm industry. From what I later learned, the agenda focused on the pending lawsuits, and the "general lack of industry response to date," which had been the source of embarrassing front-page news. While I had been crusading in vain for coordination of the industry's legal defense efforts for months, members of the new organization suddenly got enthusiastic about the idea.

The Heritage Fund would be based on a voluntary manufacturers' contribution of 1 percent of sporting sales to finance "major public relations and communications efforts and an aggressive response to the politically motivated lawsuits" against the industry. This would generate an estimated $15 to $25 million annually for a wide variety of "proactive programs" that would need to be "carefully coordinated."

But I was not welcome to help shape this policy. In other words, it would be Feldman without Feldman. The National Rifle Association would support the industry's new endeavor in every possible way—provided I was gone. The leaders who assembled in Phoenix succumbed to the NRA's pressure to cut me adrift.

Jim Baker had extracted his revenge, just as he vowed he would sixteen months before in Washington the morning of the Rose Garden ceremony.

I was at home in Atlanta on the night of March 1 when Paul Jannuzzo walked in through the front door. "Get out a bottle and pour me a drink," he said, flopping down on my leather sofa. "Pour one for yourself, too, Richie." I gave us each a stiff glass of vodka.

"Take a deep breath," Paul began. He told me that I was out, and that Bob Ricker had been named head of the new, improved American Shooting Sports Council, which in turn had been absorbed by the new larger organization with SAAMI's Bob Delfay at the helm.

Paul and I sat over our drinks, first one, then another. And then a few more. Apparently, there was some good news. The industry was offering me a severance package of $300,000. I tried to calculate the total number of hours and days, weeks, months, and years that I had struggled to build the organization and then to divide that time into the lump sum payment.

"Probably not even minimum wage," I said.

Still, I thought, clinking my ice cubes, it *had* been an interesting ride.

Politics was a rough business, and I'd been in the thick of it. I had always tried to protect America's Second Amendment rights, of which I had remained—and remain today—a strong believer. But as the firearms industry's chief lobbyist, I had also been forced to take a protective stance and seek unsentimental concessions rather than adopt the rigid absolutism that the National Rifle Association had used to its institutional advantage and the financial benefit of its senior executives and consultants.

But that institution and those leaders had won the game. With me out of the picture, I thought, they could co-opt my strategy and tactics and claim them for their own.

And this they proceeded to do.

CODA

Fairfax, Virginia, September 21, 2005: A small crowd had gathered at NRA headquarters in Fairfax, Virginia, as I entered the atrium on this warm Wednesday evening. The occasion was festive, a black-tie reception to unveil a bronze bust of the late Harlon B. Carter, the pioneering leader who had created the modern National Rifle Association.

A string quartet was playing Vivaldi. Two bars were serving cocktails. I took a glass of club soda, avoiding alcohol in order to keep my wits sharp. This was my first contact with the NRA's officials since joining Robert Glock at Governor Jeb Bush's reception during the 2003 members' meeting in Orlando. Would things get nasty again? Would someone lash into me?

I took the time to inspect the well-appointed room. This was definitely an improvement over the rather shabby lobby at the old 1600 Rhode Island Avenue headquarters. But the same venerable engraved bronze lists of Endowment, Patron, and Benefactor members hung on the walls. Squinting up, I saw my name on the roster of endowment members.

At least they haven't removed it, I thought.

Stephen Halbrook, the Second Amendment scholar and longtime NRA adviser, approached with a wide smile and shook my hand. "Hey, Richie," he said. "How are you doing? Very good to see you."

I smiled back. No lightning bolt crashed down from the atrium dome above us.

And then Maryann Carter came in, elegantly dressed in ankle-length black evening wear with a caped jacket. She seemed a bit more nervous than I remembered her, which was quite understandable since she would soon be speaking to a large group. After greeting some family members, she came right over, kissed my cheek, and thanked me for my contribution to the Harlon and Maryann Carter Fund.

"Richie, it's so good to see you again," she said, squeezing my hand.

I had gladly made the donation. *The NRA still has one thing I'll contribute to.* But I wondered if Wayne LaPierre—whom I had just learned had received almost $900,000 in total compensation the year before—had donated anything to the fund. Probably not. My research revealed that Wayne had contributed no reportable contributions from his generous pay package to the NRA's Political Victory Fund, even though the association had been dunning its members almost nonstop for years. (I'd learned from Federal Election Commission data that, since becoming executive vice president in 1991, Wayne LaPierre had never given a single reportable contribution in any two-year election cycle.)

But who would ever know, since the only public reporting of most of his income was squirreled away out of sight in the mandatory but arcane bookkeeping reports of the NRA and the NRA Foundation? Certainly very few rank-and-file members would understand how to trace Wayne's income and probably fewer still would think of questioning the integrity of their leader.

The year before the U.S. presidential campaign, the NRA had sent out one of its typical blowtorch, scare-tactic fund-raisers, this time attacking Democratic presidential candidate John Kerry for his "bald-faced lies." Kerry, the letter said, had "been on board for every rotten . . . gun-ban scheme" put forward by senators Feinstein, Schumer, and Kennedy. Like a perennial golden oldie, the fund-raiser asked for "your special contribution today of $24, $29, $36, $48, $61 or whatever you can afford to send."

These contributions, of course, were needed to make sure that gun owners would receive "the truth" to see through Kerry's lies and distortions.

Obviously, there had been nothing in the fund-raising letter about Wayne LaPierre's total compensation, which placed him in the very top echelon of national nonprofit membership organization executives.

Johnny Aquilino arrived, and we talked about Harlon Carter and the "old NRA." It had been Harlon's hard work, integrity, and dedication to the Second Amendment that had kept the association alive, out of the hands of extremists, and launched it into national prominence.

One of those ideological fanatics, Neal Knox, had died of cancer nine months earlier at age sixty-nine. He had been Carter's executive director of ILA for four years after the Cincinnati Revolution. But Neal's zealotry had driven a wedge between them. Neal had been resurrected after Harlon's death, but had finally suffered the proverbial stake through the heart in 1997 when Ackerman-McQueen served as the puppet master in the ascension of Charlton Heston to the presidency the next year. During Neal's attempted power play in the late 1990s, he had tried to expose Wayne LaPierre's and Ack-Mac's financial bloodsucking, but they had successfully taken cover beneath Charlton Heston's flowing Moses robes.

One indication of the present NRA leadership's attitude toward Neal Knox was the terse death notice that appeared in the association's *America's 1st Freedom* (the slick addition to the flagship *American Rifleman*) March 2005 edition. The quarter-page squib was at the back of the book, page 61 of 64, among minor administrative notices. A brief biographic note listed Neal's longtime "interest in guns," but made no mention whatsoever of his passion for the Second Amendment.

I was still chatting with Johnny when the NRA's secretary Jim Land arrived, spotted us, and strode over. Johnny was facing Land, but my back was to him. And he didn't recognize me until he had reached us. He was definitely taken aback to see me there, but he managed to remain polite as we exchanged small talk. As soon as it was convenient, Land murmured a "thanks for coming," and disappeared into the gathering crowd.

I looked up and saw Wayne LaPierre enter the room. On seeing me, he came right over, shook my hand, and said, "Gee, Richie, it's great to see you here. Maryann really appreciates it, and I know how fond Harlon was of you."

This was our first personal contact since the Rose Garden event of 1997 that Wayne had not appeared exceedingly nervous in my presence. In fact, he looked very sleek and comfortable in a well-tailored tuxedo that fit his now-ample figure perfectly. Any trace of the absent-minded professor had disappeared. Wayne's chipmunk cheeks had expanded, so that he now reminded me of a well-groomed, well-fed beaver who had salted away plenty of leaves and branches for the winter. I imagined that an annual salary of almost a million dollars could buy plenty of financial forage.

But more than just personal economic success bolstered Wayne LaPierre's serene presence as the undisputed public champion of America's Second Amendment rights. The National Rifle Association had been on a roll, chalking up one victory after another since 1999.

The 2000 and 2004 presidential elections were prime examples of the NRA's growing political clout. In 2000, the NRA exploited the white hot anger and frustration that gun owners and conservatives felt after eight years of Clinton/Gore firearms restrictions and bans. Between 80 and 100 million Americans owned guns. Half the households in the country had a firearm under their roofs. And the Democrats' assault weapons ban, the Brady handgun control legislation, the industry lawsuits (now part of the greater NRA fight), as well as assorted state and local regulation, had all fed the groundswell of discontent, on which the NRA capitalized.

There was a sharp difference between the two presidential candidates in 2000. George W. Bush was a Texas hunter who as governor had backed and signed a gun bill that allowed state citizens to lawfully "carry" concealed handguns in holsters or purses. To the contrary, Al Gore was perceived as an urban policy wonk, despite his Tennessee roots and past NRA support. For the association, the choice between the two candidates was clear. Kayne Robinson, then NRA's first vice president, had even crowed at a California meeting of activists that, should Bush be elected, NRA officials would have a virtual office in the West Wing. But Bush's purported lack of "gravitas" and the last minute revelation of a drunk-driving record, contributed to making the 2000 election the closest in living memory.

Florida turned out to be the pivotal state. In 1986, the Florida legislature had passed a concealed carry law. But the larger national aspects of the gun issue as divined by the NRA were still a major factor in the state. Political surveys indicated that specific gun questions and the Second Amendment in general were worth between 250,000 and 500,000 votes statewide. On Election Day, pro-gun citizens followed the lead of the NRA and voted for Bush. Ultimately, a few hundred hanging chads on punch card ballots in Palm Beach County decided the outcome of the election in Florida. But absent the gun issue—and the NRA's critical role in manipulating it—this small margin of Bush votes would not have mattered. Gore would have carried Florida by several hundred thousand votes.

But it wasn't just Florida. If Gore had won Tennessee, Arkansas, or West Virginia, he would have become president regardless of the Florida outcome. The elections in both Gore's home state of Tennessee and Bill Clinton's home state of Arkansas were very close, and once again—absent the gun issue and the NRA's grassroots activist campaign—those states would have probably gone Democratic. Instead, they went to Bush.

The real kicker was West Virginia. It was an overwhelmingly Democratic state, with a Democratic governor, and two Democratic U.S. senators. But this was where the NRA concentrated its pro-gun political messages on radio and with direct mailings. Charlton Heston visited the state and rallied activists and uncommitted voters alike. The campaign worked. West Virginia went for Bush and he became president of the United States.

What was remarkable about the 2000 campaign victory was that the NRA's pro-gun success came less than eighteen months after the April 20, 1999 Columbine High School massacre in Littleton, Colorado. There, two depressed and unstable teenagers acquired an illegal arsenal and slaughtered twelve fellow students and a teacher before killing themselves. In the national news media, the ease with which the boys, Eric Harris and Dylan Klebold, obtained their weapons became a major topic of discussion. But the NRA skillfully deflected that scrutiny. In fact, the NRA used the public and political outcry over the tragedy—the "gun grabbers" were loose again—to promote a surge in membership and contributions. Soon after

Columbine, several hundred thousand new members had joined, and total membership soared to more than 4 million by Election Day.

At the 2002 members meeting in Reno, Wayne LaPierre made the association's claim to success perfectly clear: "You are why Al Gore isn't in the White House," he told the forty-five hundred cheering delegates.

Although many political commentators had discussed the roll of the gun issue and the NRA in the 2000 presidential election, no one had exposed the critical importance of guns to the Bush victory in 2004. First, of course, the 9/11 al-Qaeda terrorist attacks had spurred a wave of gun buying nationwide. Soccer moms became "security moms" (joined by their husbands and dads). Owning firearms became much more acceptable among the suburban middle class. So the NRA was in a position to once again exploit the fear that its political opposition intended to strip Americans of their Second Amendment rights.

The renewal of the 1994 federal assault weapons ban was an issue that the NRA skillfully manipulated. Many new gun owners were not quite sure about the differences between semiautomatic pistols, semiautomatic rifles, and shotguns, and the long list of assault weapons originally banned in 1994. That confusion helped the NRA spread the fear that a Democratic White House working with a Democratic Congress would deprive Americans of their Second Amendment rights, just when they needed their guns most urgently for protection. Although few national security experts believed wild-eyed Middle Eastern terrorists were about to go berserk in quiet suburban cul-de-sacs, savagely blasting tricycles and minivans, the NRA successfully cultivated the new security moms.

Meanwhile, the NRA emasculated the antigun organizations. One of the association's most pleasurable successes was an effortless victory that they merely had to exploit. In 2000, Emory University history professor, Michael Bellesiles, published a book titled *Arming America: The Origins of a National Gun Culture*. Bellesiles contended that his research showed unequivocally that guns had never been a major part of early America's pioneering culture or the rural society of the nineteenth century. He claimed to have reached his findings after scrupulous examination of estate and probate records, which showed a very low percentage of gun ownership in nineteenth-century Americana. This historical evidence stood in stark contradiction to the NRA's ethos that firearms had long held a central place in the life of the "real" America.

Bellesiles's findings—apparently based on meticulous historical research techniques—flew directly in the face of the NRA's dogma. The book was acclaimed by nationally recognized historians such as Garry Wills and Edmund Morgan, and won the prestigious history award, the Bancroft Prize, in 2001.

Michael Bellesiles was riding high. The only trouble was that his research was a fraud, bogus. Within two years, academic investigators had discovered widespread "misconduct," which included "unethical behavior" and the "commitment of fraud" that involved intentional fabrication of research data. The documents he claimed to have consulted apparently did not exist. Other data he claimed to have entered in his computer had disappeared—stolen by hackers, he said. Nobody bought the professor's dog-ate-my-digital-homework alibi. He lost his Bancroft Prize and his job.

The NRA crowed long and loud. Here was yet another egghead antigun zealot exposed for his mendacious ways.

In 2004, Ohio, with its lode of popular and electoral votes, proved to be a decisive battleground for Bush and Kerry. What neither national campaign seemed to realize was that Ohio had also been a major decisive state over the issue of concealed handgun carry for ten years. The NRA had twice succeeded in getting the bill through the state legislature, only to have the governor twice veto it. There was no doubt that organized gun owners in Ohio backed Bush.

The NRA's anti-Kerry campaign was as ruthless in Ohio as it was nationwide. In a series of caustic ads in the NRA's publications—"If John Kerry wins, you lose"—the Political Victory Fund struck hard and often. One ad showed an effeminate clipped poodle wearing a Kerry sweater on its shaved torso and a pink ribbon on its blow-dried head, "That dog don't hunt" (which reminded me of lawyer Tim Bumann's slur against Ralph Boyd). In another ad, Kerry awkwardly clutched a shotgun on a skeet range, apparently calling to an unseen observer. His head was tilted, his mouth gaping wide. "If John Kerry thinks the Second Amendment is about photo ops, he's daffy," the text announced. Although Kerry was "here in Ohio . . . posing as a sportsman," he couldn't hide his contempt for sportsmen's rights. The ad continued to excoriate Kerry's antigun record.

In the end, Bush won Ohio by about 120,000 votes. If 65,000 votes had switched, Kerry would have won the state. A success in Ohio would have given Kerry the electoral college vote with a minority of the popular vote—just like George W. Bush in 2000.

According to analysis by knowledgeable gun rights' activists Joe Tartaro and Alan Gottlieb, the gun vote in Ohio was worth about what it had been in Florida four years before—between 200,000 and 400,000 votes. Once again, although the national media did not take notice, absent the gun issue, the outcome of the 2004 presidential election would have been entirely different—no ifs, buts, or ands!

Bush showed his gratitude to the NRA indirectly. Earlier in 2004, he had promised to sign a bill renewing the 1994 assault weapons ban—provided Congress put it on his desk. But he did not use his bully pulpit to press for the bill. At the urging of the NRA, the Republican congressional majority allowed the assault weapons ban to expire in September 2004.

In July 2005, the U.S. Senate had passed the NRA-backed Protection of Lawful Commerce in Arms Act, the purpose of which was to provide legal immunity for gun makers and dealers from being held liable for the criminal use of their legal products. The bill was moving smoothly through the House and was expected to reach President Bush's desk in October. This would be the formal end of the misguided municipal lawsuit campaign that Mayor (now Governor) Ed Rendell had initiated in 1997. The new protection act would in fact shield the firearms industry from legal harassment by the voracious plaintiffs' bar (and equally ravenous outhouse defendants' lawyers who had drooled at the lucrative opportunity to *rescue* the manufacturers).

The law would do nothing to reduce gun violence, however. I had proposed cooperative measures to bring the industry and the cities together in proactive campaigns, such as the Boston Gun Project that Ralph Boyd had championed. But we had probably been too naive in believing that reducing violence and saving lives was actually an important goal for the NRA or the mayors.

Without question, the NRA was near the peak of its power in 2005. A *National Journal* survey of seventy members of Congress found that the National Rifle Association was the "most effective" lobbying group in Washington. Of the members of Congress surveyed, twenty-five had voted for the NRA. That was almost twice the number of votes as the influential AARP and the American Israel Public Affairs Committee received—a tie at thirteen each. The top five interest groups also included the U.S. Chamber of Commerce and the National Federation of Independent Business. Interestingly, more Democrats than Republicans voted for the NRA. *Maybe*, I thought, reading the survey results, *NRA really does stand for "Never Re-Elected Again."* But while the NRA was flourishing under Wayne LaPierre's leadership, the association's financial and membership bases were slipping. In 2003, the association had to admit to an operating deficit of almost $100 million. The situation had improved somewhat, but membership had slid from its peak of more than 4 million and was wavering at the mid-3-million level.

Perhaps feeling the quiet scrape of an iceberg below the water-line, Jim Baker had once more taken a lifeboat to private industry. Reportedly outfitted with a rich settlement package (rumored to be a cool half a million annually), he was pursuing his lobbying career at the Federalist Group.

Federal affairs lobbyist and Baker protégé Chris Cox had taken over from Baker and seemed to be doing an effective job. He was certainly generating a lot of fund-raising appeals, which reached me at my new home in rural New Hampshire. My wife, Jackie, and I had first met years before at the Vermont Law School. (She had held a Massachusetts concealed carry license), and today we still get a laugh out of the NRA's appeals for cash. One appeal, calling for a fight against the dreaded "UN's Global Gun Ban Treaty" and for a fight against Hillary Clinton's reelection, asked for yet another "special contribution of $100, $250, $500." The price of poker had certainly gone up from the $15 or $20 of years before.

Besides the obvious contempt in which I held such deceitful appeals, I was still angry with myself for unquestioningly accepting the assurance of my former industry colleagues in the ASSC that I would be paid a reasonable severance package of $300,000 in 1999. I received exactly $0.00, zilch, nada. That was because Bob Delfay (with Baker's guidance) managed to smother the American Shooting Sports Council out of existence six months after I was shown the door. Bob Ricker—another candidate for Jim Baker's vengeance—also lost his job.

I went the legal route, dropping money down various rat holes, chasing my nonexistent severance pay. Ricker waited, apparently testing the temperature of a little surprise he had for the deceitful industry groups under the adage that vengeance was a dish best served cold. In February 2003, Bob Ricker was asked to provide an affidavit in a California lawsuit in which Los Angeles, San Francisco, and other cities argued that the firearms industry had "created a public nuisance" and violated state law by knowingly allowing guns to reach criminals and juveniles.

Bob Ricker's affidavit cited "corrupt dealers" who had allowed obvious "straw sales." Bob also stated that it was common knowledge among gun makers that "the diversion of firearms from legal channels of commerce to the black market" took place principally at the wholesale and retail gun sale level. "Leaders in the industry have long known that greater industry action to prevent illegal transactions is possible," he wrote. But, he continued, the industry had "resisted taking constructive voluntary action." Predictably, Bob's affidavit was called a "bomb shell." A *New York Times* editorial rather tritely called the document, "A Gun Lawsuit's Smoking Gun."

When *Gun Week* interviewed me about the affidavit, I told them Bob was "not an anti [-gun activist], although I think he's gone over to the 'dark side' a little."

Within days of Ricker's affidavit, a San Diego judge dismissed the cities' lawsuit against the industry. All this became moot, of course, when the federal immunity act passed.

This was not to say that the NRA would sail on untroubled waters indefinitely. In 2003, the Gallup Youth Survey found that the majority (54 percent) of American teens age thirteen to seventeen believed that gun laws should be stricter. Fewer (34 percent) felt that laws covering firearms should be kept as they were. And only 10 percent of these young people told the pollsters that gun laws should be made less rigorous. Girls were much more likely than boys to favor stricter gun control. That trend did not augur well for the NRA's future. Given standard age progressions, the NRA would begin running short of potential members as its staunchest supporters went on to the Great Shooting Range in the Sky. Unless, of course, the association continued to find ways to scare the living bejesus out of people. The nefarious U.N. international gun grab—would the actual grabbers descend in black helicopters?—was one example of the type of fearmongering at which the NRA excelled.

• • •

Jim Baker never showed up at the Harlon Carter reception. Just as well, because I knew there'd probably be harsh words between us if he did. As events developed that evening, Kayne Robinson, the former NRA president and the current director of general operations, (reportedly making more than $300,000), was the only official who pointedly avoided me—just as he had in Orlando in 2003. Sandy Froman, the current president, greeted me warmly. I was surprised that she even knew who I was.

Chris Cox spoke, saying that although he had never known Harlon Carter, he had hung a picture of him in his office for inspiration. How touching. Wayne's speech began off the cuff and then moved smoothly into his prepared remarks. Ackerman-McQueen had indeed groomed him well as a public speaker.

Finally, Maryann discussed Harlon's many accomplishments, and then unveiled the bronze bust. The likeness was excellent, in the warts-and-all Roman style. There was that tough jaw line, and, in my imagination at least, his glinting eyes as he spoke of the sacred Second Amendment that separated American citizens from all other people.

My evening ended with several close friends in a nearby bar. All in all, I thought, it had not been a bad day. How much of the history of the United States in the past thirty years—thousands of local and state elections, hundreds of congressional and senatorial campaigns, and the outcome of the last two presidential elections—had been directly changed by the events that Harlon Carter had put into motion in Cincinnati back in 1977?

The next morning on my flight back to New Hampshire the jet passed above lower Manhattan and I looked down to see the empty wound that the 9/11 attack had inflicted. That hole represented a conjunction of raw power and politics.

In a different context, this relationship reminded me of the role the American gun lobby, both the firearms industry and the National Rifle Association, has played and would continue to play in America's destiny.

EPILOGUE

ovember 8, 2006: I awoke late on this Wednesday morning after the midterm election, having stayed up until almost dawn watching the tectonic shift in American politics slide across the continent. The Republicans had lost the House by a hefty margin. And by that evening it was confirmed that they had also lost the Senate.

As CNN was tallying the final results, I called several friends to discuss the results. One of the questions I asked was, "What do you think the NRA will make of all this?"

"They're rollin' around like hogs in mud," Bob Ricker said. Except he did not quite say "mud."

"The NRA could not have bought themselves better results," Paul Jannuzzo said.

The National Rifle Association had *enemies* again, clearly delineated opponents in the endless struggle. And as always, it was better to fight than win. Protracted campaigns brought in new members and contributions . . . $17.63 or $11.84 . . . $100, $250, $500.

If the NRA's luck held, a ham-handed Democratic Congress would pass an expanded assault weapons ban that George W. Bush either might or might not sign—but which an incoming Democratic president definitely would. (You could almost hear the engines of the black helicopters warming up.) A reprised assault weapons ban would bring the NRA hundreds of thousands of new members and millions in contributions.

And there was an unexpected partisan twist to all this. Democrats in pro-gun districts would probably buck Nancy Pelosi's leadership and vote against a new ban in order to demonstrate to their constituents their independence—and to garner the support of the NRA.

With a Democratic Congress and the strong prospect of a Democratic White House, the NRA would indeed be in "Hog Heaven."

Fear of the gun grabbers would probably always be a hot button among the NRA's members. In the year after Hurricane Katrina when New Orleans police had confiscated firearms from armed but otherwise law-abiding citizens, the NRA milked the dramatic issue for all it was worth. The association lobbied Congress and campaigned hard for H.R. 5013, the "Disaster Recovery Personal Protection Act of 2006." The bill became law after well-publicized NRA backing. Wayne LaPierre—probably Ackerman-McQueen—voiced some smooth rhetoric around the country.

LaPierre: "Every time somebody says, 'The government is not going to knock on doors to take people's guns . . . ,' citizens should tell them 'Remember New Orleans!'"

Despite Katrina, however, most voters weren't scared that the big bad BATF would soon be taking their guns. And the NRA had little success electing pro-gun Republicans to Congress in 2006. The issue had lost its high-intensity "wedge" quality compared to the war in Iraq or illegal immigration.

So after the 2006 election, the NRA drafted an alarmist pamphlet that bore the working title "Freedom in Peril." Leaked to the media before it reached its members, the document foreshadowed how the association planned to capitalize on the Democratic control of Congress and on a future Democratic presidency:

It's inevitable that terrorists will infest America for generations to come. It's also inevitable that an anti-gun president will occupy the White House, and anti-gun forces will control the U.S. House and Senate. Unless we are well-financed to face that moment, the final disarmament of law-abiding Americans will occur beneath the shroud of anti-terrorism legislation.

A March fund-raiser from the NRA's Political Victory Fund warned that "Gun control is back on the national legislative agenda . . . . With the help from the news media led by the *New York Times*, the *Washington Post*, and the 'Big Three' TV networks, gun control extremists will . . . convince more politicians that the time is right to enact harsh new restrictions on our Second Amendment rights."

In other words, keep those contributions coming in, folks . . . $17.63 . . . $42.37 . . . $76.18 . . .

As I watched the election results roll in throughout the night and into the next day, I recalled the Contract with America. (*The Republican Revolution*, I thought, *1994–2006.*) To a large degree, the volatile issue of guns, crime, and the Second Amendment had helped keep Republican control of Congress and the White House for twelve years. Now the pendulum had swung back.

But no matter the direction of its future swing, the National Rifle Association would be prepared to reap the benefits.

●   ●   ●

On the morning of April 16, 2007, a deeply troubled young man named Seung Hui Cho used two pistols to murder thirty-one students and faculty members at Virginia Tech University in Blacksburg. He then turned the gun on himself, ending the worst civilian massacre in American history. Once again, the lineup of usual suspects argued from their cherished positions: "We need to arm students! cried the pro-gunners." We must disarm America! screamed the gun banners. This time, unlike at Columbine, the guns were not purchased at gun shows but from licensed dealers after Cho had passed the Brady background check! He had no criminal record but had been sent to a psychiatric hospital for several days in December 2005 against his will. This should have prevented his easy purchase of the guns, but there was no public record of his hospitalization.

Congress will probably appropriate millions of dollars to remedy the reporting problem, but little else is likely to change. The 2008 presidential contest is proceeding at full tilt, and no one—Republican or Democrat—wants to be viewed as in favor of any new gun control in any event and certainly not before the New Hampshire primary. The only people present in a "gun free school zone" are the victims, not the perpetrators. And why should or would homicidal psychopaths care about the consequences of their crimes when suicide is just moments away? The antigun faction tends to overreach, claiming that all gun transfers should go though a licensed dealer and be properly vetted by a panel of psychiatrists; while the pro-gun community will claim that these deaths were caused (or at least exacerbated) by foolish and futile gun controls at the university's "gun free" campus. (On this, I count myself among the pro-gun faction.)

But neither side will focus on resolving the underlying problems and offer a serious attempt at making public policy work in the best interests of the American people. After all, there's fund-raising to be accomplished here, and drawing nice clean lines with "us" and "them" to battle over makes for far more successful direct mail solicitations than actually solving problems. Hopeless? No, but the American people, gun owners and nonowners alike, need to take an active role and not leave the outcome to the professional lobbyists—that's a guaranteed prescription for stalemate.

INDEX